THE
ALL-AMERICAN
BARBECUE BOOK

Also by Rich Davis and Shifra Stein

All About Bar-B-Q: Kansas City Style

Also by Shifra Stein

Day Trips: Kansas City
Day Trips: St. Louis
Day Trips: Cincinnati
Day Trips: Houston
Day Trips: Minneapolis St. Paul
Day Trips: Baltimore
Day Trips: Phoenix Tucson Flagstaff
Kansas City: A Unique Guide to the Metro Area

Also by Rich Davis

The Secrets, Sauces, and Savvy of American Barbecue
(Home Video)

THE ALL-AMERICAN BARBECUE BOOK

Rich Davis and Shifra Stein

A SteinPress Book

Vintage Books
A Division of Random House
New York

A Vintage Original, June 1988
First Edition

Copyright © 1988 by Rich Davis and Shifra Stein
Illustrations © 1988 by Madeline Sorel

Library of Congress Cataloging-in-Publication Data
Davis, Rich.
The all-American barbecue book.
"A Vintage original"—CIP galley copr. p.
Includes index.
1. Barbecue cookery. I. Stein, Shifra. II. Title.
TX840.B3D38 1988   641.7'6   87-40477
ISBN 0-394-75842-0 (pbk.)

Designed by Matt Shamet
Composed by Lopez Graphics, Inc.,
Kansas City, Missouri

Manufactured in the United States of America
10 9 8 7 6 5 4 3 2 1

This book is dedicated to all those great barbecue experts who have taught us, shared with us, and inspired us to write a book about this special part of American cuisine; to the brave souls who have shunned the comforts of an indoor kitchen to take on the challenge and reap the rewards of outdoor wood and charcoal cookery; and finally, to our families and friends, who put up with an occasional charred start toward achieving that smoky, succulent bliss—great American barbecue. Fortunately, it's an endless journey!

Special Acknowledgment

My wife, Coleen, and I toured the barbecue belt from southwest Texas to eastern Virginia, including hundreds of spots in between. Driving across the rural and urban southern United States in our van, we covered thousands of miles together, week after week. We enjoyed it, we still speak to each other, we still eat barbecue two or three times a week, and we look forward to doing more of the same in the future. Coleen's careful note-taking and analytic tasting during this time contributed a great deal to the research of this book and is greatly appreciated by the authors.

—Rich Davis

Contents

Preface

"To be initiated into the mysteries of barbecue methods is the desire of everybody who has enjoyed communion with the product."
— *Harper's Weekly*, November 9, 1895

From the spicy smoked brisket of Texas and North Carolina's succulent chopped whole hog, to the tang and bite of crusty Kansas City and Memphis ribs, there's nothing like the simple appeal of delicious smoked barbecue. Its origins may be primitive, but one taste and you'll know that this is food fit for kings. In fact, barbecue has been served up ever since there *were* kings, even if they didn't call it barbecue.

Barbecuing is easy to learn. But common misunderstandings about it can thwart even the best intentions. By using this book as a guide, you can avoid familiar errors made by many backyard chefs and learn how to create masterpieces from the most common (and uncommon) cuts of meat. Along with the array of barbecue recipes, the delicious regional side dishes and mouth-watering desserts included here have come from prize-winning barbecuers, chefs, restaurateurs, and other professionals across the nation.

We've also included hard-to-find information regarding cuts of meat, different woods and techniques, cookers and sauces—from vinegar-based to tangy red—all of which offer an exciting range of tastes from the regions where barbecue historically reigns supreme.

Barbecue is a culinary heritage of recipes, ingredients, sauces, native woods, and methods developed originally by American Indians, black Africans, Creoles, and the English, Spanish, and early French explorers and settlers. These are the people who influenced and determined the flavors, techniques, and textures of regional barbecue in America.

The history of barbecue in the United States is truly fascinating. Over the decades several distinctive regional styles have slowly evolved. It is our intention to document the methods and recipes of these regional barbecue specialties so that they will not be lost with time and may continue to be enjoyed now and in the future.

We're very excited about what is happening to American barbecue today. This simple yet elegant "down-home" fare has captured the attention of food lovers everywhere. With its roots country-deep in tradition, barbecue has begun to emerge as one of the pillars of the "new American cuisine." The Barbecue Industry Association claims that over 66 million households now own a barbecue grill, and cites total annual sales of barbecue equipment and food in excess of $6 billion. And there is also a new sophistication associated with barbecue today. Woods such as mesquite, alder, hickory, grapevine, cherry, and applewood have become popular for home as well as restaurant use, and the design of cookers ranges from old-fashioned to high-tech, with some models selling for as much as $2,000 to enthusiasts who won't settle for less than the best.

All of this points to the fact that home cooks are beginning to recognize that barbecue is a subtle and varied kind of cooking. In no other kind of cooking does selection of fuel affect flavor so distinctly. Closed-pit barbecue tastes different from open-pit barbecue, and mesquite smoke gives a completely different flavor from maplewood smoke. Spices, sauces, meats, woods, techniques—all influence flavor and texture. The endless combinations of these factors is what helps make the *cabrito* (barbecued goat) of Brady, Texas, uniquely different from the barbecued fresh pork shoulder cooked in Lexington, North Carolina. If you've grown up with a particular style of barbecue, another region's barbecue may at first taste strange to you. Try to give the food a chance, even if your first response is, "Now that ain't barbecue like I know barbecue!" Who knows? It might be love after first bite.

Barbecue experts will testify that there are several basic elements critical to the preparation of the classic barbecue of their regions. In the following chapters, we'll explore the patchwork of styles and techniques prevalent in regional American barbecue today. On the southern Atlantic coast, whole hogs are cooked over open pits. In the Carolinas, the cooked meat is chopped fine, sprinkled with a clear, vinegar-based sauce, and served with hush puppies, slaw, and Brunswick stew. In the heart of North Carolina, sauces begin to redden and whole hog gives way to barbecued fresh ham and pork shoulder. Continuing down to South Carolina, red sauces shade to orange in ketchup-mustard combinations, then mustard gains the upper hand the farther south one goes, turning the sauces yellow. But tastes are fickle: as you cross into Georgia and Alabama, the sauces turn red again!

What whole hog is to North Carolina, pork ribs are to Memphis, Tennessee, and devotees there like their ribs served either "wet," with a hot, sweet, sticky sauce, or charcoal-cooked and dry (no sauce). At the edge of the Mississippi, pork nears the end of the river. It overflows into parts of eastern Arkansas and Louisiana, lingering at restaurants such as Couch's Corner Bar-B-Que in Jonesboro, Arkansas, where barbecued hams are served "any way the customer wants them"—chopped, pulled, or sliced—and crowned with coleslaw and a golden vinegar-based mustard sauce.

Pork meets beef where East meets West—in Kansas City, where barbecue has emerged as an eclectic food. Unlike the other barbecue regions, which tend to focus on a single kind of meat—whole hog, brisket, or ribs—Kansas City/Midwest barbecue encompasses all these favorites, serving them up with sauces that are thicker and richer than those found elsewhere.

In Texas, where brisket and hot link sausage are the stars, pork spareribs take on a supporting role. The distinctive red sauces frequently found in this part of the country are thin and soupy and are often served on the side.

As we take you on a tour of this country's regional barbecue, to places that are completely all-American in their heritage and style, we hope you'll come to understand and love this exceptional food as much as we do.

Acknowledgments

Because so many of our recipes were given to us in mega-proportions that sometimes called for hundreds of pounds of meat at a time, we had to convert much of what we researched into family-size servings. So we called in the Marines, in the form of the Greater Kansas City Home Economists in Business organization. These gallant members sliced, chopped, shredded, mixed, added, and divided beyond the call of duty. They included: Recipe Testing Coordinator Mary Holloway, Mary Dudley, Monica Haley, Debbie Hansen, Vicki Johnson, Jill Kracilcek, Susan Boothe Larson, Louise Lloyd, Joyce Lofstrom, Juanita Luthi-McKee, Kimberle Mason, Kathy Moore, Rosalie Niemi, Roberta Phillips, Loretta Polzin, Maggie Risley, Dianne Ryan, Andrea Cox Stanley, Jean Taraba, Jane Tegeler, and Roxanne Whittenburg.

Assisting the Home Economists in Business were the following: Amy Schmid, Karen Miller, Carolyn Steinfelds, Kelly Mandagere, Marilyn Dreas, Amy Van Blaricum, Teri Bahr, Carol Nichols, Sandy Behnke, Jenny Eisenbrandt, Steve Holloway, Doug Kelly, Lynn Kelly, Bob Kralicek, Mark

Lloyd, Tricia McGregor, Pat McGregor, Ken Huggins, Ivan Risley, and Kelly Holloway.

In addition to our recipe testers, we were aided in our research by the North Carolina Pork Producers Association, the South Carolina Pork Producers Association, the National Pork Producers Association, and the National Beef Industry Council, who offered special help with recipes and information. We also want to acknowledge the assistance and support provided to us by the gracious folks at the Texas Tourism Development Agency and the Memphis in May International Festival, who helped us track down good barbecue in their areas. Thanks, also, to our friend Sam Higgins, author of *I'm Glad I Ate When I Did, 'Cause I'm Not Hungry Now*, for sharing some of the recipes in his book with us and letting us ride in his pickup truck.

Then there were the experts—writers, newspaper and magazine editors, and food historians—who helped with information and recipes. These included Dr. Jose Arrom, Rosemary Brandau, Pat Gibbs, Joann Bowen Gaynor, Guy Friddell, Esther B. Aresty, Jay Gaynor, Nancy Carter Crump, Dr. Gerald Cohen, Alicia Rios, C. Anne Wilson, Lorena Walsh, Lorna Sass, Darryl Corti, Karen Hess, Pat Baldridge, Christine Arpe Gang, Carolyn Davidson, Alan Davidson, Jean Wickstrom Liles, John G. Marshall, Dr. Irving Rouse, and Dr. Sophie Coe.

Members of the Kansas City Barbecue Society, the largest functioning barbecue group of its kind in the country, offered help and recipes. Much credit goes to Ardie Davis, Rick Welch, Guy Simpson, Paul Kirk, and a host of others.

Our typing and telephone experts, Mary Johnson, Bernadette Hoyt, and Lonnie Kay Brooks, called all over the country getting updated copies of recipes and permission slips as well as typing into the wee hours to get us through our deadlines.

We want to thank our families for the special support they offered, especially Mary Spitcaufsky, whose editorial input and suggestions were greatly appreciated.

If we've left any names off our list, forgive us, please. We are truly fortunate there have been so many willing to help. To all of you we offer not only acknowledgment, but genuine thanks and appreciation for your input. As the saying goes—we couldn't have done it without you.

THE
ALL-AMERICAN
BARBECUE BOOK

Introduction

★ A BRIEF HISTORY OF BARBECUE

Barbecue has the longest tap root of any cuisine in the world. From the first time early man cooked a hunk of mastodon over live coals to the closed-pit methods popular today, there have been endless variations on the theme. We know, for example, that the Aztecs were roasting meats with wood charcoal long before the Spanish explorers arrived on their shores. And we have evidence that the early Japanese, Tibetans, and Laotians grilled their foods over open fires while Genghis Khan was rampaging through China in the twelfth and thirteenth centuries, spit-roasting along the way.

Archeological digs indicate the existence of firepits used to prepare meats as far back as 25,000 B.C. The writings of Homer indicate that the Greeks were preparing oxen, sheep, and swine by a process nearly identical to the open-pit style of today's southern barbecue long before Christ was born. Homer tells us that Achilles prepared a meal for Ajax, Odysseus, and Phoenix in which a sheep, a goat, and a pig were butchered and the pieces put on spits, salted, and roasted over live coals:

Automedon held the meats, and brilliant Achilles carved them, and cut it well into pieces and spitted them. . . . But when the fire had burned itself out, and the flames had died down, he scattered the embers apart . . . and extended the spits across them lifting them to the andirons, and sprinkled the meats with divine salt. Then when he had roasted all, and spread the food on the platters. . . .

A Greek vase from the fifth century B.C. depicts with astonishing clarity an image relating the preparation of meat for spit-roasting. The historian Elizabeth Minchin describes the image of "long strips of meat which have already been cut away from the carcass being wrapped about a spit, then roasted . . ." She points out that roasting meat was an endeavor in keeping with the "heroic" outdoor life of the average Greek male.

The Greeks taught the art of barbecuing to the Romans, and we know that both Greeks and Romans served spit-roasted meat at banquets. Later the Romans introduced this method into what is now England, and the Saxons followed their lead, roasting up great feasts.

BARBECUING IN THE UNITED STATES

As early as the 1580s John White, a member of the Roanoke Island settlement, recorded his observations of the Croatan Indians whom he saw "broyling their fishe over the flame—they took great heed that they bee not burntt." White, an artist, also gave us the first pictorial evidence we have of American Indians preparing meats over live coals. His drawings depict Indians preserving wild game and fish by smoking them on wooden frames, the same kind of frames early Spanish explorers of the Caribbean called a *barbacoa*, from the native Indian language.

The first Plymouth harvest celebration, which became our Thanksgiving Day, included roast venison and duck, as well as English-style roasting (in front of the fire, not over it), influencing the colonists' methods of food preparation.

Robert Beverley's 1705 publication, *The History and Present State of Virginia*, describes the way meats had been cooked by the Indians: "The

One of John White's illustrations of American Indians smoking fish on wooden frames, from Thomas Hariot's Narrative of the First English Plantation of Virginia, *first printed in London in 1588 and then reproduced with illustrations in Frankfurt in 1590.* Reprinted with permission of the Colonial Williamsburg Foundation.

meat was laid upon the coals [grilling] . . ." or laid "upon Sticks rais'd upon forks at some distance above the live Coals, which heats more gently and dries up the Gravy [barbecuing if we ever heard of it!] . . ."

Aside from the Indians of the Caribbean and Eastern Woodlands (those living from the Atlantic Ocean to the Mississippi River), there is evidence that other tribes knew plenty about outdoor barbecue. Plains Indians cooked over open campfires, while the tribes of the Northwest Coast grilled salmon steaks, using juniper berries for seasoning. They also used alderwood for smoking salmon, and still do today.

In *The Art of American Indian Cooking*, Jean Anderson and Yeffe Kimball indicate that the Indians of the South also used open fires for cooking. Taking "lambs and suckling pigs," they "stuffed them with apples and nuts and roasted them over the glowing coals." The authors also speculate that this Indian method of cooking eventually spread north into Maryland and

Pennsylvania, while the Spanish brought the technique (learned from the Caribbean Indians) with them when they explored the Southwest. Eventually hot *molé* sauces were used for basting in the Southwest, Anderson and Kimball suggest, and from these spicy mixtures possibly emerged some of our first "hot" barbecue sauces. The Pueblo Indians were reported to have blended fiery sauces from tomatoes and chilis and ladled them generously over roasting meats.

 # BARBECUE: WHAT'S IN A WORD?

American Indians, primarily in the southeastern United States but also in the Caribbean islands and areas of northern South America and Mexico, had long used a wooden frame upon which they placed fish and game for preservation by smoking, since the damp, hot climate made food, particularly fish, spoil quickly. So preparing food on a "barbacoa" was originally more a matter of preservation than of taste.

Most exciting to us is the discovery of the earliest usage of the word *barbacoa*. Its origins have been attributed to the Haitian and Jamaican Indians, yet an earlier direct usage has been found in *The Natural History of the West Indies*, by the sixteenth-century Spanish explorer Oviedo. In describing the natives of "Tierra Firme," the northeastern coast of mainland South America, he writes that they "trap deer and pigs with branches and traps made of nets. . . . They roast the flesh on sticks which they place in the ground like a grating or a trivet, over a pit. They call these *barbacoas*, and place fire beneath, and in this manner they roast fish also." Since the mainland was settled by natives before the islands were, we should probably attribute the origins of the Spanish *barbacoa* (and the American *barbecue*) to the Indians of South America and not to the islands, as do all English dictionaries, including the *Oxford English Dictionary*.

From the West Indian and South American Indian use of *barbacoa* to mean a wooden frame for holding meat and fish, the word gained broadened usage among the Indians: any square or oblong wooden framework supported by props; a scaffold on which Indian children sat to guard corn; a little home built on treetops or stilts; a crude platform on top of houses

One of the drawings of the Caribbean Indians from the anonymous Histoire naturelle des Indes *(the "Drake Manuscript"), depicting a young man cooking fish and game on a* barbacoa. *The original caption reads in part, "...the smoke of the fat dropping into the fire smokes and roasts the fish, which are good eating."* Reprinted with permission of The Pierpont Morgan Library, New York. MA 3900 f.109.

where grain, fruits, and other goods were placed for safekeeping. The *Diccionario de la lengua español* further informs us that Costa Rican natives used the word *barbacoa* to refer to wooden frames for growing entangling plants, while in Guatemala and Mexico it referred to a structure of green wood posts for holding roasting meats, and in Mexico it was used occasionally to mean meats roasted by that method.

We may also have the French to thank for linguistic inspiration. Their term *barbe à queue*—a phrase meaning "from beard to tail"—refers to the spit-roasting of an entire animal. But, alas for France, the *Oxford English Dictionary* clearly indicates that no documentation exists to prove that the American term derives from this phrase. The French did use the word *babracot*, apparently also appropriated from the Indians of Guiana, to describe this cooking process.

However, let's give the French credit where we can. The well-known food historian Karen Hess also points to the French *boucan*, which refers to a frame identical to the Spanish *barbacoa:* "Perhaps," states Hess, "the most curious usage . . . comes from the French West Indies where the word is *buccan, bucan,* or *boucan* . . . 'a wooden framework or hurdle on which meat is roasted or smoked over a fire.' Just so, a *buccaneer* or *buccanier* originally was 'one who dries or smokes flesh on a *boucan* . . .'" The pirates came soon thereafter!

Early English spellings included *barbecu, borbecue, barbekew,* and so on. *Barbacoa. Boucan. Barbecue.* The words are music to our ears.

★ THE SOURCE OF THE SAUCES

Tracing the history of barbecue sauces in America is difficult because there are very few barbecue sauce recipes to be found in early cookbooks. Commercial barbecue sauces were not found nationally on grocers' shelves until 1948, when Heinz put a barbecue sauce on the market. Open Pit barbecue sauce soon followed, then Kraft, and, more recently, the K.C. Masterpiece varieties and many others.

Early records indicate that colonists sometimes basted whole hogs with alternating batches of saltwater and melted butter. (A typical eighteenth-century barbecue of this sort is recreated each Labor Day weekend in Colonial Williamsburg, Virginia. As simple as the recipe sounds, the meat is truly delicious when basted this way.) A recipe for "Betty Hanford's Tomato Sauce" appears in *Beverages and Sauces of Colonial Virginia*, a compilation of recipes from 1607 to 1907 by Laura S. Fitchett, but no date for the recipe's origination is given. And the first tomato "catsup" recipe we have found is in *The Frugal Housewife* (1838) by Lydia Child.

A few recipes for true barbecue, usually open-pit style, have been passed down in English and French literature of the seventeenth and eighteenth centuries. In *Nouveaux Voyages aux Isles d'Amérique* by Jean B. Labot (1693), we found a description of a barbecued whole hog that is stuffed with aromatic herbs and spices, roasted belly up, and basted with a sauce of melted butter, cayenne pepper, and sage. The fragrant meat was sliced and served on leaves of an aromatic West Indian plant.

This distinctively French way of roasting pig—utilizing sage and melted butter for basting—was apparently brought from the French West Indies to the shores of America by early slaves and Creoles. No written record exists of the simple recipe, so the exact barbecuing and basting process for this method will never be known.

As with the American Indians, it has been difficult to unearth exact information about the contributions of black Africans and the Creoles of the Caribbean to barbecuing, since the history and cooking skills of these cultures were mostly passed down verbally rather than in writing. But we do know that both groups cooked food over live coals. In addition, the Creoles had access to the native spices of the West Indies. It is believed that some combination of the early English ketchups (which were made of vinegar and mushrooms, oysters, or walnuts, but never tomatoes) with some of the hot peppers and dry rubs used by Caribbean natives and seventeenth-century slaves, evolved to become the basis of the vinegary Eastern Carolina barbecue sauces as we know them today, with crushed red or black pepper replacing the mushrooms, oysters, or walnuts of the original ketchup.

At the opposite end of the spectrum are the tomato-based red sauces of the Midwest and Southwest. The most popular red sauces are mixtures of tomato, vinegar, hot spices, and sweeteners of some sort, and they greatly resemble the nineteenth-century American-style ketchups, to which hot Mexican chilis or African and Caribbean capsicum peppers were added.

In between the two extremes of sauces—clear vinegar and tomato-red—are the yellow sauces found in certain parts of the eastern Deep South, such as South Carolina. Their color comes from the mustard that is added to the vinegar and spices. (Maurice Bessinger, well-known barbecuer and restaurateur from Columbia, South Carolina, prefers to label this type of sauce "golden." Bessinger claims that these mustard-based "golden" barbecue sauces were created by his father and grandfather, who emigrated from Germany, where great mustards abound. Their original recipe isn't available to us, but the sauce still is, from Bessinger in Columbia, South Carolina.) There are also orange-colored sauces to be found in South Carolina, further inland on the western side of the Appalachians, in which tomato ketchup has been added to the mustard, vinegar, and spices.

Today most Americans seem to prefer rich tomato-based sauces, which come in a wide variety of flavors and consistencies. Their sales far outweigh those of any other type of barbecue sauce. The best of the new premium-grade sauces are made without gums, starches, or artificial colors or thickeners and are not only thicker and better for table use, but also tend to cling to the meat when barbecuing, which is important. For most purposes—including the majority of recipes in this book—the better commercial sauces are not only adequate but excellent.

Many food publications do not, as a matter of policy, list ingredients by brand name. When it comes to barbecue and commercial barbecue sauces, however, this policy simply doesn't make sense. Barbecue sauces, both homemade and commercial, vary so greatly by region and by the nature and proportion of their ingredients that "1 cup barbecue sauce" in an ingredients list would give the cook no idea whatsoever as to the intended flavor or consistency of the end product. For example, if you used a mustard- or tomato-based sauce where a spicy North Carolina–style vinegar-based sauce was intended, the result—in consistency, color, and flavor—would be chaos. Even in what appear to be similar barbecue sauces (for example, those containing a tomato base, sweeteners, vinegar, and spices), there are marked differences in both flavor and consistency, let alone color. And barbecue sauces with food starches, gums, artificial flavors, and other additives (even if they are labeled—and perhaps priced—as premium brands) taste different from those that do not contain such ingredients. The creator of each sauce has his or her own secret blend of spices, vinegars, and sweeteners that gives a special "something" to any dish.

Therefore, the recipes in this book list the ingredients exactly as they were provided by our sources (with suggested alternatives *of a similar type* where possible, in case a particular brand isn't available to you), in order to preserve the authenticity, region by region, of the recipes as submitted. (In some recipes, where our sources indicated that the exact type of barbecue sauce wasn't important, we've simply listed "barbecue sauce" as an ingredient.) For those of you who want to try your hand at making the basic regional sauces "from scratch," or who want to try some innovative approaches to barbecue, we've included a fantastic collection of sauce recipes.

★ OPEN- AND CLOSED-PIT BARBECUING

Barbecuing can be defined as a cooking process using live coals (from charcoal or wood) at a temperature of approximately 200°–250°F. It isn't grilling and it isn't cold smoking. It's a style of cooking that has traditionally taken place in the great outdoors.

As described in various eighteenth-century letters, diaries, and documents, the barbecue was not only a cooking method but a social and political outdoor gathering that culminated in a large and sometimes drunken feast in early colonial America. Author Rosemary Brandau has gathered some of the documents that best depict the barbecue as an early American celebration. Isaac Weld's *Travels through North America during the Years 1795, 96, 97* depicts Americans as being rather fond of "an entertainment they call Barbacue," a "large party meeting together . . . to partake of a sturgeon or pig roasted in the open air." The celebration was, unfortunately, "confined to the lower ranks . . . and it generally ended in intoxication." However, the diary of William Cabell, Jr., of Amhurst County, Virginia, included this entry:

> August 28, 1794, a Barbacue given at the Tye River Warehouse of a Beef, four Muttons, six shoats, and above sixteen Joints of Bacon and sixty gallons of Cider and nearly the same quantity of Spirits—where there was at least 500 People, all behaved Orderly and Decently. . . .

And when the cornerstone was laid for the nation's Capitol in September 1793, a huge barbecue was held in celebration.

In the Deep South, you cooked outdoors if you were poor. The wealthy had their food cooked in small, houselike structures that had open hearths similar to those used in England, where meats were roasted in front of the fire rather than over it. (In modern-day Colonial Williamsburg you can see restored kitchens operating just as they did in Revolutionary times, spit-roasting English and colonial style. But bring a fan with you, since temperatures near the open hearth often register over 120°F.) The same climate that led southern coastal and Caribbean Native Americans to smoke wild game and fish outdoors to preserve them led black Africans to cook outdoors. Also, hot climate, lack of building and cooking utensils, and other factors simply made it natural to build fires and cook outdoors, over an open pit. In time, outdoor barbecuing became so popular that local experts began to sell their products. And by the late 1800s or early 1900s, barbecue was being sold in a few restaurants.

In our travels, we've come across all kinds of barbecue establishments, from hole-in-the-wall joints in the West and Deep South, where the owners only barbecue a few days a week and close the doors when they run out of food, to large modern restaurants equipped with expensive electric motors, timers, and thermostats. The evolution of barbecue as a cooking method brought about refinements in cooking equipment and restaurant design, but it has also created some anxiety among true-blue devotees of closed-pit barbecue. The substitution of gas and electric heat sources for live coals or woods is disdained by most southern, southwestern, and midwestern barbecue purists. It's okay with them to move the process indoors or even to air-condition the kitchen, as long as you don't tamper with the original methods and techniques.

In *open-pit* barbecuing (still popular in the eastern Carolinas and some parts of the Deep South), the meat is placed, uncovered, on a rack directly over a bed of coals at a height removed enough to allow the cooking temperature at meat level to remain a constant 200°–250°F. Open-pit barbecuing has the oldest recorded history of any method of roasting or barbecuing.

Closed-pit barbecuing is a process that uses either a pit dug in the ground or a barbecue cooker on legs, with a lid that encloses the meat. The fire source is below the meat rack. Adjustable vents control the airflow. The meat is usually placed to one side of the coals so that it cooks by indirect heat. By adjusting the vents, the cook can maintain a cooking temperature of approximately 200°–250°F and an intensely smoky environment without an actual flame. Closed-pit barbecue has been used by Polynesians, American Indians (the traditional New England clambake is evidence of this), and particularly by the cowboys of the Southwest and Midwest in the nineteenth century.

Today, these "pits" have evolved into freestanding barbecue units such as the common kettle-type cookers with hoods and racks. With the hood open, you can grill steaks, hamburgers, hot dogs, or chicken, or do open-pit barbecue. With the lid closed, the fire to one side, and the food to the other, the unit becomes a closed-pit–style barbecue cooker that will maintain a low, slow cooking temperature. Another adaptation of the closed-pit barbecue on legs is the water smoker, a three-tiered unit containing a water pan between the fire and the meat. (See page 217.)

Note: If you don't own an outdoor grill and don't have the space or energy to build a barbecue pit, there's still hope. We've included in this book "barbecue" recipes that can be prepared in your oven. But we don't want to mislead you: what you'll get is not true barbecue, but rather "barbecue-flavored" dishes. Don't despair. The good news is that these tempting meals are almost as good as the real thing.

★ CHARCOAL: THAT OLD BLACK MAGIC

It was early man who discovered that charred wood produced a more dependable, even heat than uncharred wood. Eventually someone covered fire with earth to prevent complete combustion—and lo! the art of making charcoal was born. We know that American Indians used live coals for cooking, as did the early French settlers and the English who came to Virginia in 1607, bringing this technique with them. Unlike us, those first settlers didn't have the convenience of buying their charcoal in neat little bags, although the colonists did begin to manufacture charcoal by the end of the seventeenth century. Today, the majority of those who do outdoor cooking prefer the convenience of charcoal briquets to the lump charcoal used by our predecessors.

Yet charcoal briquets were not available to backyard chefs before World War II. The commercial charcoal briquet that is easily available today originated with Henry Ford, of all people. Looking for something practical to do with scrap wood (early autos had many wooden parts), Ford and Charles Kingsford developed means whereby charcoal and wood-distilled chemicals were produced from the scrap lumber. The first briquets were for sale by Ford dealers only. During the 1950s, when outdoor grills began to rise in popularity, retail grocers began to sell them as well. The Clorox Company bought Kingsford Charcoal in 1973, and the first company to sell and distribute briquets nationally was off and running. Kingsford Charcoal continues to account for the major market share of charcoal sales throughout the country.

In tandem with this development, relatively inexpensive barbecue cooking units were beginning to make their appearance in stores and catalogs across the country. The spread of backyard barbecue to suburban America began in earnest during the 1950s and 1960s, and was further enhanced by the introduction of the first national brands of barbecue sauces. From then on, American barbecue fever was on the rise.

Barbecue grew even more popular during the 1970s and 1980s, along with an interest in native American cuisine. The rapid spread of Cajun food went hand in hand with "nouvelle cuisine," which emphasized use of the freshest native produce. Open grilling of both meats and vegetables, accompanied by lighter sauces, paralleled the rejuvenation of midwestern specialties such as meat loaf, batter-fried catfish, and, of course, barbecued ribs.

Mastering the Basics

Nearly every rule about barbecuing springs from ordinary common sense. Barbecuing isn't hard to learn—just a little messy, perhaps. All you really need is patience, some practice to perfect the art, an adventuresome spirit, and this book to guide you on the path to creating great American barbecue.

★ JUST WHAT IS BARBECUE?

It's a common error to refer to grilled foods as "barbecued." Many cookbooks and magazines, probably greatly influenced by the popularity of grilling in what is called "new American cooking" or "California cuisine," frequently use the term "barbecue" when they talk about grilling. Several popular cookbooks on "barbecuing" are actually collections of a wide variety of grilled dishes, with a few true barbecue dishes included here and there. But there is a fundamental difference between the two techniques.

Barbecuing, in the proper sense of the word, is a process of slow cooking over or adjacent to live coals at low temperatures (approximately 200°–250°F). Grilling is a fast cooking process over live coals or any source of strong heat at temperatures ranging from 400°F to over 1000°F. The popular motto for traditional barbecue is "cook it slow and cook it low." In grilling, meat is seared quickly over high heat to maximize juice retention. Steaks, chops, hamburgers, fish, and marinated chicken work well with this method. The high and direct heat produces fast results, sealing in moisture and cooking the food quickly, before it toughens. Grilling is like frying, just as barbecue is similar to slow roasting.

Even early seventeenth-century English cookbooks distinguished between the hot fire cooking methods that we call grilling and the slow cooking process that evolved for roasting (barbecuing) meats. These open-hearth roasting techniques were perfected and passed down, generation to generation, by the early English settlers who cooked large cuts of meat over slow fires and by the Indians, who further modified them. Today's barbecue contest winners still slow-cook whole hogs on open pits along the southeast American coastline, using traditions handed down through the centuries.

Barbecue has many definitions. It can be used as a noun ("let's eat barbecue tonight"); as an adjective ("the meat has great barbecue flavor"); or as a verb ("let's barbecue the ribs"). It can mean an event ("let's have a church barbecue") or an apparatus ("it's time to get out the barbecue").

The Chinese method of "cold-smoking" various meats is excellent, but it, too, is distinct from barbecuing. Today's cold-smoking methods (used in Virginia and Missouri hams, for example), are quite similar to the American Indians' way of preserving meats, except that the smoke is contained within a "house." The meats are hung on open racks at an ample distance from the fire or coals so that they are smoked without actually being cooked. Meats can be smoked for hours or even days in the cold-smoker. (Some old-time methods call for three weeks of smoking.) Then they are usually hung to age and tenderize. Most smoked meats are too tough and undercooked to be used as is, and must be baked in the oven or cooked in some additional way; salt-, sugar-, and brine-cured foods must be soaked before additional cooking. Barbecued foods, on the other hand, are simultaneously smoked *and* cooked, at temperatures low enough to smoke and high enough to cook.

The simple chart below outlines the approximate temperature ranges for cold-smoking without cooking, barbecuing (smoke-cooking), grilling, and the increasingly popular "blackened" grilling at extremely high temperatures made so popular by Paul Prudhomme.

Cold-smoking (Preserving)	85°F or lower
Barbecuing (Smoke-cooking)	200°–250°F
Grilling (Sear-cooking)	300°–1000°F
"Blackening" (Very quick searing)	1000°–2000°F

In open-pit barbecue the fire source and the meat are placed at a considerable distance from one another so that the meat can cook slowly without burning. Closed-pit barbecue creates an intense smoky environment but utilizes *indirect* heat from live coals to achieve the same low temperature. Both processes occur without flames.

When it comes to barbecuing, there are certain basics that apply no matter what style of barbecue you're preparing. So before you start, here are some important things to remember before you put the meat on the grill.

1. Smoke it slow and keep the fire low.
Authentic American barbecue requires patience and a slow hand. Barbecuing is neither grilling nor cold-smoking, and it can't really be done with gas or electric fires, although you can use gas and electric fire-starters to get the coals going.

To barbecue right, you use low heat (200°–250°F) and smoke from live wood or charcoal fires so that the meat is simultaneously smoked and cooked. Use open-pit methods for lightly smoked meat and closed-pit methods for heavily smoked meat. It is nearly impossible to close-pit barbecue a whole beef brisket in less than 8 hours, and many a prize-winning brisket will barbecue for as long as 24 hours. This slow cooking process may require basting to keep the meat moist, depending upon the kind of meat and the flavor desired. Many experts, though, will smoke a brisket for 24 hours without basting or moving the meat and serve it crunchy on the outside, moist and tender on the inside.

2. Use high heat only when grilling or searing meat.
Searing is sometimes recommended as the first step in a barbecue recipe, before the meat is slow-cooked. Place the meat directly over a hot fire. Cover the grill and leave the air vents open; the oxygen flow will increase the heat. After searing, reduce the heat and barbecue. You may want to use liquid marinades to tenderize some cuts of meat, as well as add seasoning.

3. Don't trim the fat off the meat before you barbecue it.
In traditional barbecuing it's essential that you leave the fat on the meat during barbecuing so that it will continually moisten and baste the meat as its melts. (In a sense, the fat takes the place of a spit or rotisserie.) Position the meat as far from the fire as possible to keep it at a cooking temperature of 200°–250°F. With the fat left on, turning is usually not necessary unless the meat becomes too brown on the underside.

After the meat is cooked, excess fat should be trimmed off before it is served. There is almost always a large amount of fat on a whole cooked brisket. After the cooking process has been completed and the meat has cooled, simply trim away the fat by raising the upper layer of the cooked brisket and slicing out the excess. Then slice the remaining meat. There will be enough "crust" left on the brisket to give everyone a taste of both the juicy, well-done interior and the crisp, smoky exterior.

Fat is essential for producing a flavorful and juicy result when barbecuing. Remember, however, that during the hours of cooking, the fat drips away. For health-conscious people this dripping off is an important factor, since cooking meat this way and trimming away the fat results in less animal fat in the final product than pan-frying the same cut of meat. This natural juice–basting principle applies to open-pit as well as closed-pit barbecuing. A whole hog with the skin and fat left on continually bastes itself, producing a rich flavor and smooth texture. When the meat is chopped, all the fat is sectioned out and thrown away. And thanks to fat, perfect Kansas

City–style barbecued ribs will have a touch of crisp coating on part of the outside of the rib while still being moist next to the bone.

Crust and juice—that's the art of barbecue. We can teach you the "how," but you must perfect the art.

4. Traditional American barbecued meats are almost always well-done.
In nearly all heavily smoked barbecue, the pinkness that you see when the meat is sliced runs *from the outside in*, and is a result of the slow smoking process, not undercooking. (The pinkness of undercooked meat runs from the center out, disappearing toward the surface.) The interior of a properly barbecued rib, for example, should remain moist, with a pinkness toward the outside blending into a crusty exterior. (There are a few exceptions to this rule: some contemporary barbecuers first grill, then slowly barbecue a whole beef tenderloin or boneless prime rib roast, leaving the interior a medium pink or even a rare red. This might be called *nouvelle* barbecue, and it *is* delicious.)

5. Select the right cooker.
There are a variety of barbecue cookers on the market from which to choose, including the popular kettle and rectangular units. Many barbecue aficionados recommend using a *water smoker*. This is a closed unit with a pan at the bottom to hold the charcoal. Above the charcoal is another pan that contains water and sometimes liquid seasoning agents. Above this is the grillwork that holds the meat. This type of smoker has recently become quite popular and can produce excellent smoke-flavored barbecue, especially with dry meats like turkey. Water smokers also tend to intensify smoke flavor. Meats take longer to cook in these units, because the temperature at the top level is lower and the smoke heavier. The only drawback to this method, according to several barbecue contest winners, is that too much heat under the water pan tends to steam the meat and can eliminate the crusty exterior. This can be avoided by removing the water for the last hour of cooking.

Others insist that the *oil drum cooker* makes the best barbecue, having no water unit at all. When building the fire and positioning the meat on the grill in this type of cooker, be careful not to place the meat directly over the coals unless it's at a safe distance.

You can also put an aluminum pan of water in the center of a round unit and build the charcoal fire around the edges, then position the meat above the water pan. The illustration shows how to barbecue for many hours without burning the meat, leaving the interior moist and delicious. (See the Equipment and Supplies chapter at the end of the book for more information on the wide range of combined barbecue and grilling units available today. See also pages 165-67 for instructions on building an open-pit barbecue unit.)

6. Take the weather into consideration when barbecuing.

It's simply common sense, yet many a novice forgets to allow for the state of the weather when barbecuing. A brisket barbecued in summer with the sun bearing down on it will cook far more rapidly than on a cold, blustery day. The meat may tend to dry out, since the unit is being heated by both the sun and the charcoal, so be careful to check the temperature and baste more frequently if necessary. Barbecuing outdoors in winter (which many people do regularly) eliminates the external heat source, so additional charcoal or a longer cooking time is needed to make up the difference. You must also take the wind into consideration. A good barbecue unit will be reasonably well sealed so that it will smoke and slow-cook with only the vents providing the airflow needed to maintain the fire. But if it's windy out, some air will force its way into the various crevices of the cooker. Therefore, hot, blustery summer days will tend to increase the cooking temperature, but cold winter air will tend to lower it.

By learning to control your barbecue unit even when you can't control the elements, you'll be able to produce the kind of barbecue you want all year long.

7. Learn when and how to use sauces.

There are great differences between sauces, marinades, bastes, and dry rubs. Barbecue *sauces* are liquid seasonings applied to food *just before or during eating*. *Marinades* are liquid seasoning mixtures in which foods are soaked *before cooking*. *Bastes* are marinades and other liquid mixtures applied *during the cooking process*. (Some marinades double as bastes.) *Dry rubs* are mixtures of dry seasonings that are applied *before the barbecue process begins.* All enhance that famous barbecue taste, but each has specific uses.

A common error novices make is to put red tomato and sweet barbecue sauces on the barbecue before or during the entire cooking process. Although most people would not consider cooking asparagus *in* Hollandaise sauce, many see nothing wrong with marinating or continuously basting barbecued meats with tomato-based sauces. To barbecue pros, this is sacrilege! Marinate in vinegar-based liquid or use a dry rub, yes. But a red table sauce? Definitely not. Tomato-based and heavily sweetened barbecue sauces tend to burn and turn black and are intended to be served *alongside* cooked meat, or used during final basting. This is not the case with vinegar- or wine-based basting liquids.

Barbecue sauces are generally served at the table so that diners can add them to their plates as desired. Many pros, however, baste the meat during the last 30 to 45 minutes of cooking with their favorite barbecue sauces. This seals the meat and provides an excellent aroma and taste, producing a crust and flavoring the barbecued meat without giving it a chance to burn. We recommend this technique in many cases. A few barbecue chefs brush on a tomato-based sauce mixed with honey throughout the cooking process, to provide flavor and moisture. But this is a good idea only if the fire is low enough and you prefer a bit of charring on the outside of the meat. Don't forget to check the meat regularly to see that it doesn't burn.

There is great debate among professional barbecuers about pre-seasoning and basting. There are purists who add nothing to the meat, letting the barbecue process itself produce all the flavor they need. Some cooks use no seasonings at all during the cooking process, adding them only after the meat is sliced and served. Others use seasoned dry rubs before the barbecuing begins. Some barbecuers paint on the sauce during the last 30 minutes, and still others baste off and on with non-sugar, acidic bastes. The use of salt is another great source of debate. Some swear that any dry rub containing salt will suck the juices right out of the meat. Yet some prize-winning pros use a sugar and salt mixture before barbecuing and get great results. Our experience shows that salt and a dry rub, when used during true, low-heat barbecuing, add great flavor and do not dry out the meats as some predict.

8. Make the best use of wood.

Your selection of woods for barbecuing should depend on availability, cost, and flavor. Mesquite burns quickly and produces the hottest fire. Hickory is the most readily available and produces a heavy smoke flavor. Fruitwood has a mellow taste. Never use pine or other resinous soft wood. When grilling, add the water-soaked wood chips or chunks directly to the coals.

Place a pan of water on the grill of a closed unit, if you wish, to add moisture and maximize smoke flavor and juiciness. To provide continuous moisture, put the water pan over the fire, opposite the meat. Many barbecuers employ only the "dry" method for smoking ribs, though, using no water pan at all to produce the crusty, blackened rib tips.

Wood chips and sawdust are fine for grilling; chunks and logs are best for barbecuing. The longer the wood soaks, the better the smoke. Small chips should sit in water for at least 30 minutes; big chunks of wood, for several hours before cooking. (For more information on woods, see page 32.)

9. Use charcoal briquets for best results.

Charcoal briquets of the best quality burn more evenly, and longer, than wood. Woods can be great, but they are expensive, and require close, expert tending of the unit.

Allow the charcoal to ash down completely, until a light whitish coating covers the charcoal. This allows for the hottest, most even temperature. A small charcoal fire in a closed unit provides an excellent heat source as well as a means of producing smoke from the wood. Heat doesn't escape as it does with open barbecuing, and a little fuel goes a long way.

You can start with between twelve and twenty-five briquets in the unit. This should last from 1 to 2 hours. Add more briquets as needed. (One of the most common errors of the novice barbecuer is to build much too large a fire. Bigger is not better where a barbecue fire is concerned.) Serious barbecuers use cookers equipped with a firebox, a contraption that provides for easy loading of additional charcoal and wood. (See page 30 for more information on charcoal.)

10. Bring meat to room temperature before cooking.

Except when preparing seafood, fish and fowl, adhere to this rule for the most dependable results.

★ QUICK TIPS FOR BETTER BARBECUING AND GRILLING

Vegetables and Fruits

Once you master the technicalities, you can forge ahead, putting your creativity to work. The beauty of barbecue rests in its simplicity. For example, you can prepare a variety of vegetables by wrapping them in foil and placing them directly on charcoal briquets inside a closed barbecue unit. You'll need to add more briquets for cooking meats and vegetables together than for cooking vegetables alone.

All you need for a feast is the vegetable itself, heavy-duty aluminum foil, salt and pepper, oil and butter. We recommend using peanut oil or clarified butter, since they will not smoke or burn at higher temperatures.

Wash and oil the vegetables and wrap them with foil. With a fork, pierce larger vegetables such as potatoes, cucumbers, squash, and eggplant to prevent them from exploding when roasting over the coals. When removing foil watch out for steam!

Using the following methods, you can turn out a variety of beautifully prepared vegetables:

Baked potatoes: Clean the potato and coat it with peanut oil. Pierce it in several places with a fork. Wrap in foil and place directly on hot charcoal. Turn every 10 or 15 minutes for about 45 minutes to 1 hour, or until potato is tender all the way through. Discard the foil and eat the potato with butter or margarine, salt, and pepper.

Squash (butternut, etc.): Wash and oil the squash, pierce with a fork, and wrap in foil. Place directly on hot coals, turning occasionally. After an hour remove the squash and discard the foil. Halve the squash, remove the seeds, and add butter, salt, and pepper for a delicious treat.

Corn on the cob: Pull the husks back (do *not* tear off and discard). Remove the silk. Soak the exposed corn in ice water for half an hour. Wipe dry, brush with butter, and sprinkle with salt. Replace the husks and wrap the corn in aluminum foil. Place the corn directly on the coals for 30 to 40 minutes, rotating every 10 minutes.

Onions: A whole onion can be prepared without wrapping in foil. Simply trim off the end of a very large onion and *bury* it right in the coals. Do not rotate it during cooking. After about an hour, remove the onion with tongs and discard the charred outer skin. Inside will be a smoky, delicious onion, ready to eat.

Frozen vegetables: Place the block of vegetables on a piece of foil approximately three times its size. Season with butter, salt, and pepper. Wrap and seal well. Place on a hot grill for 30 minutes. Remove and serve.

Stuffed vegetables: Vegetables such as squash, potatoes, whole onions, green peppers, and tomatoes can be cleaned and hollowed out and filled with a stuffing of seasoned, minced vegetables. Top with butter and wrap in foil. Place on grill or directly over hot coals and roast for 30 minutes to 1 hour, depending upon the size and kind of vegetable used. (See the index for specific recipes.)

Fruit: Apples and other whole fruits can be cored and filled with a mixture of sugar, seasonings, coconut, and so forth. Wrap the stuffed fruit in foil, place on the grill, and cook for about 20 minutes, or until tender.

You can also skewer fruits, whole or in pieces, just as you would vegetables. Season to taste, baste with butter, and cook on a hot grill.

Fish and Shellfish

Using a wire grilling basket will net you a better fish every time. In fact, any food that easily disintegrates (hamburgers, too) could use a wire basket.

To cook *whole fish* on a grill, place them about 5 inches from a medium-hot bed of coals (approximately 300°F). The rule of thumb is to cook about 10 minutes per inch of thickness, measuring the fish at the thickest part. If you prefer to wrap the fish in foil, figure 15 minutes per inch.

Don't forget to oil the basket or grill as well as the fish prior to cooking, so that the entire fish can be removed intact, without pieces of fish clinging to the basket. Cleanup's easier that way, too.

For *smoked fish*, make a solution of ¼ cup kosher salt per quart of water. Place fish fillets or steaks in a glass, plastic, or other non-corrosive container. Pour the salt water over them and place in the refrigerator over-night. Place the fish in a wire grilling basket and let stand for at least ½ hour before grilling, or until dry to the touch.

A water smoker is best for smoking fish. When the fire is right and the water pan is full, simply place the oiled fish on the oiled grill and cover it. Smoke for 1 to 2 hours, depending on thickness.

Smoked oysters and clams are easily prepared and delicious to eat. Always buy the freshest seafood available. Clean and rinse the shellfish, shuck them in the usual way, and drain off the excess liquid, leaving them on the half shell. Put a drop or two of vegetable oil on each oyster. Season as desired. Let them smoke for 1 hour on a closed-pit grill, using hickory wood for flavor.

Skewered Foods

Skewered foods such as shrimp, cherry tomatoes, mushrooms, and so on, are most attractive if they are left whole. If you want to cut up the vegetables, make sure all the pieces are about the same size.

Arrange the food on skewers, alternating wedge-shaped cuts of meat with flat or round pieces of vegetables. Season as desired. Place on the grill over medium heat and baste with oil or butter, turning occasionally.

If the meat takes longer to cook than the vegetables you are using, you can speed up the process by cutting the meat into long, thin strips and weav-ing them onto the skewers in an S-shaped design, placing the vegetables in between. Some foods, such as shrimp, need only a very brief grilling time, as opposed to larger vegetables, such as small, whole onions, which may need to be briefly parboiled prior to grilling. You can also place the meat on one skewer and the vegetables on another and time it so that both are cooked the appropriate amount of time.

Breads and Baked Goods

Slice a whole loaf of French, Italian, or sourdough bread and spread the slices with herb or garlic butter. Reassemble the loaf, wrap it in foil, and place it on the grill for around 20 to 30 minutes. (See directions on package.) You can also heat pre-cooked brown-and-serve rolls on the grill. Unbaked frozen bread loaves should be allowed to rise according to the manufacturer's directions, then baked in a loaf pan on a covered grill over medium (250°F) indirect heat for approximately 20 minutes.

For tasty Texas-style toast, butter thick slices of bread or halved large buns and place directly on the grill. When the bread starts to turn golden brown, it's ready (although you may prefer to make yours darker, with the grill marks showing).

Frozen pizzas and fruit pies can be wrapped in foil and placed on the grill. Consult the package directions for temperatures and adapt your cooker accordingly. Biscuits and rolls can also be baked this way as long as they are enclosed in disposable foil pans or heavy-duty aluminum foil.

Fatty Foods

When barbecuing meats that are excessively fatty, such as duck, goose, or bacon, place a small aluminum pan directly under the food to catch the drippings, thus avoiding frequent flare-ups.

Spit-Cooking

One of the things that surprises us is that Americans have neglected to include the spit in their barbecue repertoire. Certainly the rotisserie has been used upon occasion, but it isn't really popular for indoor or outdoor barbecuing. Yet spit-roasting has long roots in many cultures.

The earliest colonists had large open hearths with fires arranged to accommodate a spit for roasting in front of the fire rather than over it. This way the juices that dripped from the meat could be collected in a pan for basting, and then for making a sauce. This arrangement is quite sensible, since barbecuing tends to dry out meats, whereas spit-roasting and basting help to keep them moist. By rotating the spit, the meat is basted on all sides continuously, which enhances the flavor.

By placing an aluminum pan under the meat, you can continuously intensify the flavor as well as prevent flare-up caused by fat dripping into the coals. This is important, particularly for turkey or other drier meats, since the loss of juices frequently leads to a grainy, dry meat that tends to crumble when sliced. Nearly all of the barbecue recipes in this book—closed-pit and open-pit—may be done with an electric spit or rotisserie. Whenever possible, we encourage you to use this method, and we offer the following tips for successful spit-roasting:

1. Remove excess fat before placing meat on the rotisserie, to avoid flare-ups.

2. Fix the meat firmly on the spit so that it will not spin loose or slide off as it cooks. Make sure that the meat is well balanced around the spit so that it will turn evenly. (Test by turning the spit in your hands to see if it is overloaded in any direction and readjust as necessary.) Tie any loose appendages such as the wings and thighs of fowl to the main body of the meat, using butcher string.

3. Insert a good meat thermometer in the center of the meat, away from bone or fat. Stay at least an inch away from the spit rod. Make sure that the thermometer is positioned so that it can be read clearly as the meat turns and will clear obstacles such as the lid, grill, and charcoal.

4. Make sure that the spit motor has adequate power to turn a piece of meat of the size and weight you intend to cook. The manufacturer's instructions should clarify this.

5. Place a drip pan under the meat to collect the juices for basting and to prevent flare-up. Add additional flavorings such as spices, fruit juices, wine, vinegar, etc., to the drip pan as desired.

6. If you are using sugar- or tomato-based sauces, apply them to the meat only during the last 30 minutes of cooking.

7. Remove the meat from the cooker when it is 5° *below* the desired

doneness. Do not remove the spit until the meat has cooled for at least 15 minutes. The meat will continue to cook on the inside via the metal spit during this time. Standing gives it a chance to reabsorb its juices. Then remove the spit, slice the meat, and serve it with the accumulated juices, which can be thickened or seasoned additionally with spices and butter if desired.

★ MEATS

Beef brisket and pork ribs are two of the most common cuts for barbecuing in the Midwest and Texas. Before you barbecue them on the grill, though, here are some things worth knowing.

Brisket

The *brisket* is the underside chest muscle from beef cattle, and is tough enough to need tenderizing. You can use a wet, acidic marinade before cooking to help break down the fibers, or you can cook it very slowly, which will accomplish the same thing.

A whole brisket usually weighs anywhere between 5 and 12 pounds untrimmed, depending on the size of the animal. It has a thick end or "point" and a thin or "flat" end. The brisket is covered with fat on one side and has another larger layer of fat that extends inside the point end. The fat acts as a natural baste and adds an excellent taste to the meat as it cooks. Once the meat is done, the fat should be trimmed away and discarded.

Rib Talk

Your choice of *ribs* for barbecuing is determined by the location of the ribs and their weight and size. If you're confused about barbecued pork ribs and the various names used to identify them, and want to know just how spareribs differ from loin ribs, country back ribs, and baby back ribs, refer to the drawings.

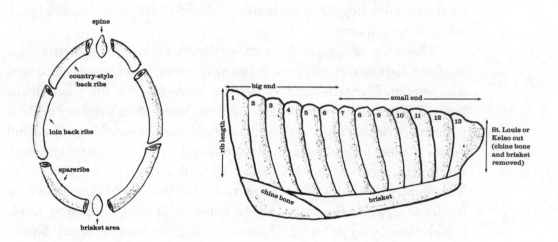

The three main rib cuts—country back, loin, and sparerib.

A slab of spareribs, intact and untrimmed.

Spareribs, which come from the underside and sides of a hog, are the most popular cut of ribs. The entire side of ribs is called a *slab*. A whole slab of spareribs can be cut in half, giving you the smaller, or "short end," ribs on one half and the larger, or "long end," ribs on the other. There is more meat and less bone on "short ends," so they are usually somewhat more expensive in restaurants. Untrimmed spareribs are great, but they have the most bone, gristle, and fat. That's why they are the cheapest rib cut.

When the chine bone and brisket are trimmed off the spareribs, what is left is the *St. Louis*, or *Kelso*, cut (see illustration). If you cut the St. Louis section in half, you again have the long and short ends. If left whole, you have an entire slab of St. Louis–cut spareribs. They cost more, but we recommend this trim of spareribs.

Loin pork ribs, generally the preferred cut, look somewhat like the trimmed St. Louis cut, but require no trimming because they lie between the spareribs and back ribs and have no gristle. They are the most expensive ribs, and the meatiest.

Baby back ribs are just that—ribs from a younger hog. The entire slab weighs less than two pounds. The true "baby backs"—and the best—are from the loin ribs.

Back ribs or *country-style back ribs* are short, spine-split ribs from the back bones of a hog. They are bony, but they do have larger hunks of pork where there is meat.

The lower weight of the entire slab distinguishes the better ribs, regardless of whether they are loin ribs or spareribs. Lower weight indicates a higher ratio of meat to bone. Whole, untrimmed slabs of either loin ribs or spareribs are weighed and labeled as follows: whole slabs weighing under 2 pounds are called "two and down," followed by slabs weighing "three and down," "three to five," and "five pounds and over." Therefore, loin pork ribs (meatiest cut) 2 pounds and down (meatiest weight) are the choicest. The country-style back ribs are also meaty, but have thicker bones and are harder to separate. Spareribs are next in line, with well-trimmed St. Louis or Kelso cuts being preferred. These are the most commonly served "barbecued ribs." Still, if you can afford it, the small loin ribs are tops for meat and have no gristle.

That's rib talk, translated.

★ CHARCOAL: THE SMOLDERING ISSUE

Today, the availability of charcoal briquets has made outdoor cooking a national pastime. As consumers have discovered, though, the quality of charcoal briquets can vary greatly. Most commercial briquets are packaged in 10- and 20-pound bags and may contain a blend of hardwood charcoal, anthracite or sawdust, a lighting ingredient, and starch binders. Sometimes sodium nitrate or lime is added for easier ignition, but better-quality charcoal does not have these ingredients. The greater the percentage of hardwood charcoal, the better the charcoal briquet. Check carefully and you'll find some briquets that are 100 percent hardwood, without additional materials. These are the best, but they may start more slowly. Lump charcoal—pure carbonized wood (with no additives) that has not been pressed into briquets—is occasionally available. It's easy to light and quick to ignite, but it burns out faster than briquets.

Charcoal provides more even heat than wood logs, is easier to start, and has a more consistent quality, since woods are sometimes moist, or still green. Yet many experts prefer all-wood barbecue and have mastered the tricks. One of us (Rich Davis) used mesquite logs exclusively in preparing the barbecue for the Sally Field and James Garner movie, *Murphy's Romance.*

Some of the new charcoal briquets are already impregnated with lighter fluid and are very convenient, since they require no other mechanisms for starting. In a recent comparison conducted in Hawaii of different charcoals (as reported by Jay Hartwell in the *Honolulu Advertiser*), Kingsford's "Matchlite" self-starting charcoal briquets rated very high on ease of starting, and were "the first to be ready." Some charcoal has bits of wood (commonly mesquite) embedded in it to provide wood flavor, so additional chips don't have to be added to the fire. Aside from the charcoal briquets commonly found in supermarkets, there are more unusual types available, including mesquite and oak plain slab charcoal (found in only a few regions).

You may use any charcoal at all for barbecuing, but you should first become familiar with how easily it starts, how long it burns, and how even it keeps the temperature. Of all the charcoals, mesquite burns the hottest, and is therefore best for grilling. But mesquite has a quirky habit of popping and shooting off little sparks, while hickory and oak quietly and calmly smolder away. In other words, charcoal can vary as greatly as the people who use it. But it's still best for barbecue.

Experts often test whether a charcoal fire is ready for cooking by holding their hands about 5 inches from the firebed. They count seconds, using the "one thousand one, one thousand two" method. If they have to remove their hands in 1 or 2 seconds, the fire is hot enough for grilling; 3 to 4 seconds indicates medium heat for slower grilling; 5 seconds is a slow fire. For beginners, the safest and surest way is to place an oven thermometer on the grill at meat level.

If you find that your fire is not hot enough, you can raise the heat by pushing the coals closer together with a pair of tongs, or by opening the vents, or by tapping the ash off the charcoal. If it is *too* hot, lower the temperature by closing the vents or spreading the charcoal away from the meat. Spraying the fire with a little water naturally cools it down, as does lowering the heat source away from the meat, where possible, or raising the meat. *Remember that every time you open the hood during closed-pit barbecuing, you lose both smoke and heat.* It takes approximately 10 minutes to restore a standard-size cooker to its original temperature and smoke concentration. Antsy barbecuers need longer cooking times!

Ember Cooking

Some recipes call for placing foods directly on the hot coals, with some sort of husk or skin (or aluminum foil) used to protect them from charring. Corn on the cob, some thick steaks coated in coarse salt and cracked peppercorns (scraped off after cooking), baked potatoes—even bananas (coated with butter and brown sugar and wrapped in foil)—can be cooked this way. Imagine barbecued dessert!

 THE RIGHT WOODS, AND HOW TO USE THEM

A wide variety of wood can be used for grilling and smoking meats, and modern transportation makes it easy to obtain nearly any variety you want. Wood such as hickory and mesquite is sold at most supermarkets and gourmet grocers, in both chunk and chip form. The chunks or chips are usually soaked in water and added to a charcoal, gas, or electric fire, where they provide smoke (not heat) to flavor grilled or barbecued foods.

For the purposes of barbecuing, you'll want to use hard woods, rather than soft, resinous ones. There are a few other points about using wood that you'll need to understand before you begin barbecuing:

Wood in the form of sawdust or small chips burns fast when placed on the grill, imparting a light, smoky flavor that enhances a quick-seared steak or other food that doesn't need long cooking. These small particles of wood tend to flame and burn up quickly, so they are more appropriate for grilling than true barbecuing. It's important to soak them in water for at least 30 minutes before using so that they'll smolder for a while on top of the fire instead of burning up immediately. When using a gas grill, wrap the soaked chips in aluminum foil poked with holes to keep them from flaring up or clogging the vents with ashes. Place directly on the flames, being careful not to block the gas flow.

For most barbecuing, you need wood in a form that will produce smoke for several hours, so use larger chunks or even small segments of logs. Soak the chunks or logs in water for several hours. (Many barbecuers advise letting large chunks soak overnight.) The size of the wood depends on its purpose, just as the variety of wood you select depends on the flavor you want.

In traditional open-pit barbecue, log fires are started in a small pit away from the cooking pit itself, and the logs are allowed to burn down to embers before they are shoveled directly under the whole hog. The separate fire is continued while the hog cooks so that more embers can be added as needed. (When choosing logs for large barbecues, select greener woods that will burn slower and produce more smoke.) In open-pit barbecuing with charcoal, a secondary bed of charcoal is started and maintained in the same way so that coals can be added to the cooking pit as necessary to keep meat-level temperatures at approximately 200°–250°F. (See pages 165-167 for more on open-pit barbecuing.)

With any given wood, you naturally want to choose a compatibly flavored barbecue sauce. When using hickory wood, buy a hickory-flavored barbecue sauce. The same goes for mesquite. Most premium-grade sauces have a basic or "original" flavor that can be used with any wood.

Every region has its favorite fuel, including:

Alderwood gives a great taste when smoking salmon, but it is not commonly available outside of the Northwest.

Maplewood and corncobs are commonly used in the Northeast, where there is easy access to both. The excellent flavor this combination produces is imparted to some of the famous hams and Canadian bacons that come out of Vermont.

Many common *fruitwoods* are excellent for barbecuing. The most popular and most widely available are *apple, peach,* and *pear. Grapevine clippings* and *cherry wood* also give a good flavor when mixed with other woods. If you're lucky enough to have a contact at a local fruit orchard, you might ask if, after the trees are pruned, you can have the clippings, which are an excellent source of smoke. Smaller clippings can be tossed on the grill when cooking hamburgers or steaks. Soak the larger pieces in water and use them when barbecuing.

Sassafras and *sassafras root* are found in southern Missouri and other parts of the South. The good news is that they impart an unusually delicious flavor to barbecue; the bad news is that they're hard to obtain elsewhere. In addition, certain chemicals contained in sassafras tea are considered health hazards. Although we know of no specific studies on the smoking of foods with sassafras wood or root, you may want to weigh this information carefully before using these materials for barbecuing.

Hickory and *oak* are also native to southern Missouri and most parts of the South, and are traditionally the most popular woods for barbecuing. Hickory is an excellent hardwood that burns slower than softer woods and produces an excellent smoke flavor. Often oak and hickory are used in combination for smoking a Carolina-style whole hog.

Pecan wood is hard to find, and only certain parts of the South seem to have it in abundance. Pecan-smoked foods have a particularly delicate flavor. In addition, pecan doesn't seem to produce the sooty residues that other woods do. It is also excellent for grilling.

Mesquite is most commonly available in arid areas of the Southwest. One of the hardest woods known, it produces a distinct smoky flavor and burns hotter than other hardwoods; hence it is best for grilling. (It's currently one of the "in" woods in the nouvelle Southwest and California cooking.)

Kiawe is the Hawaiian name for an extremely hard wood that botanists say is identical to mesquite. (Its seeds were originally brought to Honolulu in 1828.) Nevertheless, Hawaiians prefer it to mesquite, although one tester at a Hawaiian barbecue said, "You gotta be a connoisseur and eat chicken for three years before you can tell the difference."

★ LIQUID SMOKES, DRY RUBS, WET MARINADES, AND TABLE SAUCES

Liquid Smokes

There are many varieties of liquid smoke, including hickory- and mesquite-flavored products. Some serious barbecuers eschew them, but they do come in handy when you can't cook outdoors.

Natural liquid smoke is made by burning wood over water, which is then processed and filtered to remove noxious or bitter-tasting particles. One hundred percent purified liquid smoke is approved by the FDA and can be a pleasant seasoning for "indoor-barbecued" beans, turkeys, hams, ribs, and other foods; some bona fide barbecue recipes call for it as well. Liquid smoke is not a substitute for a table sauce, and shouldn't be consumed "raw" at all, since it has a bitter taste. (None of the recipes in this book call for *artificial* liquid smoke, and we do not recommend its use.)

Liquid smoke can be combined with water, in a ratio of two parts water to one part liquid smoke, to make a marinade for "indoor-barbecued" meats. Place the meat in a noncorrodible glass, stainless steel, ceramic, or plastic container; heavy-duty, sealable plastic bags are fine. (Never use aluminum or other corrodible metals for marinating.) Place in the refrigerator and let stand for 30 minutes to an hour, turning occasionally. Whole turkeys and large roasts can soak, refrigerated, for several hours. Remove the meat and cook as desired, using an overhead fan, since there will be a strong smoke smell. You'll get a pleasant smoky flavor, although it really doesn't match the taste of an honest-to-goodness hunk of real barbecue.

Dry Rubs

Dry rubs are sometimes called dry marinades, which may seem like a contradiction in terms; both refer to a mixture of spices that is rubbed on meats before cooking, particularly in Southwest- and Midwest-style barbecue. Dry rubs are also excellent for indoor barbecuing. Some of them include powdered smoke, which gives foods an approximation of outdoor wood flavor, even when you're cooking indoors.

Some people use dry rubs on everything. The most common ingredients are salt, pepper, and sugar, followed by varying amounts of paprika, chili powder, garlic powder, and other seasonings, such as cayenne, cumin, and powdered mustard. Some experts like to brush sweet basil over a dry rub to enhance the flavor of lamb. Many cooks brush the meat with a thin layer of prepared mustard before applying a dry marinade. (Mustard contains vinegar, which is a natural tenderizer.) A mustard that is both hot and sweet works well with a rub that includes brown sugar and paprika. But for every chef who swears by the paprika, brown sugar, and spices combination, there's another who seasons his ribs, chicken, and pork with only pepper, or nothing at all. These purists insist that the true barbecue taste comes exclusively from a controlled cooking temperature and the smoking process.

Among those cooks who do use dry rubs, salt is the one ingredient that invariably sparks debate. Several barbecue contest winners caution against its use, claiming that it's a natural toughener and will dry out slow-cooked meat. But others swear by their prize-winning mixes of salt and sugar. We have tasted and prepared excellent barbecue using dry rubs with both salt and sugar. Experiment for yourself and see how you like it. Inventing your own concoctions takes practice, so it's probably a good idea to start with some of the many recipes for wet and dry marinades included in this book.

"Wet" Marinades

According to Webster's, one definition of barbecue is "to cook in a highly seasoned vinegar sauce." In the southern states, where whole hog barbecue is a way of life, vinegar-based "wet" marinades are indispensable. Barbecuers in the Carolinas, Arkansas, Tennessee, Mississippi, Kentucky, and other areas of the South use these mixtures for basting, and pour them into the belly cavity during the last hours of barbecuing a whole hog. Marinades can also be mixed in with or sprinkled over the cooked meat, although many are too pungent to be used as "dipping" sauces.

Traditionally, wet marinades are thin mixtures of vinegar and spices that tenderize the meat from the outside in (instead of burning onto it as a crust, the way sweet tomato-based table sauces do). Some barbecue purists frown on the inclusion of ingredients like beer or soy sauce in their marinades, nor would they use a baste of melted butter and wine. Such ingredients may produce an excellent taste, but those who use them are sometimes viewed as "city folks."

The beauty of a wet marinade is that it can tenderize tougher cuts of meat, such as flank steak and brisket, making them taste like a rich man's bounty. Marinades also work well for pork, chicken, fish, beef tenderloin, and wild game. The secret is to marinate the meat well before putting it on the grill, remembering that fish, shrimp, and skinless chicken require less time than a whole roast. Baste the meat throughout the cooking process for really tasty results.

Our experience has shown that liquid or dry marinades containing tenderizers such as papaya tend to make the meat mushy if it's left in the marinade for any length of time. But if the meat is taken out too quickly, the marinade doesn't have an opportunity to permeate it. Therefore, we don't recommend these types of marinades for barbecuing.

Here are some guidelines for cooking with "wet" marinades:

Beef brisket should marinate overnight prior to barbecuing outdoors slowly at 225°F. Baste every 30 minutes with the wet marinade until done (at least 8 to 10 hours). *Beef roasts* and *whole loins* may be marinated in a wide variety of wine- or vinegar-based marinades that can also be used for basting. Dozier's Market in Fulshear, Texas, uses a simple marinade baste of one part vegetable oil to eight parts vinegar to produce their superior pecan-smoked barbecue.

Pork ribs should marinate for at least 2 hours. Smoke them on a low fire (200°–225°F) for about 3 or 4 hours, basting them every 30 minutes or so.

Chicken should be marinated for 1 or 2 hours, then grilled on a medium fire (300°F). Dip the pieces in the marinade every time you turn them.

Lamb chops should be marinated for 2 hours, large roasts and legs for several hours or overnight. Barbecue at 200°–225°F until done, then finish off with a final squeeze of fresh orange juice.

Trout and *other whole fish* can marinate for 30 minutes to 1 hour and then be barbecued over a low fire (200°F), but *fish steaks* and *seafood* are best quickly grilled over high heat, since they tend to dry and toughen if slow-smoked. A water smoker is particularly effective for producing tender barbecued fish (see page 217).

Table Sauces

The majority of successful table sauces are variations on the theme of a tomato base (in the form of tomato concentrate or ketchup) plus sweeteners such as brown sugar, corn syrup, or molasses, mild and hot spices, vinegar, and occasionally liquid smoke. Among the recipes in this book you'll find outstanding red barbecue sauces, as well as vinegar- and mustard-based sauces, dry rubs, and wet marinades. But if you prefer the convenience of ready-made sauces, there are plenty from which to choose, and many of the recipes in this book call for specific brands favored by our sources.

★ COLESLAWS

Of all the side dishes typically served with barbecue, coleslaw is the most popular. During our tour of regional America we came across six basic varieties of coleslaw.

The most common was a mixture of cabbage and mayonnaise or whipped salad dressing, along with a bit of vinegar, sugar, and milk. Another combination included vinegar and celery seed in an oil base. There was also a pure vinegar base, with or without sugar, to which celery seed and salt had been added.

In addition to these three basic dressings, we found other varieties in the South. In North Carolina we were served something called "barbecued" coleslaw, which was always pink because it was flavored with barbecue sauce. In the Midwest, we found people like Mrs. Virginia Gregory, who makes her slaw by putting chopped cabbage into a boiled, seasoned salt brine and letting it sit overnight so that it pickles slightly. This makes a crisp, slightly vinegary coleslaw with a delicate flavor. We also came across a Kansas City slaw made with a boiled dressing of vinegar, egg, and milk or sour cream, plus spices.

The best coleslaws we ate were made from fresh cabbage. And by fresh, we don't mean it was bought that day at the grocery store. The cabbage we ate had been picked recently and had no brown leaves or dark stems. It still had a natural crispness and was quite sweet, with a slightly hot taste. The traditional coleslaw recipes included in this book were made using fresh cabbage, and we don't recommend using any other kind.

★ WHAT TO DRINK WITH BARBECUE

You can drink anything with barbecue. All around, the safest choice is water; the most unsavory is milk. In between lie the three favorites—beer, iced tea, and soft drinks. Since barbecue is usually spicy, and sometimes (not always) salty, one usually consumes more fluid with it than with most other foods. That's at least one reason we suggest light-on-the-alcohol, high fluid intake with barbecue.

Wine with barbecue? Why not? There are a number of wines that taste fine with barbecue. Our friend Darryl Corti of Corti Brothers wineries in Sacramento, California, recommends generally young, medium-bodied, fairly fruity red wines such as the Zinfandels, Gamets, Pinots, and some of the Cabernets. Three eastern seaboard wines that Darryl recommends are Cynthiana, an American hybrid, and Baco Noir and Foch, two of the French-American hybrids.

One of our favorites is a fine Chianti; its dry, puckery impact contrasts nicely with the smoky, juicy barbecue. Another is white Zinfandel, the pale-pink variety. The editors of the Time-Life series book *Outdoor Cooking* suggest that the most practical wine to serve with barbecue is a rosé, such as Tavel from Provence or the Cabernet or Pinot rosés from California. The white wines they suggest range from French Muscadets for fish and shellfish to German Piesporters and California Chardonnays.

Your own taste and preferences should rule the day. We fondly still prefer iced tea, colas, and beer.

GOOD NEWS FOR HEALTH-CONSCIOUS CALORIE COUNTERS

Like most health-conscious Americans, we've tried to keep up to date on the latest findings about cholesterol and calories. We asked the National Beef Council and the National Pork Producers Council to give us their latest findings. The information they supplied may dispel some common misconceptions.

We learned that beef and pork are not all that high in cholesterol. Three ounces of slowly cooked, lean, well-trimmed beef contains 76 milligrams of cholesterol. The same amount of roasted barbecued chicken with the skin *removed* contains exactly the same 76 milligrams, and the identical amount of plain grilled shrimp has 129 milligrams. Pork, now being touted as "the other white meat" by the National Pork Producers Council, contains 80 milligrams of cholesterol per 3-ounce serving. And less than a third of the fat in pork is saturated, which is an important consideration for those watching their fat intake. Whichever you choose—seafood, chicken, beef, or pork—the meat should be lean and as fat-free as possible.

People counting calories should know that 3 ounces of cooked lean beef has only 189 calories, compared to 200 calories in an equal amount of lean pork. Three ounces of fried chicken (with skin) tops both, at 246 calories. As far as nutrition is concerned, beef and pork, as well as chicken and seafood, are rich in essential nutrients.

If you're wondering whether or not to barbecue, you might take into consideration the fact that cooking meat slowly at low temperatures in a closed pit allows much of the fat to drip away. You don't have to take our word for it: see for yourself. Put a drip pan under the meat you're barbecuing. Most of the fat collects in the pan, leaving the meat relatively fat free. Finally, you can simply trim off any remaining fat before serving, for an even leaner piece of meat. For the health conscious, that's food for thought.

THE REGIONS

★ A BARBECUE ODYSSEY

Most of the information and many of the recipes in the regional barbecue sections of this book were gathered firsthand as we traveled throughout the country collecting information, quotes, and recipes.

One of us (Rich Davis), in addition to a lifetime devotion to barbecuing, creating sauces (he originated the K.C. Masterpiece barbecue sauces), and sampling barbecue across the country, embarked with his wife upon a personal tour of regional barbecue "hot spots." Averaging five restaurants a day, six days a week for nearly two months, the well-fed couple collected sauces, copied records and recipes, and recorded conversations in cities and rural areas throughout the Sunbelt.

The other of us (Shifra Stein), a former restaurant critic and noted food and travel writer, ate her way through Memphis, Kansas City, and parts of Texas and North Carolina with such zeal that she devoured half her not inconsiderable weight in ribs each day. Interviewing restaurateurs and barbecue contestants throughout the areas, she was able to compile a fascinating picture of regional barbecue in America today.

Not only were the excursions enlightening, but they helped confirm our faith that Americans are enthusiastic about barbecue. In most places we were warmly received, and although we weren't sure owners and chefs would part with their recipes readily, we found that once they understood what we were trying to do, they were happy to help.

In Kansas City, restaurant owners and barbecue contestants opened their homes and their hearts to us, offering us their advice and recipes, many of which are included in this book.

In Memphis, we spent a sauce-drenched weekend writing about and sampling delicious barbecue at the city's famed "Memphis in May" barbecue contest. (Rich has taken on the welcome chore of judging the contest several times in years past.) After gorging ourselves there, we managed to find room to tackle the ribs at such famous restaurants as Charlie Vergos's Rendezvous and Gridley's.

Sam Higgins of Arlington, Texas, author and barbecue aficionado, personally escorted us to every significant barbecue place we could visit in Dallas, Fort Worth, and Arlington. His wife, Becky, a first prize–winning cook herself, served us not only Sam's unbeatable smoked brisket, but also her simple and elegant coleslaw.

Richard Reynolds of the Texas Tourism Development Agency guided us through the Hill Country, where we sampled barbecue in the small German towns outside Austin. In Lockhart, we gorged ourselves on hot link sausage at Kreuz Market, and there experienced our first bottle of cherry-sweet Big Red soda. In the German-Czech community of Taylor, Texas, Rudy Mikeska introduced us to his version of German potato salad and led us to the town's annual church supper, where we sampled and were given recipes for even more potato salad, sausage, and sauerkraut—by then a welcome break from our usual fare of beans and coleslaw.

In North Carolina we traveled throughout the state, gathering information at barbecue championship cook-offs and from experts like Willis Peaden and restaurant owners such as Bill Ellis in Wilson and Wayne Monk in Lexington—who gave us two exactly opposite opinions on how to prepare "the best" North Carolina–style barbecue!

In beautiful Columbia, South Carolina, we spoke with Maurice Bessinger, owner of Maurice's Piggy Park, and his son Lloyd, who were happy to help out with historical references and tours of the restaurant.

As we traveled, we found that most regional barbecue restaurants were family owned and operated. We met husband and wife teams, such as Isaac and Juanita Brannon of Shawnee, Oklahoma; father and daughter teams, like Ernest Alexander and daughter Pamela of Atlanta, Georgia; and extended family operations that included descendents of the three King brothers who founded restaurants scattered throughout Virginia.

We dined in two-room, three-table, freestanding roadside barbecues such as Johnnie Baldwin's in Seminole, Oklahoma, and at large, commercial restaurants such as Luther's in Houston, Texas.

Throughout the South, we never saw a naked wall. Even the most smoke-blackened partition had *something* hanging on it. Philosophical signs abounded ("Why should we worry about a depression when we managed to go broke during the boom?"), and in many places pictures of Jesus hung side by side with graven images of Elvis Presley and John Wayne.

In parts of Texas where hunting is a favorite pastime, the interior of many restaurants greatly resembled a taxidermist's, replete with stuffed bears (Angelo's in Fort Worth), wild boar heads (Gaylen's in Arlington), and even an occasional hippo head (Riscky's in Fort Worth).

We personally sampled barbecue as well as side dishes and desserts in more than two hundred barbecue restaurants across the country. We attended barbecue contests across the South and Midwest, where we nibbled on as much prize-winning pork and beef as we could possibly ingest. (It was a tough job, but somebody had to do it!)

We realized that we may have taken our love of barbecue to extremes, especially since one of us (Rich Davis) won first place in the 1980 American Royal Barbecue Contest for his barbecued pork tenderloin recipe (see page 59). But this is what comes of really enjoying one's line of work.

We found in each region a uniqueness that set it apart from the rest. Each area had its own style of combining meats, sauces, woods, and accompaniments. Almost all of it was delicious, yet distinctly different.

So we invite you to share in our experience, and we hope that you'll enjoy preparing and sampling the food that put regional America on the culinary map.

Midwest

★ KANSAS CITY: A HEARTLAND HAVEN FOR BARBECUE

They say good barbecue is all a matter of personal taste. We agree that some of the best barbecued brisket comes out of Texas, and outstanding barbecued pork can be found in the Carolinas. But it's in the Midwest, and particularly in Kansas City, where you get both barbecued pork and brisket, as well as chicken and lamb of equal caliber. While barbecue is prevalent all over middle America, Kansas City is the city that most typifies the use of the unique sauces, sandwiches, and traditions of the heartland. The barbecue found in this Midwest mecca has made missionaries out of visitors and fanatics out of residents, some of whom can't go a week without a fix of the smoky, tangy stuff.

If you want to know what's so special about Kansas City barbecue, we'd be happy to enumerate its virtues: just hold on to your taste buds. Imagine thin slices of slowly smoked barbecued beef brisket piled high on a cushion of plain white bread and slathered with thick, brick-red sauce. Top with another slice of bread, hickory-smoked ham, more sauce, sliced dill pickle and, yes, one last piece of bread. At least four inches high, this mouth-watering creation is the haute cuisine of the heartland.

What exactly *is* Kansas City barbecue? The answer probably lies somewhere in the roots of this river town, which became, from the early 1900s on, a melting pot of sauces and traditions brought north from the heart of Texas and the open-pit grills of the South, giving rise to Kansas City's famous barbecue sauces. From these sauces, combined with distinctively midwestern barbecuing techniques, Kansas City barbecue has emerged as a unique, yet eclectic kind of cooking.

Barbecue flourished in the urban ghettos of Kansas City during the thirties. This was a time when blues and jazz were synonymous with the beef and ribs served up in the back rooms of speakeasies. Most barbecue places were black owned and operated, and many remain so today. On the famed streets of Vine, Brooklyn, and Highland, where boarded-up buildings and crumbled concrete now mark the passage of better days, black entrepreneurs such as Charlie and Arthur Bryant, George and Ollie Gates, and others took humble food and elevated it to greatness.

But the evolution of Kansas City barbecue really took off in the early years of the Depression, when a long, lean fellow called Henry Perry started selling slabs of open-pit–barbecued ribs on the streets of Kansas City to make ends meet. His barbecue caught on, and he eventually passed his style and techniques down to two young brothers, Charlie and Arthur Bryant.

When Charlie Bryant died in 1952, Arthur took the reins, operating out of his present location at 18th and Brooklyn. Thus began the legend of "King" Arthur, whose barbecue has become a favorite with presidents (Harry Truman and Jimmy Carter), and other well-known figures from writer Calvin Trillin to Emperor Haile Selassie of Ethiopia, who visited Bryant's back in 1937. His visit was the only time anyone can recall when the countermen were awed enough to use tongs to handle the meat. But most barbecue mavens will attest that the countermen's touch is an essential ingredient in the taste of the ribs anyway.

When Arthur Bryant passed away in 1982, some mourned openly for the old days, when you could slide all the way to your chair on the grease-encrusted floor of his establishment. These days, the floors at Bryant's are cleaner, the beef leaner, and the fries crisper and still sizzled in lard at 400°F (which requires extra juice from the Kansas City Power and Light Company). But the old Formica-topped tables remain, along with the same secret recipe for the cayenne-flavored sauce. Some folks say it isn't as hot as it used to be, but that isn't all bad! All you need is a mouth big enough to hold the big-enough-for-two beef sandwich and the huge plate of fries served here.

Once the food of the poor and unemployed, barbecue has risen to new heights; it has even become fashionable and has been a key part of what is now being touted as the new American cuisine. In Kansas City, many barbecue restaurant owners have moved to the suburbs and doubled their business. Today there are nearly sixty restaurants serving up barbecue in Kansas City, and there's a veritable profusion of sauces and styles from which to choose. Along with such old-timers as Bryant's and Gates's are such popular eateries as Hayward's, Bobby Bell's, the Smoke Stack, Rosedale's, Quick's, and the K.C. Masterpiece Barbecue and Grill Restaurant.

Most of these joints are the roll-up-your-shirt-sleeves-and-dig-in kind of places. Rosedale's, for example, is nestled near the railroad tracks and warehouses of a largely industrial district and is a popular luncheon spot where beef and beer go together like champagne and caviar. The restaurant, which opened over half a century ago, serves up to 2,000 pounds of smoked meats on weekends. The owner makes a thin but potent sauce that many admirers swear is the best in Kansas City. But then, they haven't met the fans of the Smoke Stack, which, in addition to the usual fare, also serves a variety of pit-barbecued fresh fish. Other "don't miss" establishments include Stephenson's Old Apple Farm on Old Lee's Summit Road, where hickory and applewood produce fine smoked meats. And when it comes to traditional but upscale barbecue, K.C. Masterpiece Barbecue and Grill has earned a reputation as one of the best places in town to get superior hickory-smoked ribs, succulent slices of pork tenderloin, and pecan wood–grilled specialties at reasonable prices.

While barbecue restaurants abound in Kansas City, there are those inventive and intrepid residents who prefer to make their own smoke ovens. Everything from barrels and refrigerators to cement blocks are used at Kansas City's famous barbecue contests.

In early October the American Royal Livestock, Horse Show and

Rodeo hosts a barbecue competition that brings professional and amateur chefs from around the country to vie for blue ribbons, and the thousands of observers who show up each year get to dine on the contestants' entries. From whole hog barbecue and beef brisket to chicken, smoked fish and ribs, the American Royal Barbecue Contest is the place to find out firsthand from the pros how to fix Kansas City barbecue. Held in conjunction with the American Royal Contest is the Diddy Wa Diddy National Barbecue Sauce Contest, where hot and mild commercial sauces and bastes and dry rubs go head to head in competition. (See the list of barbecue contests, page 229.)

Midsummer, in suburban Kansas City, it's the rapidly expanding Lenexa, Kansas, annual barbecue contest, which is also the official State of Kansas barbecue contest. They'll have to go some, though, to top the historic Kansas barbecue of 1850 at which six whole cattle, twenty hogs, and more than fifty sheep, pigs, and lambs—nearly four tons of meat—were roasted, served, and devoured. Now, *that's* barbecue!

Kansas City barbecue would never have been possible without the flavorful native woods for smoking. As with any cooking method, native products and ingredients provide the basis for a regional style. It's not that hickory or oak, pecan or apple are necessarily the best woods to use. It is merely that whatever hardwood is most accessible—in the Midwest, indigenous hickory and oak—becomes an integral part of local cuisine and accounts for the distinctive taste of the region's barbecue.

Missouri hardwood—hickory in particular—is essential to Kansas City's barbecue success, and the state is one of the nation's largest producers of hardwood charcoal and charcoal briquets. But it takes more than charcoal briquets to produce a hickory-smoked flavor; many barbecuers place soaked chunks of hickory over hickory-based charcoal to get a stronger flavor. Fortunately, wood is now transported from one region to another, making it possible for folks almost anywhere to purchase nearly any wood available in the world for barbecuing. And several firms now package and ship many different kinds of wood chips.

The range of Kansas City's spicy barbecue sauces is virtually unlimited. A sampling of sauces available in supermarkets and restaurants around the city reads like a local and national who's who of the barbecue business. There are probably more varieties of barbecue sauce available in Kansas City than in any other city in the United States. (One local supermarket carries more than sixty varieties and sizes of barbecue sauce.) Add to this the local barbecue restaurants that sell their sauces on the premises, and you've got a virtual Valhalla for lovers of the stuff.

Very few midwesterners use the pure eastern Carolinas type sauce, consisting primarily of peppers bottled in vinegar. The vast majority of midwestern barbecue sauces are red sauces, variations on the theme of a tomato base (in the form of ketchup or tomato concentrate), plus vinegar, sweeteners, hot spices and, occasionally, natural liquid smoke.

In this book you'll find outstanding prize-winning recipes for barbecue sauces, as well as for dry rubs and wet marinades. But many barbecuers buy ready-made sauce, sometimes adding their own distinctive ingredients. Kansas City devotees enjoy such an unparalleled choice of commercial sauces that they know they could eat barbecue for a month without exhausting the possibilities. When you start talking about sauce, Kansas City folks start seeing red. The issue of who's got the best barbecue sauce is a favorite local topic of conversation. And seldom do two barbecue fans agree. There are those who swear by Arthur Bryant's paprika-spiced concoction. Others love Gates & Sons' peppery and piquant version. But in the 1970s and 1980s, a native Kansas City barbecue sauce came on the scene, and it has become the most popular barbecue sauce in the city's history. K.C. Masterpiece barbecue sauce, available in five flavors, accounts for nearly one of every two bottles of barbecue sauce sold in Kansas City.

Most chefs would rather surrender the keys to their cars than give away the secret of a red sauce. And while a practiced taste bud can discern cayenne, sage, or cumin, even though individual spices are not labeled on bottles of commercial sauce, the proportions of the ingredients are a key to the final taste. Creating a great red sauce is indeed a work of art. So use the recipes compiled here, and you may find yourself crowned the Beethoven of barbecue.

 **MEATS**

Rich Davis's Kansas City BBQ Ribs:
The Basic Method

Fixing Kansas City barbecue isn't difficult at all, once you've mastered the basic rules. Try this simple, basic rib recipe to get the hang of the method. Soak several chunks (not chips) of hickory in water for several hours.

Start your charcoal briquets (for lighting instructions, see pages 224–226) and let them ash down—they should be white on the outside—before you place the meat on the grill. Do not spread the charcoal out as for grilling; leave it in a pile to one side of the grill.

Prepare a *dry rub* of the following proportions: 2 parts sugar, 1 part salt, 1 part ground black pepper, and 1 part paprika. Rub on all sides of 3 whole slabs of loin pork ribs (preferably no more than 2 pounds each).

When the coals are ready, place the hickory chunks on top. (They will smoke throughout the cooking process, giving the meat a delicious, distinctive flavor.) Place the ribs fat side up in the smoker or grill, on the side away from the fire. Close the lid, leaving the vents barely open. Do not open the lid except to add more briquets or wood chunks. An oven thermometer should register 200°–225°F at meat level. Some smoke should continue to seep out around the edges of the smoker and through any cracked vents at all times, but don't allow the fire to flare up. (If the wood flares when you add briquets, close the lid tightly to quench the flame; if that doesn't work, spray the fire lightly with water, aiming away from the meat. Flames are no-no's in barbecuing.)

Smoke the ribs at 200°–225°F for 4 to 5 hours. To encourage self-basting, you can stack the ribs and rotate their positions from time to time; you don't need to turn them over unless the fire has gotten too hot and over-browned a side near the coals.

Turn the ribs fat side down during the last 30 minutes of cooking and baste generously with barbecue sauce (Rich uses K.C. Masterpiece) using about ½ cup sauce per side. Let smoke until done.

Let the ribs cool down enough to handle. Serve with additional barbecue sauce on the table.

SERVES 6.

Rich Davis's Hickory-Smoked Barbecued Ribs

2 whole slabs of loin baby back pork
   ribs (approximately 4 pounds)
Prepared yellow mustard
Ground black pepper
Hungarian paprika

Dark brown sugar
K.C. Masterpiece Barbecue sauce
Salt

Lightly rub prepared mustard all over the ribs. Sprinkle lightly with black pepper (no salt) on both sides. Sprinkle generously with paprika on both sides. Crumble dark brown sugar over both sides of the ribs and press into the meat.

Place ribs on the rack of the grill, fat side up, away from the charcoal fire on which water-soaked hickory chunks are smoking. Do not place the ribs directly over the fire, since they must smoke for 4 to 5 hours at 200°– 225°F. Check the fire occasionally to be sure the ribs aren't cooking too fast. There's no need to turn the ribs during cooking, although you may want to restack them occasionally to ensure even cooking.

During the last 30 to 45 minutes of cooking, *salt the ribs*, then coat the top side generously with barbecue sauce. Serve when cool enough to handle. (These ribs are also delicious served cold the next day.)

SERVES 4.

Steve Stephenson's Barbecued Ribs

Stephenson, owner of Steve Stephenson's Apple Tree Inn, and his father, Lloyd, who owns the award-winning Stephenson's Old Apple Farm, swear by a mixture of apple and hickory wood for barbecuing.

1 cup salt
1 cup commercial seasoned salt
1 cup paprika
5 or 6 slabs pork spareribs
    (approximately 15 pounds)

Sauce
2 14-ounce bottles ketchup
3 tablespoons prepared horseradish

3 tablespoons salad mustard (hotter
    than regular mustard)
2 tablespoons Worcestershire sauce
1 tablespoon lemon juice
1 teaspoon celery seed
1/4 teaspoon onion salt
1/4 teaspoon cayenne pepper
1/4 teaspoon liquid smoke
1/4 teaspoon garlic juice

Let the coals run almost to white before you begin cooking the ribs.

Mix all the seasonings together on a large plate. Starting at one end of a slab of ribs, cut between each rib, almost all the way through. Lay each slab in the seasoning mixture, pressing as much of it into the ribs as you can. Flip them and repeat on the other side.

Lay the ribs on the smoker or grill. Let them cook 15 minutes on one side, then turn them over for 15 minutes on the other side. Continue to turn them every 15 minutes until the ribs pull apart easily—about 2 1/2 hours at 225°F.

Combine all the sauce ingredients. Heat and serve with meat.

SERVES 10 TO 14.

Simpson and Davis's Championship Barbecued Spareribs

Guy Simpson and Marvin Davis have won a number of barbecue contests with their own blend of dry seasonings.

1 slab spareribs (approximately 3 pounds)	Celery salt
	Ground black pepper
Liquid smoke	1 12-ounce can beer
Garlic salt	Barbecue sauce of your choice

Pull off the membrane that covers one side of the ribs and the fatty meat portion. (This takes some practice, but with the help of a needle-nose pliers, you should be able to grasp one corner of the meat and pull it off in one shot.) Sprinkle the skinned ribs lightly with liquid smoke and rub it in by hand. Lightly sprinkle the remaining ingredients over both sides of the ribs. Place the ribs on a smoker or pit, using indirect heat, and cook for around 2½ hours, or until the bone is exposed about ½ inch. Turn the ribs every 45 minutes and keep them moist by dabbing them with beer every now and then; the more moisture, the better the ribs. During the last 30 minutes, baste with your favorite barbecue sauce.

SERVES 2 OR 3.

Rich Davis's Barbecued Crown Roast of Pork

Whole crown roast of pork (about 6 pounds)	Dried rosemary
	Minced garlic
Prepared mustard of your choice	K.C. Masterpiece barbecue sauce,
Granulated brown sugar	any label

Coat the roast with your favorite mustard, rubbing it generously on all sides with fingers. Then sprinkle granulated brown sugar over the mustard and press into meat. Finally, coat heavily with the rosemary and minced garlic.

Barbecue the meat in a charcoal barbecue unit with soaked wood chunks on the coals. Cook at 225°F to well-done, about 5 or 6 hours. During the last hour, baste with barbecue sauce. (The roast can also be baked in an oven preheated to 250°F.) Test for doneness with a meat thermometer, to a register of 160°F. Remove, let stand 10 minutes, carve, and serve with additional barbecue sauce.

SERVES 8.

Dick Mais's Prize-Winning Honey-Smoked Pork Loin

Barbecue contest winner Dick Mais recommends smoking this pork loin over a combination of hickory and mesquite. He also believes that the finest way to enjoy the pork loin is with a southern-style mustard-based sauce or one that contains such ingredients as apple cider vinegar, onions, soy sauce, sugar, and blended peppers. (See recipes in the Southeast section.) You can also try it with a red Kansas City sauce.

1½ cups honey	½ cup prepared mustard, such as
1 3- to 6-pound pork loin	Rooker's (a Kansas City brand)
(preferably Canadian)	Any dry rub (see pages 70-71)

Heat the honey until it's the consistency of water, but don't let it boil. Using a large-bore needle and syringe, inject the pork loin with the honey in at least four different sites. Cover the loin with the prepared mustard and the dry rub. Wrap the loin in aluminum foil and let marinate in the refrigerator for at least 6 hours.

Remove the loin and allow it to reach room temperature. Smoke the meat, preferably at 175°F, for 12 hours. If your oven temperature is hotter, keep the heat as low as possible and smoke for 6 to 8 hours. If you like a red sauce, use your favorite brand to glaze the loin during the last 30 minutes of cooking.

SERVES 6 TO 12.

Paul Kirk's Creole-Smoked Sausage

Paul Kirk, Grand Champion of several regional barbecue contests, has earned the title of Kansas City's "Baron of Barbecue." A purveyor of barbecue products, Kirk runs a mail order business: The Recipe Exchange Products Company, P.O. Box 14406-A, Kansas City, Missouri 64152.

7 pounds boneless fresh pork	1/2 teaspoon cayenne pepper
2 large onions, minced	1 tablespoon dried parsley flakes
1 clove garlic, pressed	1/2 teaspoon ground allspice
2 tablespoons salt	1/4 teaspoon powdered bay leaf
2 teaspoons ground black pepper	1/4 teaspoon grated nutmeg
1 teaspoon crushed red pepper	
1 teaspoon paprika	5 yards sausage casing

Grind the pork, using the coarse blade of the meat grinder. (Or have your butcher pre-grind it.) Add the onions, garlic, and the remaining seasonings, and mix thoroughly. Regrind. (Keep the sausage meat as cold as possible when preparing it.) If you can, let the sausage sit in the refrigerator overnight. Stuff into casings and smoke or barbecue. If this sausage is not hot enough for your taste buds, add more crushed red pepper and cayenne, a little at a time. You may want to "try" a little of the sausage meat, pan-frying it before you stuff it into the casing.

SERVES 10 TO 12.

Simpson and Davis's Barbecued Sausage

This recipe, submitted by Guy Simpson and Marvin Davis, took first place in the sausage division at the American Royal Barbecue Contest.

4 pounds pork butt

4 teaspoons salt

4 teaspoons sugar

3 teaspoons rubbed sage

1 teaspoon grated nutmeg

2 teaspoons ground black pepper

1/2 cup water

8 feet sausage casing

Have the pork butt ground coarse. Mix the remaining ingredients together, add to the meat, and work in, using your hands. Stuff the sausage into the casings and put it in the barbecue oven on low heat (225°F) for 2 1/2 hours, turning once. For best results, do not use direct heat.

SERVES 8.

Otis Boyd's Famous Hot Link Sausage

Otis Boyd is the owner of Boyd's Barbecue in Kansas City.

2 1/2 pounds ground pork
(shoulder cut)

2 1/2 pounds ground beef (brisket, round, or sirloin)

2 teaspoons dried sage

2 teaspoons crushed red pepper

2 teaspoons paprika

2 teaspoons ground cumin

2 teaspoons dried sweet basil

2 teaspoons aniseed

2 teaspoons dried oregano

Dash salt and ground black pepper

Mix the meats with the spices. For sausage links, attach 2 1/4-inch sausage casings to the stuffer nozzle on a hand meat grinder. Stuff the casings to the desired length, cut the links, and secure the ends with string. Barbecue at 225°F for 2 hours or slow-smoke at 185°F for 4 hours. For sausage patties, form the meat mixture into a roll and cover with wax paper. Slice the roll into patties and peel off the wax paper. Patties can be fried or grilled.

MAKES 5 POUNDS SAUSAGE; SERVES 8 TO 10.

Rich Davis's Barbecued Whole Tenderloin

This recipe won first prize at the Colorado Beef Growers' Contest, using a whole beef tenderloin, and first prize at the American Royal Barbecue Contest in 1980, using whole pork tenderloin. It is now served at the K.C. Masterpiece Barbecue and Grill Restaurant in Overland Park, Kansas, a suburb of Kansas City.

3 large pork tenderloins (or 1 whole *trimmed* beef tenderloin), at room temperature (approximately 6 to 7 pounds)

Marinade
1 cup soy sauce
1/3 cup Oriental toasted sesame oil
3 large cloves garlic, minced
1 tablespoon ground ginger

1 teaspoon MSG (monosodium glutamate) (optional)

Sauce
1 19-ounce bottle K.C. Masterpiece barbecue sauce, any label
1/3 cup soy sauce
1/4 cup Oriental toasted sesame oil
1 large clove garlic, finely minced

Prepare the marinade: In a small bowl, mix together the soy sauce, sesame oil, garlic, ginger, and MSG (if used). Place the tenderloins in a glass or enameled pan, pour the marinade over, cover with plastic wrap (or seal in a heavy plastic bag), and let marinate overnight in the refrigerator.

Place the tenderloins on a charcoal grill with moistened hickory added, over indirect low fire (225°–250°F). Barbecue with lid closed, turning every 15 minutes and basting with marinade, approximately 1 1/2 hours for pork (for beef, until done to taste).

Prepare the sauce: Mix together the barbecue sauce, soy sauce, sesame oil, and garlic in a small saucepan and heat well. Serve the sauce with the meat.

Note: For indoor barbecuing, cook in an oven preheated to 300°F, following the basting directions above, to desired degree of doneness. Use a meat thermometer for best results.

SERVES 8.

Rich Davis's Barbecued Prime Rib Roast

1 prime rib roast with 4 ribs
   (approximately 5 to 6 pounds)
1 cup sugar
1/2 cup salt

1/2 cup ground black pepper
1/2 cup paprika
K.C. Masterpiece barbecue sauce,
   any label

The roast should be at room temperature. Mix together the sugar, salt, pepper, and paprika to make a dry rub. Coat the roast generously with this mixture. Barbecue in a closed charcoal unit at 200°–225°F. (Do not place the meat directly over the coals.) Add water-soaked wood chunks to assure a smoky cooking environment. Cook for 3 to 4 hours, to preferred doneness (140°F for medium-rare), using a meat thermometer to check. During the last hour of cooking, baste with barbecue sauce. Let stand 10 minutes, carve in thick slices, and serve with additional barbecue sauce for dipping.
    SERVES 6.

Betty Goss's Beef Tenderloin

Betty is surrounded by men—her husband and four sons—who all claim that she fixes the best barbecued beef they ever tasted.

1 whole beef tenderloin (5 to 7
   pounds), trimmed
1/2 cup (1 stick) butter, melted

1 19-ounce jar barbecue sauce
2 teaspoons garlic salt

Marinate the tenderloin overnight in a mixture of the butter, barbecue sauce, and garlic salt. Remove the tenderloin, saving the marinade. Grill the tenderloin for 15 minutes on each side over a hot fire with soaked hickory chips added for flavor. Remove the tenderloin and place it in a roasting pan lined with aluminum foil. Pour the reserved marinade over the tenderloin, fold the foil over, and seal it tight. Cook for 1 hour at 300°F, or to an internal temperature of 140°F for medium rare. (Cook for a shorter time if you want it rarer.) Use a meat thermometer to obtain an accurate reading, inserting the thermometer into the meat and wrapping the foil tightly around it.

SERVES 6 TO 8.

American Restaurant's Barbecued Leg of Lamb

This recipe is simple and the sauce is worth the trouble. It's not traditional Kansas City barbecue, but it is one of the best "nouvelle" barbecue sauces we've tried. The dish is served (with advance notice) at Kansas City's renowned American Restaurant.

1 whole 10-pound leg of lamb, bone in	3 12-ounce bottles beer
1 tablespoon salt	1 bottle white wine
1 tablespoon ground black pepper	8 pounds charcoal
4 cloves garlic, minced	3 pounds applewood chips
2 teaspoons paprika	3 pounds cherry wood chips
3/4 cup fresh chopped rosemary	3 pounds mesquite wood chips

Rub the leg of lamb with the herbs and seasonings, making sure that they are evenly distributed.

Place the wood chips in a large basin and soak in cool water for 1 hour. Place the beer and wine in a metal cake pan. Light the charcoal and let burn until the coals are red. Distribute several handfuls of the mixed wood chips on top of the coals. Set the pan of beer and wine on top of the chips and replace the grate on the grill.

Place the leg of lamb on the grate and cover tightly with the grill lid or aluminum foil, so that a minimum of smoke escapes. Add two handfuls of wood chips every 20 minutes or so to keep the smoke going. Cook until the internal temperature of the leg of lamb is 125°F, or the lamb reaches desired degree of doneness (approximately 3 hours, depending on the heat of the coals). Serve sliced thin, with Natural Rosemary Barbecue Sauce (see below).

SERVES 8 TO 10.

Natural Rosemary Barbecue Sauce

20 pounds lamb shank bones

3 medium onions, peeled and coarsely chopped

6 carrots, peeled and coarsely chopped

1/2 bunch celery, coarsely chopped

1 1/2 cups chopped fresh rosemary

1 1/2 cloves garlic, crushed

10 bay leaves

1/4 cup chopped fresh thyme

2 1/2 cups Hunt's chili sauce

2 cups red currant jelly

3 yellow banana peppers

1/2 cup red wine (optional)

2 tablespoons cornstarch (optional)

Have butcher select good fresh shank bones and have them split or cut on the bandsaw. Place bones in a heavy roasting pan and brown at 425°F until dark brown, 30 to 45 minutes. Transfer bones to a heavy stockpot that holds at least 2 gallons; set aside. Place the onions, carrots, and celery in the roasting pan and bake at 425°F until very brown, stirring every 10 minutes. Add the vegetables to the stockpot with the bones. Cover with cold water and add the rosemary, garlic, bay leaves, and thyme.

Place the pot over high heat and bring to a boil. Reduce the heat and simmer for 6 hours or more. (The longer it cooks, the better the flavor.) Strain out the bones and vegetables and add the chili sauce, currant jelly, and banana peppers to the stock. Simmer over low heat for 1 hour. Sauce should be thickened naturally by this time, but if it seems thin, mix the red wine with the cornstarch, stir in, and cook a few minutes longer.

MAKES ABOUT 8 CUPS.

★ POULTRY AND GAME

Hyatt Regency Peppercorn Duck Club
Smoked Duck

This recipe was specially created for the American Royal Barbecue Contest and can be ordered (upon advance request) at the Kansas City Hyatt Regency's Peppercorn Duck Club.

1 4- to 4½-pound duckling	½ cup salt
1 teaspoon each dried rosemary, fennel seed, aniseed, garlic powder, white pepper, and paprika	Hickory chips

Trim the duck: remove tail, neck flap, wing tips, and knuckles on the legs. Add seasonings to salt and mix well. Rub seasonings all over outside of duck and put 1 tablespoon of the mixture inside the duck.

Soak hickory chips in water for at least 30 minutes and sprinkle on hot coals. The chips will smolder and impart an excellent taste to the duck, which will turn a natural golden red.

Smoke the duck on a banked fire away from the flame for 2½ hours at 200°–225°F. You'll know when the duck is done by pushing on the leg; if it moves freely, it's finished. The internal temperature on the thigh should reach 160°–165°F.

SERVES 2 TO 4.

Dick Mais's Kansas State Championship Cornish Game Hens

2 cups orange juice
3 tablespoons Cointreau
1/4 cup (1/2 stick) butter

4 Cornish game hens
1 cup honey
Paprika

Mix orange juice, Cointreau, and butter over low heat until well blended. Using a large-bore needle and syringe, inject mixture into each side of the breast and thighs of each bird. Add honey to remaining mixture and use for basting.

Smoke 4 to 6 hours on very low heat (200°–225°F) over well-soaked mesquite and pecan woods. Thirty minutes before they are finished, sprinkle the hens with paprika.

SERVES 4.

Buffalo's Barbecued Squirrel

This recipe comes to us courtesy of John F. "Buffalo" Gattenby of Kansas City, who barbecues in his famous refrigerator-turned-smoker (see page 000).

1 squirrel or rabbit, dressed, washed
    and patted dry
1 cup Heinz 57 sauce

1 cup honey
Hickory, cherry, and applewood
    chips

Soak a mixture of hickory, cherry, and applewood chips in a bucket all night before you smoke the meat. (Fresh game should be prepared immediately.) Cook at 200°F in an aluminum tray and baste continually with juices until the meat is tender (at least 1 to 2 hours). Glaze with a mixture of Heinz 57 sauce and honey 20 minutes before you take the meat off the grill.

SERVES 1 OR 2.

Carolyn Wells's Venison Ribs

In that mysterious macho sport of barbecue, few women have dared enter the male domain of competition. But Carolyn Wells is an exception. Wells claims she can pit her ribs against anybody's and has the trophies to prove it.

Slab of venison ribs
½ cup vegetable oil
¼ cup chopped onion
1 teaspoon salt
2 teaspoons Worcestershire sauce

1 bottle Lambrusco
1 bottle Wicker's barbecue sauce
   (or other Carolina vinegar-based
   sauce)

Place the ribs in a pan. Combine the oil, vinegar, chopped onion, salt, Worcestershire sauce, and wine, and pour over ribs. Cover tightly and marinate for 4 days in the refrigerator, turning twice a day. Drain the ribs, place them on a grill at low heat (200°F), and cook for 4 hours, basting with barbecue sauce from time to time. Enjoy with corn on the cob.

SERVES 3 OR 4.

 FISH AND SEAFOOD

Jessica Kirk's Prize-Winning Smoked Catfish

Jessica Kirk is a Kansas State Championship barbecue sauce winner whose simple recipe for catfish hooked the taste buds of the judges.

1 4- to 6-pound whole catfish
Vegetable oil

Salt

Clean and gut the catfish and brush it with oil. Salt lightly. Jessica oils a cheesecloth liberally, ties a knot at one end of it, slips in the catfish, head-first, and hangs it with the tail end up in a drum smoker (see page 221). Slow-cook (at 200°–225°F) for 4 hours. You can also cook the catfish on a piece of aluminum foil or in a wire grilling basket in a closed grill.

SERVES 4.

Dick Mais's Smoked Trout

¹/₄ cup salt
2 cups packed brown sugar
3 cups water

2 8-ounce trout
¹/₂ cup (1 stick) butter
2 tablespoons lemon juice

Combine the salt, 1 cup of the brown sugar, and 2 cups of the water, and let the trout soak in this mixture for 8 hours. Heat the butter, the remaining cup of water and brown sugar, and the lemon juice over low heat until well blended. Smoke the fish over low heat (200°–225°F) for about 2 hours, basting frequently with this mixture. (Dick Mais recommends using apple and mesquite wood for best results.) Trout has a tendency to stick, so oil the outside of the fish and wrap it in cheesecloth.

SERVES 2.

Michael Edmondson's Smoked Trout

Chef Michael Edmondson has been a prize-winning contestant at various midwestern barbecue contests. He says this recipe works well with salmon, swordfish, perch, or oysters. Whatever fish you use, you'll get best results with a water smoker, which helps retain moisture.

1 cup kosher salt
¹/₄ cup coarsely ground black
   pepper
1 tablespoon aniseed
¹/₂ cup sugar
¹/₄ cup mustard seed

10 trout fillets, unskinned
1 medium onion, sliced thin
1 carrot, sliced thin
2 stalks celery, sliced thin
5 tablespoons dried dillweed

Combine the seasonings and sprinkle the trout with this mixture. Place half the onion, carrot, and celery in the bottom of a 9 x 13-inch glass baking dish. Put a layer of trout on top of the vegetables. Cover with remaining vegetables and the dill. Refrigerate for 2 days. Smoke at 200°F until done (about 2 hours). Discard vegetables and serve.

SERVES 5 OR 6.

Kiki Lucente's Barbecued Fish in Cajun Sauce

Kiki Lucente and her husband, Richard, are the proud owners of one of Kansas City's more popular Cajun restaurants, Kiki's Bon Ton Maison.

Sauce
2 medium onions
3 cloves garlic
2 tablespoons chopped fresh parsley
³/₄ teaspoon Louisiana hot sauce
¹/₄ cup vegetable oil
1¹/₂ teaspoons salt

1 cup sauterne wine
1 tablespoon lemon juice
3 tablespoons Worcestershire sauce
1 8-ounce can tomato sauce

4 pounds red snapper or bass fillets

Make the sauce: Put the onions, garlic, parsley, and hot sauce in a blender. Add just enough water to blend. Pour the mixture into a saucepan and add the oil. Cook over low heat for about 40 minutes. Add the salt, wine, lemon juice, Worcestershire sauce, and tomato sauce. Simmer about 1 hour, covered, adding water if needed.

Place the fish on a sheet of heavy-duty aluminum foil and pour the barbecue sauce over fish. Seal foil and place on grill with hood, if possible. Cook for 1 hour over a low fire (225°–250°F), turning every 20 minutes.

Remove fish from foil and place directly on grill for 10 minutes. Turn and cook another 10 minutes, basting with sauce.

SERVES 6.

Deb-Bob's Famous Mahi-mahi

This recipe comes to us courtesy of Chef Michael Edmondson. It also works well with swordfish.

2 cups soy sauce
1 cup pineapple juice
1 cup apple juice
2 whole star anise
1-inch piece fresh ginger, peeled
    and crushed

1 orange, peeled, quartered, and
    sliced thin
2 cloves garlic (or to taste), crushed
1 small onion, peeled and chopped
2 pounds Mahi-Mahi fillets, whole or
    cut into pieces
Dry rub (see pages 70–71)

Combine all the ingredients except the fish in a saucepan. Simmer for 30 minutes. Let cool overnight.

Pour the sauce over the fish; the fish must be covered completely. Marinate in the refrigerator, covered, for 24 to 48 hours.

Remove fish from marinade and sprinkle with dry rub. Smoke fish at 200°F for 1 1/2 to 2 hours, or until done. This is also good grilled over hotter coals.

SERVES 3 OR 4.

Rich Davis's Grilled Skewered Shrimp
and Vegetables

16 fresh large shrimp, peeled and
    deveined
2 large sweet red peppers, cut in
    large cubes
6 small sweet onions, cut in large
    cubes
12 large fresh mushrooms
Soy sauce

Sauce
1/3 cup fresh lime juice
1/3 cup honey
1/3 cup Durkee's Dressing (or
    substitute Dijon mustard)
1/4 cup (1/2 stick) butter, melted
Toasted sesame seeds

Brush the shrimp and vegetables with soy sauce. Thread on 4 skewers, alternating shrimp and vegetables. Mix together the sauce ingredients. Baste the skewered shrimp and vegetables with the sauce and grill over hot coals, approximately 2 to 3 minutes on each side, basting continuously. Remove, sprinkle with toasted sesame seeds, and serve with a dish of the remaining sauce for dipping.

SERVES 4.

Vintage Swine's Championship-Winning Barbecued Shrimp

This recipe appears courtesy of Kansas State Grand Championship winners Jim Roberson and his barbecue team.

Sauce
1 15-ounce can tomato sauce
1 cup Wicker's barbecue marinade
   (or other Carolina vinegar-based
   sauce; see pages 173–177)
1/2 cup brown sugar
1 tablespoon lemon juice
2 tablespoons Worcestershire sauce
1 to 2 tablespoons prepared
   horseradish

2 pounds jumbo shrimp
1 cup (2 sticks) unsalted butter,
   melted
1 cup Wicker's barbecue marinade
   (or other Carolina vinegar-based
   sauce; see pages 173–177).
3 cloves garlic, minced

Make the sauce: Combine all the ingredients in a saucepan. Cook over low heat until sauce is reduced by half.

Clean, devein, and butterfly the shrimp. Combine with the butter, marinade, and garlic, and let marinate for several hours in the refrigerator.

Cook the shrimp over a hot fire for 3 to 5 minutes. (If cooked longer, shrimp will toughen.) Serve with the sauce.

SERVES 2 OR 3.

★ SAUCES AND RUBS

Feel free to experiment with these rubs. For example, you could omit the salt, cut ingredients in half, or add seasoned garlic, celery, or onion salts. Keep trying until you get a combination that works for you.

Cowtown Cookers' Basic Barbecue Rub

John Schlosser and the Cowtown Cookers have won several barbecue competitions using this rub.

2 cups sugar
1 1/2 cups commercial barbecue
    seasoning
3/4 cup salt
1/2 cup seasoned salt

1/2 teaspoon garlic powder
1/2 teaspoon paprika
1/2 teaspoon cayenne pepper
1 tablespoon mustard seed

Combine all the ingredients and mix well. Sprinkle generously on meat and rub it in. Let sit at least 30 minutes before cooking.

MAKES ABOUT 5 CUPS.

Paul Kirk's Basic Barbecue Rub

2 cups sugar
1 cup commercial barbecue
    seasoning

1/2 cup salt

Combine all the ingredients and blend well. Rub heavily on meat before barbecuing.

MAKES 3 1/2 CUPS.

Paul Kirk's Texas Barbecue Rub

1 cup salt
1 cup ground black pepper

1 cup paprika

Mix ingredients well and rub on meat before barbecuing.
    MAKES 3 CUPS.

Rich Davis's Basic Dry Rub

½ cup granulated brown sugar
½ cup coarsely ground black
    pepper
½ cup paprika

¼ cup chili powder
¼ cup salt
2 tablespoons garlic powder

Mix together and rub over meat prior to barbecuing.
    MAKES ABOUT 2 CUPS.

Dick Mais's Southern-Style Vinegar Marinade
and Baste

2 cups apple cider vinegar
1 cup K.C. Masterpiece "spicy"
    barbecue sauce

2 tablespoons lemon juice
1 tablespoon dry mustard

Combine all the ingredients in a saucepan and simmer mixture over low
heat until well blended. Cool. Pour over meat and marinate up to 24 hours
in refrigerator. This mixture acts as a natural tenderizer.
    MAKES ABOUT 3 CUPS.

Dick Mais's Chicken and Fish Marinade and Baste

2 tablespoons Dijon mustard
2 tablespoons lemon juice

$^{1}/_{2}$ cup (1 stick) butter
1 teaspoon Lawry's seasoned salt

Combine all the ingredients in a saucepan and simmer mixture over low heat for 10 minutes. Cover chicken or fish with the cooled marinade and let stand for 30 minutes. Use the reserved marinade for basting.

MAKES ABOUT $^{3}/_{4}$ CUP.

American Restaurant's All-Purpose Natural Barbecue Sauce

Another recipe from Kansas City's American Restaurant, courtesy of chef Ken Dunn.

10 pounds chicken backs, washed
3 onions, peeled and coarsely chopped
1 bunch celery, coarsely chopped
8 carrots, peeled and coarsely chopped
$^{3}/_{4}$ cup chopped fresh thyme
3 cups chopped fresh basil
10 bay leaves

3 cloves garlic, crushed
1 tablespoon whole black peppercorns
2 cups red currant jelly
2 cups Hunt's chili sauce
4 yellow banana peppers
$^{1}/_{2}$ cup white wine (optional)
2 tablespoons cornstarch (optional)

Place the chicken backs in a heavy roasting pan and roast in a 425°F oven until dark golden brown. Pour off grease from pan. Place backs in a heavy-bottomed stockpot. Place the vegetables in the pan in which the backs were cooked and put in a 425°F oven. Brown well, stirring about every 10 minutes.

Add the browned vegetables to backs and cover with cold water. Bring to a boil over high heat, then lower heat, add the thyme, basil, bay leaves, garlic, and peppercorns, and simmer for 6 hours or more. Strain stock and discard bones and vegetables. Put stock back in pot and add the currant jelly, chili sauce, and yellow banana peppers. Simmer for at least 1 hour. If the sauce needs thickening, combine the wine and cornstarch, stir in, and cook a little longer.

Note: A nice variation on this sauce is to take the roasted chicken backs and smoke them on the charcoal grill with hickory or applewood chips before placing them in the stockpot. This will add a natural smoky flavor to the sauce.

MAKES ABOUT 5 CUPS.

Jeanne Bunn's Barbecue Sauce

Mrs. Bunn, of Prairie Village, Kansas, has been making this recipe for over twenty years and it still works every time!

1/4 cup chopped onion
2 tablespoons vegetable oil
2 cups ketchup
1/3 cup honey
1/4 cup Worcestershire sauce
1 teaspoon to 1 tablespoon prepared
  horseradish mustard, to taste
1/2 teaspoon liquid smoke

1 teaspoon white vinegar
1/4 teaspoon garlic salt
1/4 teaspoon cracked black pepper
1/4 teaspoon crushed dried rosemary
1/4 teaspoon crushed dried thyme
1/4 teaspoon crushed dried oregano
1/4 teaspoon dried savory
2 drops Tabasco sauce

Sauté the onion in the oil until tender. Add the remaining ingredients. Simmer, uncovered, for 10 to 15 minutes.

MAKES ABOUT 2 1/2 CUPS.

Cowtown Cookers' Basic Barbecue Sauce

This one's courtesy of John Schlosser.

1 32-ounce bottle ketchup	1 teaspoon garlic powder
1 cup dark molasses	2 1/2 tablespoons dry mustard
1 1/2 tablespoons Tabasco sauce	3 tablespoons white vinegar
1 1/2 medium onions, chopped fine	3/4 cup packed brown sugar
1 large green pepper, chopped fine	1/4 cup liquid smoke
1/2 cup lemon juice	1/4 cup Worcestershire sauce

Combine all the ingredients in a large, heavy pot. Add 1/2 cup water to the empty ketchup bottle, swirl around, and add to pot. Bring mixture to a boil, stirring constantly. Reduce heat and simmer until onion and peppers are tender (about 2 hours).

MAKES ABOUT 6 CUPS.

Frank Pellegrini's Maple Barbecue Sauce

Frank is an amateur barbecuer who has come up with this unique and delicious sauce.

1 medium onion, chopped	1 cup maple syrup
1 tablespoon butter	1/2 teaspoon salt
1/2 cup white vinegar	1/2 teaspoon MSG (monosodium glutamate) or Accent (optional)
1/4 cup sugar	
3/4 cup "original" K.C. Masterpiece barbecue sauce (or other Kansas City tomato-based barbecue sauce)	1/4 teaspoon crushed whole black peppercorns
	1/4 teaspoon paprika
	1 cup beer (preferably Michelob)
4 cups ketchup	1/2 cup wine vinegar (optional)
1/4 cup brown sugar	5 cloves garlic, minced

Sauté the onion in the butter until tender. Add the white vinegar and sugar and bring to a boil. Let stand for 5 minutes, then add the remaining ingredients. Stir well and return to a boil. If sauce is too thick, add about 1 cup water. (If wine vinegar is used, do not add water.) Use at once or store in a covered jar in the refrigerator.

MAKES ABOUT 8 CUPS.

Linda Thomason's Boss Hawg's Sauce

2 cups ketchup
1 tablespoon paprika
¹/₂ tablespoon garlic powder
¹/₂ tablespoon onion powder

¹/₂ tablespoon ground black pepper
¹/₂ tablespoon brown sugar (or honey, to taste)
¹/₄–¹/₂ cup white vinegar (to taste)

Combine all the ingredients in a saucepan and bring to a boil.

MAKES ABOUT 2 CUPS.

 **INDOOR BARBECUE**

Rich Davis's Barbecued Cocktail Sausage Links

1 19-ounce bottle "original,"
    hickory-, or mesquite-flavored
    K.C. Masterpiece barbecue sauce
2 teaspoons garlic powder

4 tablespoons red currant jelly
36 bite-sized smoked and completely
    cooked sausage links

Heat the barbecue sauce in a saucepan. Add the garlic powder and currant jelly, stir thoroughly, and heat. (Do not boil.) Add the sausage links and transfer to a chafing dish over *lowest* heat. Stir occasionally to prevent sticking or burning. Serve as a snack, party food, or as a quick and easy main course.

MAKES 8 TO 12 COCKTAIL SERVINGS.

Rich Davis's Indoor Barbecued Beef Brisket

1 4- to 5-pound beef brisket
Salt and ground black pepper
1 medium onion, diced
3 cloves garlic, minced
1 jalapeño pepper, stemmed, seeded,
   and minced
2 cups hickory- or mesquite-flavored
   K.C. Masterpiece barbecue sauce

1/4 cup white vinegar
1/4 cup Worcestershire sauce
2 tablespoons brown sugar
1 teaspoon salt
2 tablespoons liquid smoke

Salt and pepper the meat to your satisfaction. In a large Dutch oven, sear on all sides over high heat. Reduce heat and add enough water to cover. Add the onion, garlic, and jalapeño pepper. Bring to a boil, then lower heat and simmer, covered, for 2 hours. Remove meat and reserve pan juices.

Preheat the oven to 250°F. Return the brisket to the pot. Mix the barbecue sauce with the remaining ingredients and pour over brisket. Cover and bake for 4 hours.

While the brisket is cooking, place the reserved pan juices in a saucepan and reduce to 1/3 volume over medium-high heat. Set aside and keep warm.

Remove the brisket from the pot and let stand 15 minutes before slicing. Pour the reduced pan juices over the sliced brisket and serve.

Serves 6 to 8.

Art Siemering's Indoor/Outdoor Ribs

Art Siemering is the food editor of the *Kansas City Star* and a devoted fan of barbecue.

4 pounds pork ribs or beef short ribs
1/2 cup strong-flavored beer
1/4 cup light molasses
2 teaspoons commercial gravy
   seasoning (such as Kitchen
   Bouquet or Maggi)

1 teaspoon liquid smoke
1 teaspoon Oriental toasted sesame
   oil (no other oil will do)
Any Kansas City tomato-based
   barbecue sauce

Place the ribs in a large roasting pan. Pour the beer around the ribs and cover tightly with a lid or heavy-duty aluminum foil. Bake at 400°F for 1 hour.

In a small bowl, combine the molasses, gravy seasoning, liquid smoke, and sesame oil; set aside. Remove the ribs from the pan and pat dry with paper towels. Brush the meat with the sauce and grill over hot coals for 6 minutes, or until ribs are well charred. (To finish the ribs in the broiler, place them on the rack, meaty side up, and brush generously with the sauce. Place the rack 4 to 6 inches from the heat and broil 4 to 5 minutes or until browned to taste. Turn and brush with more sauce and broil until done.) To serve, spread each portion over two slices of bread; paint generously with barbecue sauce.

SERVES 4.

Mrs. Kitty Berkowitz's Indoor Baby Back Ribs

Kitty Berkowitz, a barbecue aficionado, is the aunt of Kansas City mayor Richard Berkley. Her barbecued ribs are delicious, with an outdoor smoky flavor.

4 pounds baby back ribs
1/4 cup liquid smoke
1/4 cup tomato sauce
3/4 cup Old Southern Hickory Smoke
    barbecue sauce (or other

hickory-flavored tomato-based
    barbecue sauce)
1 teaspoon salt

Place the ribs in a large roasting pan. Mix the remaining ingredients together and pour over both sides of the ribs. Let stand 1 hour.

Preheat oven to 500°F. Bake the ribs, uncovered, for 10 minutes. Reduce the temperature to 250°F, cover with aluminum foil, and cook 2 hours, basting occasionally. Remove and let cool before serving.

SERVES 4.

K.C. Masterpiece Barbecued Sloppy Joes

Salt and ground black pepper to taste

1 1/2 pounds lean ground beef

1 large onion, chopped

2 cups K.C. Masterpiece barbecue sauce, any flavor

2 tablespoons prepared mustard

8 hamburger buns, split

Salt and pepper the ground beef. Sauté it with the onion in a large skillet over medium-high heat, until the meat is no longer pink and the onion is tender. Drain off excess fat. Stir in the barbecue sauce and mustard and bring to a boil. Reduce heat and simmer for 10 minutes to blend the flavors and thicken the sauce. Spoon over the bottom halves of the buns and top with the remaining halves.

SERVES 8.

Jerry Vincent's Barbecued Chili

Jerry Vincent is Hospitality Management Program Director at Johnson County Community College.

1 pound ground beef

1 cup chopped onion

1 cup "spicy" K.C. Masterpiece barbecue sauce (or other Kansas City tomato-based barbecue sauce)

2 16-ounce cans peeled whole tomatoes, broken up, with their juice

1/4 teaspoon cayenne pepper

1/2 teaspoon garlic powder

3 tablespoons chili powder

1 tablespoon ground cumin

1/2 teaspoon white pepper

1 tablespoon salt

1 teaspoon paprika

1 15 1/2-ounce can red, pinto, or kidney beans

1/4 cup white vinegar

Brown the ground beef and onion in a heavy skillet. Drain off excess fat. Add the remaining ingredients, including the liquid from the beans, and simmer for 30 minutes.

SERVES 3 OR 4.

Variations: Add 1 12-ounce can corn kernels, drained, or top with shredded Cheddar cheese.

If you would like a slightly thicker chili, mix 1 tablespoon Wondra flour with 1 tablespoon of water, add the chili, and simmer until thickened.

Rich Davis's Barbecued Meat Loaf

1¹/₂ pounds lean ground chuck
¹/₂ pound lean ground pork
1 cup chopped onion
1 cup chopped green pepper
2 thick slices dry toast, crumbled
1 egg, beaten
³/₄ cup "spicy" K.C. Masterpiece
   barbecue sauce

3 tablespoons Worcestershire sauce
   (preferably Lea & Perrins)
1¹/₂ tablespoons minced garlic
2 tablespoons chili powder
Salt and ground black pepper to
   taste
1 6- to 8-inch piece fully cooked
   smoked sausage

Thoroughly combine all the ingredients except the smoked sausage. Place the mixture on wax paper and flatten enough to place the sausage down the center. Wrap the mixture around the sausage and shape to form a meat loaf with the sausage in the center. Place in a loaf pan. Make a slight groove in the top and pour in additional barbecue sauce. Bake in a preheated 375°F oven (or on a hot covered barbecue unit) for 1 hour. Remove and let cool 10 to 15 minutes. Turn loaf out of pan and slice; top servings with additional barbecue sauce.

SERVES 4 TO 6.

Ruth Davis's Barbecued Sausage Balls

Ruth Davis is the mother of Rich Davis. She and her late husband, Chick, taught Rich everything they knew about barbecue. These sausage balls are still served at the the family restaurant, Kansas City's K.C. Masterpiece Barbecue and Grill.

1 pound bulk sausage	2 tablespoons brown sugar
1 egg, beaten	1 tablespoon white vinegar
1/3 cup bread crumbs	1 tablespoon soy sauce
1/2 teaspoon rubbed sage	
1/2 cup hickory-flavored K.C. Masterpiece barbecue sauce	

In a large bowl, combine the sausage, egg, bread crumbs, and sage. Shape into small balls. Brown the sausage balls in an ungreased heavy skillet. Drain off excess fat. Mix together the barbecue sauce, brown sugar, vinegar, and soy sauce, and add to the skillet. Simmer over low heat for 20 minutes.

SERVES 6 TO 8.

Rich Davis's Barbecued Sausage Casserole

This is the classic baked bean casserole recipe. It creates a sensation every time you serve it. People even have fun at company picnics after eating this dish!

2 16-ounce cans pork and beans, drained of excess liquid	1/2 cup brown sugar
3/4 cup K.C. Masterpiece barbecue sauce, any label	1 tart apple (such as Jonathan), peeled, cored, and chopped
2 tablespoons golden raisins	6 small fully cooked smoked sausages
1/2 medium onion, chopped	

Combine all the ingredients except the sausages in a flat, 2-quart baking dish. Top with the sausages. Bake, uncovered, in a preheated 350°F oven (or on an outdoor grill-smoker) for 1 hour.

SERVES 6.

Rich Davis's Barbecued Stuffed Cabbage Rolls

This is a great party dish. For a smaller group, reduce quantities by half.

3 pounds lean ground beef
1¹/₂ teaspoons salt
1 teaspoon cracked black pepper
1 tablespoon minced garlic
¹/₂ cup cooked rice
2 tablespoons Worcestershire sauce
¹/₂ cup chopped green bell pepper
1 12-ounce can Ro-Tel tomatoes and chilis, drained and chopped

3 cups chopped onion
2 eggs, lightly beaten
¹/₂ cup crushed plain soda crackers
2 or 3 heads fresh cabbage (enough to yield 36 large leaves)
3¹/₂ cups "original" K.C. Masterpiece barbecue sauce (or other Kansas City tomato-based barbecue sauce)

In a large bowl, mix together by hand the ground beef, rice, Worcestershire sauce, green peppers, tomatoes and chilis, 1 cup of the onions, and the eggs and crackers.

Cut out and discard hard center of the cabbages. (We like to cube the cores and dip them in barbecue sauce for an easy, crunchy, cold hors d'oeuvre.) Place the cabbages in a large kettle and pour boiling water over to cover. Simmer over low heat until the leaves can be easily removed, about 6 or 7 minutes. Leaves should be soft and pliable, but not flabby.

Preheat oven to 350°F. Roll the meat mixture by hand into sausage-like shapes, about 3 inches long and 1 inch thick. Place each meat roll on a cabbage leaf and fold the leaf over the stuffing, tucking in the ends to seal. You will have about 3 dozen stuffed leaves.

Thoroughly grease two 9- by 13-inch oblong roasting dishes or baking pans. Spread the remaining 2 cups chopped onion over the bottom of the pan. Place the cabbage rolls in neat rows on top of the onion, seam side down.

Pour 3 cups of the barbecue sauce evenly over the rolls, and cover the pan tightly with aluminum foil. Bake for 1 hour. Remove foil (watch out for the steam!) and baste the rolls with the pan juices. Uncover and bake for an additional 15 minutes. Serve with the remaining ½ cup sauce spooned over.

SERVES 12 TO 15.

Rich Davis's Oriental Barbecued Chicken Nuggets

This is a skillet dish that makes great party fare; it can also be served as a main course.

1½ pounds chicken breasts, boned and skinned	1½ teaspoons ground black pepper
1 cup white vinegar	1 teaspoon salt
1 cup water	1½ teaspoons paprika
1 tablespoon Oriental toasted sesame oil	1½ teaspoons garlic powder
1 teaspoon Tabasco sauce	½ cup vegetable oil
½ cup flour	Oriental Barbecue Sauce (see below)

Cut the chicken breasts into 1- or 2-inch cubes. Mix together the vinegar, water, sesame oil, and Tabasco sauce, and place the chicken nuggets in this marinade for 30 to 40 minutes only. Remove and pat dry.

Mix together the flour and seasonings and coat the nuggets with this mixture. Pour the vegetable oil into a heavy 12-inch skillet and place over high heat. Add the coated nuggets to the hot oil and brown on all sides for approximately 10 to 15 minutes, or until done. Remove the nuggets and drain on paper towels. Place on a platter or in a chafing dish. Serve immediately, with individual cups of Oriental Barbecue Sauce for dipping.

SERVES 6.

Oriental Barbecue Sauce

1 19-ounce bottle K.C. Masterpiece
    barbecue sauce (original, or
    hickory- or mesquite-flavored)

¹⁄₂ cup soy sauce
¹⁄₄ cup Oriental toasted sesame oil
1 tablespoon ground ginger

Combine all the ingredients in a small saucepan. Simmer, without boiling, for 5 minutes.

MAKES ABOUT 3 CUPS.

Rich Davis's Barbecued Shrimp Cocktail

1 cup water
1 cup white vinegar
2 ounces (4 tablespoons)
    commercial shrimp boil spices
1 pound fresh or frozen shrimp

Sauce
²⁄₃ cup "original" K.C. Masterpiece
    barbecue sauce (or other Kansas
    City tomato-based barbecue
    sauce)
2 tablespoons mayonnaise
1 tablespoon prepared horseradish
    (or to taste)

Place the water, vinegar, and shrimp boil spices in a pot. Bring to a boil. Drop in the shrimp, return to a boil, and boil for 2 minutes for small shrimp, 3 minutes for large shrimp.

Make the sauce: In a small bowl, combine the barbecue sauce, mayonnaise, and horseradish. Chill.

Remove the shrimp to a platter to cool. Cover and refrigerate for 3 to 4 hours. Remove from shell and devein. Place the shrimp in a dish, cover with the sauce, and serve cold.

SERVES 4 TO 6.

The Great American Barbecued Bird

For a holiday or any great meal, roast the Great American Bird with a great American barbecue sauce.

Prepare your turkey for roasting in the usual manner. Prepare your favorite bread stuffing, substituting barbecue sauce for half the broth or other liquid.

Stuff turkey and roast as usual. During the last 30 minutes of roasting, baste turkey with additional barbecue sauce. Pass a bowl of warm barbecue sauce at the table.

American Restaurant's Barbecued Shrimp over Kansas Wheat Pilaf

Selected as a representative of the Midwest in the "Taste of America" reception for the 1985 inaugural week celebration, the American Restaurant served more than twelve thousand shrimp during the three days of this prestigious event. The holder of the Mobil Four-Star, Holiday-Travel, and Cartier dining awards, the American Restaurant offers this taste of Kansas City barbecue.

Presidential Barbecue Sauce
1/4 cup minced onion
1/4 pound carrots, minced
6 cloves garlic, peeled and minced
1/4 cup minced celery
1/4 cup vegetable oil or 4 tablespoons
 (1/2 stick) butter
1 1/4 cups chili sauce
1 1/4 cups ketchup
1 1/3 cups tomato puree
1/4 cup canned tomatoes, broken up,
 with juice

2/3 cup red currant jelly
1/3 cup tomato paste
1/2 pound veal bones, smoked with
 apple and cherry wood on
 barbecue grill or smoker until
 golden brown
1/4 cup fresh sage
1/4 cup fresh thyme
1/4 cup fresh marjoram
2 teaspoons whole black
 peppercorns
2 teaspoons ground cumin

¹/₃ cup dried sage
¹/₄ cup chili powder
¹/₄ cup paprika
Salt to taste
Ground black pepper to taste

2 tablespoons malt vinegar
4 whole bay leaves

6 to 8 jumbo shrimp per person

Sauté the onion, carrots, garlic, and celery in the oil or butter until tender in a heavy-bottomed saucepan. Add the remaining ingredients and simmer for 2 to 3 hours. Press through a strainer. Makes 4 cups sauce, enough for 24 jumbo shrimp.

Peel and devein the shrimp. Place the shrimp in a saucepan and add sauce to cover. Bring to a simmer and cook 4 to 6 minutes, just until shrimp are cooked through. Do not overcook or shrimp will get very tough. (Freeze or refrigerate any leftover sauce for use another time.) Serve over Kansas Wheat Pilaf (see below).

Kansas Wheat Pilaf

Wheat pilaf also makes a wonderful bed for chicken breasts or your favorite casserole. It is similar to rice pilaf, except that the wheat will absorb far more liquid than rice and will have a crunchier texture.

2 cups hard red Kansas wheat
 berries (available in health or
 natural food stores)
12 cups hearty chicken stock (made
 with necks and backs)
¹/₂ cup raw pumpkin seeds, toasted
 to light golden brown

¹/₂ cup (1 stick) unsalted butter
1 tablespoon plus 1 teaspoon minced
 garlic
Kosher salt
Ground black pepper

In a heavy-bottomed saucepan place the wheat berries and 8 cups of chicken stock. Simmer slowly over low to medium heat, stirring occasionally until tender, about 3 to 4 hours. (Add water if necessary.)

While the wheat is cooking, make chicken glaze: Place 4 cups of chicken stock in a saucepan over medium heat. Simmer until no more than 2 tablespoons of the syrupy mixture remains. This will take about 2 hours.

Place the butter in a skillet and melt. Add the garlic and cook over medium-low heat for 3 minutes. Add the chicken glaze and stir thoroughly. Add the cooked wheat, mix thoroughly, and simmer for 5 minutes. Add the pumpkin seeds. Season to taste with kosher salt and freshly ground black pepper before serving.

SERVES 6.

Jim Flynn's Southern-Style Barbecued Shrimp

Jim is a Kansas City food broker who loves heartland barbecue.

1/2 cup chopped onion
1/2 cup chopped celery
1 clove garlic, minced
3 tablespoons vegetable oil
1 16-ounce can (2 cups) tomatoes, chopped
1 cup "spicy" or "original" K.C. Masterpiece barbecue sauce (or other Kansas City tomato-based barbecue sauce)
1 1/2 teaspoons salt

1 teaspoon white vinegar
3/4 teaspoon chili powder (increase to 1 1/2 teaspoons if not using "spicy" sauce)
1 tablespoon Worcestershire sauce
Dash Tabasco sauce
1 teaspoon cornstarch
1 pound raw jumbo shrimp, cleaned and shelled
1/2 cup chopped green pepper

Sauté the onion, celery, and garlic in hot oil until tender. Add the tomatoes, barbecue sauce, and seasonings. Simmer, uncovered, 45 minutes. Mix the cornstarch with 2 teaspoons water and stir into sauce. Cook and stir until mixture thickens. Add the shrimp and green pepper. Cover and simmer until done, about 30 minutes. Serve over a bed of rice.

SERVES 4 TO 6.

★ SIDE DISHES

Rich Davis's Microwaved Stuffed Mushrooms

24 medium mushrooms
1 tablespoon melted butter or
    margarine
1/4 cup chopped green onion
1/3 cup K.C. Masterpiece barbecue
    sauce, any label (or other Kansas
    City tomato-based barbecue
    sauce)

1/4 cup chopped cooked ham
1/4 cup fine dry bread crumbs
1/2 teaspoon garlic salt

Wash the mushrooms; remove the stems, cut off and discard the tough bottoms, and finely chop the rest. Mix the chopped stems in a small microwave-proof bowl or casserole with the butter and green onion. Microwave on high power until tender, 1 1/2 to 2 minutes. Stir in remaining ingredients, except mushroom caps. Mound the mixture in the mushroom caps.

Arrange 12 caps on a paper towel–lined plate, placing the larger caps around the outside. Microwave until hot, 1 to 2 minutes, rotating the plate after half the cooking time. Repeat with the remaining 12 caps. Serve immediately.

MAKES 24 APPETIZERS.

Rich Davis's Barbecued French Onion Dip

1 8-ounce container prepared
    French onion dip
3/4 cup hickory- or
    mesquite-flavored K.C.

Masterpiece barbecue sauce
(or other hickory- or mesquite-
flavored Kansas City tomato-
based barbecue sauce)

In a small bowl, mix together the onion dip and barbecue sauce until well blended. Serve with assorted raw vegetables or chips.
MAKES ABOUT 2 CUPS.

Admiral Joe Yon's Barbecued Cream Cheese

Joe is a retired admiral who likes the smooth richness of cream cheese combined with the spicy bite of barbecue sauce.

1 8-ounce package cream cheese
K.C. Masterpiece barbecue sauce
  (or other Kansas City tomato-
  based barbecue sauce)
Crackers

Place the cream cheese on a tray. Pour the barbecue sauce generously over the cream cheese. Serve with crackers and a knife for spreading.

Rich Davis's Cold Raw Veggies with Hot Oriental Dip

For a spicy treat that's different, this hot dipping sauce with cold veggies is great! It makes a no-fat, no-cholesterol party tray that is really a sensation.

1 recipe Oriental Barbecue Sauce
  (page 83), heated
1 bunch broccoli, cleaned and cut
  into bite-size pieces
1 head cauliflower, cleaned and
  broken into bite-size pieces

2 large carrots, peeled and cut into
  2-inch sticks
2 large stalks celery, cut into 2-inch
  sticks

Pour the hot sauce into a small heatproof dipping bowl in the center of a large tray. Surround the hot dip with the cold veggies and serve.
SERVES 8.

88

Rich Davis's Devilishly Good Barbecued Eggs

4 hard-boiled eggs
1/4 teaspoon salt
2 tablespoons "spicy" K.C.
   Masterpiece barbecue sauce
   (or other spicy Kansas City
   tomato-based barbecue sauce)

2 tablespoons mayonnaise
2 teaspoons finely minced dill pickle
Finely chopped parsley

Cut the eggs in half lengthwise and remove the yolks. Mash the yolks with the salt, barbecue sauce, mayonnaise, and dill pickle. Stuff the egg whites with this mixture. Sprinkle with finely chopped parsley, chill, and serve.
    SERVES 4 TO 8.

Rich Davis's Baked Onion Surprise

Large, flat-bottomed onions (allow 1
   onion per serving)
Butter

Lawry's seasoned salt, or mixture of
   salt and dried oregano and sweet
   basil

Trim away the outer layers of the onions until they are shiny and smooth. Cut off the tops and hollow out the centers about 1 inch deep. Fill the cored center with a large pat of butter and the seasoned salt (allow 1/2 teaspoon per onion). (Be creative and experiment with other seasonings.) Wrap each onion tightly in greased aluminum foil. Place in barbecue cooker or oven (heated to 300°F) and cook for 45 to 50 minutes, or until tender. Remove from the oven or cooker, using a mitt to protect your hand, fold back the foil (watch out for the steam), and serve the onions in their natural juices.

Rich Davis's Saucy Tomato Soup

1 11-ounce can tomato soup
3 tablespoons K.C. Masterpiece
    barbecue sauce, any label (or
    other Kansas City tomato-based
    barbecue sauce)
2 tablespoons minced dill pickle

Prepare the soup according to label directions. Add the barbecue sauce and minced dill pickle. Stir well, heat, and serve with garlic toast.
    SERVES 2.

Paul Kirk's Bayou Hot Slaw

1 medium head cabbage (2$\frac{1}{2}$ to 3
    pounds), shredded and chopped
1 large onion, minced
1 large green pepper, minced
1 small sweet red pepper, minced
4 stalks celery, sliced thin
$\frac{1}{2}$ cup vegetable oil
1 bay leaf
2 tablespoons flour

$\frac{1}{2}$ cup sugar
1 cup water
1$\frac{1}{4}$ cups white vinegar
1 teaspoon Worcestershire sauce
$\frac{1}{2}$ teaspoon white pepper
$\frac{1}{2}$ teaspoon dry mustard
$\frac{1}{2}$ teaspoon garlic powder
$\frac{1}{4}$ teaspoon cayenne pepper

Place the first five ingredients in a large salad bowl and mix well. In a saucepan, heat the oil and bay leaf and stir in the flour, but don't let it brown. Add the sugar and water, stirring until thickened. Pour in the vinegar and the rest of the ingredients, stirring until you have a smooth, thick sauce. Cool to lukewarm and pour over the slaw. Toss and mix well. Chill and serve cold. (If you want a hotter slaw, add more cayenne pepper.)
    SERVES 6.

Virginia Gregory's Country Coleslaw

If you prefer a creamy coleslaw, mix in some whipped salad dressing or mayonnaise before serving this.

1 medium-large head cabbage, shredded (about 8 cups)
2 medium onions, diced (about 2 cups)
3 tablespoons chopped canned pimento, drained

6 tablespoons minced green pepper
3/4 cup white vinegar
1 cup sugar
1/2 teaspoon celery salt
1 heaping tablespoon salt
1 teaspoon celery seed

Mix all the ingredients together well. Add boiling water just to cover and let stand 1 hour. Pack into jars and chill in refrigerator overnight. Drain and salt lightly before serving.

SERVES 6.

Rich Davis's "Barbecue" Coleslaw

1 medium head cabbage, shredded (about 5 cups)
1 medium onion, chopped
1/2 medium green pepper, chopped
1 2-ounce jar pimentos, drained and diced

1 cup sugar
3/4 cup white vinegar
1 tablespoon salt
1/2 teaspoon celery salt
2 cups tomato juice

Mix all the ingredients except the tomato juice together. Heat the tomato juice to boiling, then pour over cabbage mixture just to cover. Cool and refrigerate for 1 or 2 days. Drain off excess liquid before serving.

SERVES 6 TO 8.

Rich Davis's Coleslaw with Boiled Dressing

$^{1}/_{2}$ teaspoon celery salt
$^{1}/_{4}$ teaspoon garlic salt
1 teaspoon dry mustard
$^{1}/_{8}$ teaspoon ground black pepper
$^{1}/_{4}$ teaspoon salt
$^{1}/_{4}$ teaspoon paprika

2 tablespoons sugar
$^{1}/_{2}$ cup water
1 egg
$^{1}/_{3}$ cup cider vinegar
4 cups shredded cabbage

Dissolve the celery salt, garlic salt, dry mustard, pepper, salt, paprika, and sugar in the water. Set aside. Beat the egg lightly in a small, heavy saucepan. Place over low heat, and immediately beat in the vinegar and dissolved spice mixture, stirring constantly until the mixture thickens, about 5 minutes. Chill. Pour over the shredded cabbage and toss well.

SERVES 3 OR 4.

Jim Williams's Coleslaw

This is an unusual coleslaw that we like. For a variation, add 1 teaspoon salt and increase oil to $^{3}/_{4}$ cup.

1 medium head cabbage, shredded
$1^{1}/_{2}$ medium tomatoes, seeded and chopped
1 medium cucumber, peeled, seeded, and chopped
1 medium green pepper, chopped
1 carrot, peeled and chopped
1 cup sliced radishes

$^{1}/_{4}$ teaspoon garlic salt
$^{1}/_{4}$ teaspoon ground black pepper
$^{1}/_{8}$ teaspoon white pepper
$^{1}/_{2}$ cup vegetable oil
$^{1}/_{4}$ cup white vinegar
$^{1}/_{4}$ to $^{1}/_{2}$ teaspoon salt (optional)
$^{1}/_{4}$ teaspoon MSG (monosodium glutamate) or Accent (optional)

In a large bowl, mix together the cabbage, tomatoes, cucumber, green pepper, carrot, and radishes. In a small bowl, mix together the remaining ingredients. Toss this dressing with the vegetables.

SERVES 6.

Rich Davis's Fresh Cilantro New Potato Salad

2 pounds small red new potatoes
Enough chicken broth to cover
   potatoes (approximately 4 cups)
²/₃ cup chopped sweet onion
¹/₂ cup minced celery
2 tablespoons minced fresh cilantro

4 hard-boiled eggs, whites chopped
   and yolks crumbled
Lawry's seasoned salt
Cilantro Mayonnaise (see below)
Salt
Ground black pepper
Paprika

Scrub the potatoes. Cut in half, but leave the skins on. Place the potatoes in a large saucepan, add chicken broth to cover, and bring to a low boil. Simmer until potatoes are tender but not mushy, approximately 15 to 20 minutes. Pour off the chicken broth and reserve for soup or another use. When the potatoes are cool enough to handle, cut them into bite-size pieces. (Peel them first, if you prefer.) Add the onion, celery, cilantro, and egg whites. Sprinkle lightly with Lawry's seasoned salt and add salt and black pepper to taste. Add the Cilantro Mayonnaise, turning gently, until the potatoes are coated and moist. (You may need to add a splash of the reserved chicken broth to moisten.) Transfer to a serving dish and sprinkle with the crumbled egg yolks and paprika. Refrigerate until serving.

   SERVES 6 TO 8.

Cilantro Mayonnaise

2 egg yolks, at room temperature
¹/₂ teaspoon salt
Dash cayenne pepper
1 teaspoon dry mustard
2 tablespoons white vinegar

1 cup vegetable oil
2 tablespoons half and half
3 tablespoons chopped and packed
   fresh cilantro

Whip the egg yolks in a blender until foamy. Add the salt and cayenne pepper. With blender running, add the mustard and vinegar, then slowly add the vegetable oil. When thick, add the half and half and cilantro, and blend well.

MAKES ABOUT 1½ CUPS.

Variation: Substitute ½ cup minced dill pickle for the cilantro in the salad, and substitute 1 teaspoon dried dillweed and 2 tablespoons minced fresh watercress for the cilantro in the mayonnaise.

Paul Kirk's Creole Potato Salad

5 pounds red potatoes
¼ cup vegetable oil
¼ cup white vinegar
1 medium onion, finely chopped
6 stalks celery, finely chopped
6 green onions, thinly sliced
1 tablespoon minced parsley
6 hard-boiled eggs, mashed fine

¼ teaspoon Louisiana hot sauce
1 pinch ground thyme
¼ teaspoon salt
¼ teaspoon white pepper
2 cubes chicken bouillon
1 cup mayonnaise or commercial
  whipped salad dressing

Boil the potatoes until tender, drain, and cool until they can be handled easily. Peel and cut to desired size. Place in a bowl, pour in the oil and vinegar, and mix well. Add the onion, celery, green onions, parsley, and eggs. Mix gently. Add the hot sauce, thyme, salt, and pepper. Dissolve the bouillon cubes in 2 tablespoons water. Pour over salad and toss gently. Add the mayonnaise and mix again. Serve chilled or at room temperature.

SERVES 10 TO 12.

Dick Mais's Bandalero Baked Beans

1 16-ounce can pork and beans, with liquid
1 16-ounce can pinto beans, drained
1 16-ounce can red kidney beans, drained
1 16-ounce can butter beans, drained
1 16-ounce can navy or Great Northern beans, drained

1 cup chopped onion
1 cup "spicy" K.C. Masterpiece barbecue sauce (or other Kansas City tomato-based barbecue sauce)
1 cup chopped smoked sausage or barbecued beef or pork
1 tablespoon liquid smoke (optional)

Preheat oven to 325°F. Combine all the ingredients in an ovenproof dish and bake for 1½ hours. (If you use leftover barbecue, omit liquid smoke.)
MAKES ABOUT 8 CUPS, TO SERVE 10 TO 12.

Steve Stephenson's Barbecued Beans

2 16-ounce cans pork and beans, with liquid
1 12- or 16-ounce can tomatoes, drained
1 cup apple cider
½ cup ketchup
½ cup packed brown sugar

½ medium onion, chopped
2 tablespoons prepared horseradish
1 tablespoon Worcestershire sauce
1 teaspoon seasoned salt
1 teaspoon dry mustard
½ teaspoon ground black pepper
¼ teaspoon Accent

Preheat oven to 350°F. Mix all the ingredients in a shallow 3-quart baking pan. Bake for 1½ to 2 hours.
SERVES 6 TO 8.

Judith Epstein's Non-Kosher Indian-Style Baked Beans

³/₄ pound sliced bacon
2 31-ounce cans pork and beans
¹/₂ cup packed brown sugar
2 tablespoons minced onion
2 tablespoons chili powder
2 tablespoons prepared yellow
   mustard

2 teaspoons liquid smoke
1 cup barbecue sauce of your choice
¹/₂ cup dark corn syrup
¹/₂ cup molasses

Preheat oven to 325°F. Fry the bacon until almost done; drain on paper towels. When cool, tear into small pieces. Pour off a little of the juice from the canned pork and beans, discard the little pieces of pork fat, and combine with the bacon and all other ingredients in a 2- or 3-quart ovenproof casserole. Bake for 1 hour and 15 minutes, uncovered. (You can also cook the beans in a crock-pot for 6 or 7 hours on the low setting.)
SERVES 6 TO 8.

Note: Use the amounts given as a guideline. You may want to use a little less or a little more, depending on your personal taste. If the barbecue sauce you use is spicy, you may want to cut down on the chili powder. If the sauce is smoky, you might want to use less liquid smoke. Taste as you go along and see what happens.

James Williams's Western Beans

2 16-ounce cans pinto beans,
   drained
¹/₂ medium onion, chopped
¹/₂ green bell pepper, chopped

¹/₄ cup brown sugar
¹/₄ cup prepared mustard
³/₄ cup molasses

Combine all ingredients well, pour into a 2-quart casserole, cover, and bake for 1 hour at 350°F.

SERVES 6 TO 8.

Steve and Shirley's Barbecued Baked Beans

Steve and Shirley Bernard are fine cooks who gave us their original recipe for this dish, which we modified. It's the most popular bean dish on the menu at the K.C. Masterpiece Barbecue and Grill Restaurant.

2 16-ounce cans pork and beans, drained
3/4 cup K.C. Masterpiece barbecue sauce, any label
2 tablespoons golden raisins
1/2 cup packed brown sugar
1 tart apple (such as Jonathan), peeled, cored, and chopped
1/2 small onion, chopped
1 teaspoon Oriental toasted sesame oil
3 strips bacon, cut in half (or substitute 2 tablespoons butter or margarine)

Preheat oven to 350°F. Combine all the ingredients except the bacon in a 2-quart baking dish. Top with the strips of bacon or butter or margarine. Bake, uncovered, for 1 hour.

SERVES 6 TO 8.

Microwaved Barbecued Bean Casserole

4 slices bacon, cut into 1-inch pieces
1 medium apple, cored and chopped
1 small onion, chopped
2 16-ounce cans pork and beans, drained
3/4 cup K.C. Masterpiece barbecue sauce, any label (or other Kansas City tomato-based barbecue sauce)
1/2 cup packed brown sugar
1/4 cup golden raisins

Place the bacon in a 2 1/2-quart microwave-proof casserole. Cover with wax paper. Microwave on high power until bacon is browned and crisp, 4 to 6 minutes. Remove bacon and drain. Discard all but 1 tablespoon drippings from casserole. Add apple and onion to casserole and stir well. Microwave on high power until tender, 2 to 3 minutes.

Return bacon to casserole and add the remaining ingredients. Cover with wax paper. Microwave until hot and bubbly, 8 to 10 minutes. Stir halfway through the cooking time.

SERVES 6.

Variation: Add 1 12-ounce package cooked smoked sausage links, cut into ½-inch slices (about 3 cups) along with the pork and beans. Increase the cooking time by 2 minutes.

Jason's Fried Corn

Jason Stein is the teenage son of author Shifra Stein and is, at his tender age, already an aficionado of barbecue.

¼ cup (½ stick) butter or margarine	1 teaspoon garlic powder
2 12-ounce cans yellow corn kernels, thoroughly drained	1 teaspoon lemon pepper seasoning
	1 tablespoon McCormick Salad Supreme (optional)
2 jalapeño peppers, seeded and chopped	Salt
	Ground black pepper

Melt the butter or margarine in a heavy skillet and fry the corn and jalapeños until brown. Add the seasonings and salt and pepper to taste. Corn should be hot and chewy and stick to, and in between, your teeth if it's made right. Supply toothpicks as necessary.

SERVES 4.

Dick Mais's Corn on the Cob

6 ears fresh corn	Salt
1 cup milk	Ground black pepper
½ cup (1 stick) butter	

Shuck and clean the corn. Soak twelve paper towels in the milk. Spread butter on corn, and sprinkle with salt and pepper to taste. Wrap in milk-soaked towels (two towels per ear) and then in aluminum foil. Place on moderate grill for 45 minutes. (Do not place directly over fire.)

SERVES 6.

Lindsay Shannon's Avery Island Potato Pancakes

Lindsay Shannon is an expert backyard chef whose name is synonymous with blues and barbecue in Kansas City.

6 medium red potatoes	Salt
1/2 cup (1 stick) butter	Ground black pepper
1 cup (approximately) milk or half and half	2 eggs
1/2 cup flour	3 to 5 drops Louisiana hot sauce or Tabasco sauce
2 medium onions, grated (optional)	Additional flour for dredging

Place the potatoes in a heavy pot, add water to cover, bring to a boil, and simmer until they are tender (poke them with a 2-pronged fork to test). Pour off the water and mash the potatoes, adding the butter, milk or half and half, flour, onion, salt, and pepper a little at a time. Stick your finger in the potatoes to taste, then add more butter, milk, salt, or pepper if needed. (They should have a thick, mashed potato consistency.) Cover pot and put in refrigerator to chill.

Break the eggs into a bowl and mix in the hot sauce to taste. When the potatoes are cold, shape them into patties, dip them into the egg mixture, and dust with flour. Brush a cast-iron skillet with butter and place over medium-high heat. Fry until both sides of potato pancakes have a crust. Serve hot with barbecued ribs.

SERVES 4.

Serena Hammer's Crimson Sauerkraut

2 27-ounce cans sauerkraut,
   including juice
1 1/2 10 1/4-ounce cans undiluted
   tomato soup
1/2 cup packed brown sugar (plus a
   bit more)

3 tablespoons schmaltz (rendered
   chicken fat) or butter, melted
White sugar to taste

Preheat oven to 350°F. Mix together the sauerkraut, tomato soup, and brown sugar. Rinse out the soup cans with a little water and add. Spoon into a greased 3-quart casserole. Bake, uncovered, for 30 minutes. Reduce the temperature to 300°F and bake another 1 to 1 1/2 hours. Toward the end of the baking time, add white sugar to taste.

SERVES 10 TO 12.

Paul Kirk's Dirty Rice

1/4 cup vegetable oil
2 cups Uncle Ben's converted rice
1 bay leaf
4 cups water
1 green pepper, diced
1 sweet red pepper, diced
4 stalks celery, sliced
1 small onion, minced
1/2 small tomato, diced
1 clove garlic, pressed

1 teaspoon Worcestershire sauce
1 teaspoon crushed red pepper
1/2 teaspoon dry mustard
1/2 teaspoon white pepper
1/4 teaspoon ground cumin
2 chicken bouillon cubes
1/2 pound ground beef
Salt
Ground black pepper

Heat the oil in a 3-quart saucepan with a tight-fitting lid. Add the rice and bay leaf. Stir and sauté until the rice is light brown. Add the rest of the ingredients except the ground beef, bring to a boil, and stir well to make sure that the bouillon cubes dissolve. Cover and turn the heat off. Let sit undisturbed on the burner, without uncovering, for 30 minutes or longer.

In a heavy skillet, sauté the ground beef until well browned. Season to taste with salt and pepper. Just before serving, fold the ground beef into the rice. Serve hot.

SERVES 8.

K.C. Masterpiece Barbecue and Grill's "Dirty Rice"

Rich Davis II suggests this version for people who don't like their "dirty rice" to include chicken livers. This excellent recipe comes courtesy of chef Brad Nordgulen.

1/2 pound ground beef
3 ounces hot pork sausage
1/2 teaspoon minced garlic
1/4 teaspoon cayenne pepper
1/2 teaspoon ground sage

1/2 teaspoon salt
1/2 teaspoon ground black pepper
3 tablespoons finely minced celery
3/4 cup finely chopped onion
6 cups cooked rice

Sauté the ground beef, sausage, and seasonings together over medium-high heat until well browned. Add the celery and onions and continue to cook until they are transparent. Add the rice, stir well, and serve.

SERVES 6 TO 8.

Sautéed Apples

2 1/2 tablespoons margarine or butter
4 sweet, red Jonathan or Winesap
    apples (Granny Smiths are too
    tart, Delicious too mushy),
    washed, cored, and sliced

2 tablespoons brown sugar
1/2 teaspoon ground cinnamon
1/4 teaspoon ground nutmeg

Melt the margarine in a large heavy skillet, add the apples, and sauté over low heat until the apple skins are soft and tender. Sprinkle with the brown sugar, cinnamon, and nutmeg and serve warm. This goes well with pork chops.

SERVES 4.

Ann's Spicy Jalapeño Corn Bread

Ann McAdam is a dear friend and a fearless cook who will try out any new recipe idea.

1 15- or 17-ounce package corn
   bread mix
2 eggs
1 cup water
1 4-ounce can jalapeño peppers,
   drained and chopped

1 8¾-ounce can creamed corn
3 tablespoons chopped onion
1 cup grated Cheddar cheese
1 teaspoon chili powder (optional)

Preheat oven to 425°F. Grease a 9-inch-square pan. Mix all the ingredients together. Pour batter into pan and bake for 40 minutes.

SERVES 6 TO 8.

Carolyn Wells's Corn Bread

3 cups cornmeal
2 teaspoons baking powder
1 teaspoon baking soda
1 teaspoon salt

½ cup Wicker's wet marinade (or
   other Carolina vinegar-based
   barbecue sauce)
1½ cups buttermilk
3 eggs, lightly beaten

Preheat oven to 425°F. Mix together the cornmeal, baking powder, baking soda, salt, and marinade. Add the buttermilk and eggs. For thick servings, pour into a deep-dish 9x12-inch baking pan. For crisp cornbread use a shallow pan or cookie sheet.

Bake for 25 to 35 minutes, or until golden brown and firm.

SERVES 8 TO 10.

Grandma Davis's Homemade Dinner Rolls

1 cake yeast
1 cup milk, scalded and cooled to
   lukewarm
⅓ cup sugar
½ cup (1 stick) butter, melted

3 eggs, separated
Dash salt
4 cups flour
Additional melted butter

In a large mixing bowl, dissolve the yeast in a little of the milk. Let stand 5 minutes. Mix in the remaining milk, the sugar, and the butter. Beat the egg yolks with the salt and add. Mix in the flour. Beat the egg whites until stiff, and fold in. Cover and refrigerate overnight.

Divide the dough into four parts and roll out each to a ¼-inch thickness. Cut each portion into twelve triangles, approximately 3x2x2 inches (or make fewer and larger triangles if you want larger rolls). Brush each triangle with melted butter and roll up, starting with the large end. Place 3 inches apart on a buttered or Teflon-coated baking sheet. Let stand 2 hours at room temperature.

Preheat oven to 350°F. Bake the rolls for 10 to 12 minutes, or until golden brown.

MAKES 3 TO 4 DOZEN ROLLS.

 **DESSERTS**

Paul Kirk's Peanut Butter Custard Cake

A recent finalist in the Rich's Whipped Topping Contest, Paul Kirk's recipe for Peanut Butter Custard Cake came in thirty-sixth out of seven thousand entries. The recipe, in one form or another, has also won several national, state, and local awards, including the Georgia Peanut Commission's Chef's Recipe Contest.

2 envelopes unflavored gelatin

3/4 cup orange juice

1 cup crunchy peanut butter

1/4 cup flour

1 cup plus 3 tablespoons sugar

1/4 teaspoon salt

2 cups half and half

3 eggs, separated

1 hard, stale angel food cake

1 cup heavy cream, whipped

1/2 cup roasted peanuts, chopped

Dissolve the gelatin in the orange juice. Place the peanut butter, flour, 1 cup sugar, salt, and half and half in the top of a double boiler. Heat, stirring, until well blended and thickened. While hot, stir in the gelatin mixture and the egg yolks. Cool.

Beat the egg whites until stiff. Beat in 3 tablespoons sugar. Fold the egg whites into the custard.

Break the cake into bite-size pieces. Layer the cake pieces with the custard in a greased 10-inch tube mold or angel food cake pan. Refrigerate overnight.

Unmold the cake. Top with whipped cream and garnish with the peanuts.

SERVES 12.

Paul Kirk's Sauerkraut Sour Cream Spice Cake

Paul Kirk's unusual Sauerkraut Sour Cream Spice Cake won him second place at the Kraut Packers National Chef's Recipe Contest in New York. And the gentleman is a whiz at barbecue, too!

2 cups packed brown sugar

1/2 cup solid vegetable shortening

3 large eggs

2 cups sauerkraut, drained and
    chopped fine

2 teaspoons ground cloves

2 teaspoons ground cinnamon

2 teaspoons ground allspice

2 1/2 cups flour

1 teaspoon baking soda

1/4 teaspoon salt

1 1/4 cups sour cream

Icing

1 cup packed brown sugar

1/2 cup (1 stick) butter, at room
    temperature

1/4 cup heavy or light cream

1 cup chopped pecans

Cream the brown sugar and shortening. Beat in the eggs, one at a time. Add the sauerkraut and spices, and blend well. Mix together the flour, baking soda, and salt, and add to the batter alternately with the sour cream.

Preheat oven to 375°F. Pour batter into a greased 9x12-inch cake pan and bake for approximately 30 to 45 minutes, or until a knife inserted in the center comes out clean. Turn out and let cool on a rack.

Make the icing: Cream together the brown sugar and butter. Add the cream a little at a time until the icing is smooth.

Spread the icing over the cool cake and sprinkle with the pecans. Place under the broiler just until the icing starts to bubble.

SERVES 10 TO 12.

Thunder Thighs' Indian Bread Pudding

The sister of author Shifra Stein, Judith Epstein (a.k.a. Thunder Thighs) has lost twenty-five pounds since the final editing of this book. We wish to announce that, although she no longer carries the weight for which this recipe is named, she still puts out one heck of a fabulous dessert.

1 loaf bakery-style egg bread (not white bread), sliced
1/2 cup (1 stick) butter
2 cups sugar
3 cups very hot water
1 teaspoon vanilla

2 teaspoons ground cinnamon
2 cups raisins
1 pound mild Cheddar or longhorn cheese, grated
Heavy cream (optional)

Toast the bread lightly and cut off the crusts. Butter on one side and place the slices buttered side down in a greased 9x13-inch glass baking dish. (You should have two layers.) Set aside.

Pour the sugar into a deep, heavy saucepan and place over medium-high heat, stirring constantly, until it melts and becomes a dark caramel color, about 8 minutes. Remove the pan from the heat and, taking care to protect against splattering, slowly pour 3 cups of very hot water in a slow stream into the melted sugar. (At first the sugar will sizzle and harden into lumps, but it will dissolve as the mixture is stirred.) Keep stirring over medium-low heat until completely dissolved, then add the vanilla and cinnamon. Simmer for 1 to 2 minutes more.

Sprinkle the raisins over the bread, and then sprinkle the grated cheese over the raisins. Carefully pour the sugar syrup over all, making sure that all the cheese is moistened with the syrup.

Bake in a preheated 350°F oven for 30 minutes. (Do not let it get too done!) Serve warm, with cream poured over if you don't mind a few extra calories.

SERVES 12.

Marilyn Moore's Sweet Potato Pie

3½ pounds (6 to 8 medium) sweet
   potatoes
Butter
1 cup (2 sticks) butter or margarine,
   melted
4 large eggs
2 cups sugar

½ cup milk
½ cup flour
1 tablespoon grated nutmeg
2 teaspoons ground cinnamon
1 tablespoon baking powder
3 8-inch deep-dish (or 4 regular)
   unbaked pie shells

Wash the sweet potatoes, pat dry, and rub with butter. Put in a saucepan and cover with water. Bring to a boil, turn down the heat, and simmer until tender. Drain the sweet potatoes and let them cool until you can handle them. Peel and cut into ¼-inch slices across the grain of the potato.

Mix together the butter, eggs, milk, and sugar, and add to the sweet potatoes. Sift together the flour, nutmeg, cinnamon, and baking powder. Stir into the sweet potato mixture. Preheat oven to 350°F. Pour the sweet potato filling into the uncooked pie shells. Bake for 40 minutes, or until the filling is firm.

MAKES 3 8-INCH DEEP DISH (OR 4 REGULAR) PIES.

Lindsay Shannon's Sweet Potato Pone in Early Times Sauce

3 cups grated raw sweet potatoes
1/2 cup sugar
1/4 cup unbleached white flour
2 eggs
1/2 cup dark molasses

1/2 to 1 1/2 teaspoons grated nutmeg, to taste
1 teaspoon vanilla
1/4 cup (1/2 stick) butter, melted

Preheat oven to 350°F. Place the potatoes, sugar, flour, eggs, molasses, nutmeg, and vanilla in a large bowl. Pour the melted butter over and mix well. Pour the mixture into a cast-iron skillet for best results. Bake for around 50 minutes, or until firm. Serve warm, topped with Early Times Sauce if you have a really sweet tooth.

Lindsay Shannon's Early Times Sauce

1/2 cup Early Times bourbon (only Kentucky bourbon will do)
1/2 cup (1 stick) butter

1 egg
1 cup sugar

Cut the butter into small pieces and place in a double boiler over hot water until it melts. Combine the egg and sugar in a small bowl and add this to the butter. Stir with a wooden spoon until the sugar dissolves completely and the sauce thickens, about 2 minutes. (Don't let the sauce boil.) Remove from heat and let cool to room temperature. Then slowly mix in the bourbon.

SERVES 6.

Coleen Davis's Wild Huckleberry Pie

Rich Davis's wife, Coleen, is a whiz with desserts. Her excellent recipe for wild huckleberry pie wins raves every time.

Crust
3 cups sifted all-purpose flour
2 teaspoons salt
1/2 teaspoon baking powder
1 teaspoon sugar
3/4 cup vegetable oil
1/4 cup plus 2 tablespoons cold milk

3/4 cup sugar
1/4 cup flour
2 teaspoons quick-cooking tapioca
1 tablespoon lemon juice
2 tablespoons butter
Milk
1/2 teaspoon sugar

Filling
1 quart fresh wild huckleberries (or
    other berries) in season

Make the crust: Sift the dry ingredients together. Pour the oil and cold milk over the dry ingredients all at once. Mix gently, just until blended. Divide into two parts. Roll each part out to a 10- or 11-inch circle. Fit one crust into a 9-inch pie pan. Prick the dough all over. Save the second part of the dough for the top crust.

Make the filling: Mix together the berries, sugar, flour, tapioca, and lemon juice. Pour into prepared crust. Dot with the butter.

Preheat oven to 450°F. Cover filling with top crust and make small decorative slits in the dough. Brush the crust with milk and sprinkle with the 1/2 teaspoon sugar. Bake for 10 minutes, then reduce the temperature to 350°F and bake another 25 to 30 minutes. Pie should be golden brown, with juice bubbling onto the crust. Serve warm.

MAKES 1 9-INCH DOUBLE-CRUST PIE.

Aunt Mary Kay's Cheesecake

This recipe is courtesy of Amy Schmid of Lenexa, Kansas.

Crust
1 3/4 cups fine zwieback cracker
    crumbs (about 20 crackers)
1/4 cup finely chopped walnuts

1/2 teaspoon ground cinnamon
1/2 cup (1 stick) butter, melted
2 tablespoons confectioners' sugar

Filling
4 eggs, well beaten
2 8-ounce packages cream cheese, softened
1 cup sugar
$1/4$ teaspoon salt
2 teaspoons vanilla
$1/2$ teaspoon almond extract
3 cups sour cream

Glaze
1 10-ounce package frozen strawberries, thawed
1 to 2 tablespoons water
1 tablespoon cornstarch
$1/4$ cup sugar
1 or 2 drops red food coloring (optional)

Make the crust: Thoroughly combine the cracker crumbs, walnuts, cinnamon, melted butter, and confectioners' sugar. Press onto the bottom and sides of a 9-inch springform pan. (The sides should be about $1^{3}/4$ inches high.)

Preheat oven to 375°F.

Make the filling: Combine the eggs, cream cheese, sugar, salt, vanilla, and almond extract in a mixing bowl; beat until smooth. Blend in the sour cream. Pour this mixture into the crumb crust. Bake for about 35 minutes, or just until set. Remove and let cool, then chill thoroughly for 4 to 5 hours. (Filling will be soft.)

Meanwhile, make the glaze: Crush 1 cup of the strawberries and place in a small saucepan. Add the water and simmer for 2 minutes; pass through a sieve. Mix the cornstarch with the sugar and stir into the hot berry mixture. Bring to a boil, stirring constantly, and cook until the mixture is thick and clear. Add the red food coloring if desired. Cool to room temperature.

Place the remaining strawberries atop the chilled cheesecake; pour the glaze over. Chill for about 2 hours.

SERVES 10.

Southwest

 BARBECUE: TEXAS SOUL FOOD

In the Deep South, at the edge of the Mississippi River, whole hog barbecue winds down to a trickle, wandering into parts of eastern Arkansas, Louisiana, and Missouri before gradually giving way to beef as the meat of choice in the great Southwest.

Like the whole hog barbecue east of the Mississippi, brisket, beef clod (upper shoulder), hot link sausage, and even goat are preferred in the Southwest, with pork spareribs assuming a secondary role. You can also find chicken and even wild game. But, for the most part, beef is to Texas what pork is to the Carolinas.

Texans will travel long distances for a taste of their favorite barbecue. No matter what the temperature or inconvenience, you'll see long lines in front of Sonny Bryan's in Dallas, Louie Mueller's in Taylor, and Goode Co. in Houston. Each Labor Day weekend, many folks head to Brady, Texas, south and west of Fort Worth, to eat barbecued *cabrito* (goat) at the World Championship Barbecue Goat Cook-Off. And there are many people who will actually fly into Austin and drive the short distance to Lockhart's Kreuz Market to pick up a supply of link sausage, a specialty of Taylor and other German towns located in the central Texas Hill Country surrounding Austin.

Texas-style pit barbecue, part of the traditional cuisine of the Southwest, evolved out of the broad expanse of central Texas's open range, and eventually moved westward to New Mexico and Arizona and north to Oklahoma. The arid, sun-scorched terrain may have seemed inhospitable to some, but not to the people who made this part of the country their home.

The agrarian Pueblo Indians of the Southwest who inhabited the region before the visits by European explorers included the Hopi, Zuni, Papago, Tano, and Pima. The Indians farmed the land, growing *maize* (corn), from which they made bread and tortillas. Their gardens produced beans and squash, and they used the piñon pine and mesquite bush for fuel. In the sixteenth century, the Spanish explorers came, bringing with them horses and longhorn cattle along with new foods such as garlic, onions, tomatoes, sausage, rice, avocados, and citrus fruits, which the Indians adapted to their own cooking. As Spanish and Indian cuisines mingled, Mexican cooking evolved, and with it *frijoles* (beans), corn tortillas, and guacamole.

In the mid-1800s, the first American cowboys, lured by the promise of steady work provided by this vast cattle country, took to the Lone Star State like sauce to meat. A hungry cowboy required "stick-to-the-ribs" food on arduous cattle drives and roundups, and, next to his horse, the chuck wagon became his best friend. This rolling-pantry-on-wheels was manned by a cook who had to be an expert with steaks and chili-laced stews, since cowboys needed to eat three square meals a day. The well-paid chef earned his keep, cooking over an open fire with scanty equipment and a food supply that contained staples such as cured pork, salt, lard, flour, cornmeal, cane sugar syrup, dried beans, coffee, and sourdough starter used for making biscuits and hotcakes.

Most meals were prepared on-the-go, but at the end of the trail, when the herd was in, a steer was cooked up over an open fire. Ernest Bracewell, owner of South Side Market in Elgin, Texas, tells how they did it in his father-in-law's trail-ridin' days:

The cowboys would dig an open pit in the ground and build a hardwood fire. Then they'd skewer the whole beef carcass on a spit made from a wooden pole, which acted as a rotisserie.

The cook would attach a crank to the end of the pole, put the meat over the coals, and keep the fire going until the meat was done clear through.

Chuck-wagon chefs came up with some sauces of their own, which were strongly influenced by now-native wild chilis, onions, cumin, garlic, peppers, and paprika, typical of the seasonings used by the Indians and Mexicans. In fact, it is reported that some range chefs would plant peppers and onions along the cattle trails so that at a later time they would be available for harvesting. The pit method and their ingredients were probably the origins of the style of barbecue so prevalent in South and West Texas today.

As Texas-born Sam Higgins relates, "Out on the range they'd cook a whole cow in a whole day in a hole." Well known in Texas as a barbecue aficionado, author, chef, and caterer, the Arlington-based Higgins experimented with forty different smokers before he wound up using his own creation, a contraption that consists of two metal bathtubs hinged together. The bottom tub contains the grill, and the top tub acts as a lid and vents the smoke. Higgins claims he can cook up to fifty slabs of ribs on his smoker at a time, enough to feed one hundred people.

"Good barbecue," he says, "is cooked the way a cowboy dances, slow, easy, and often. It's as tender as a lady's heart, as moist as her good-night kiss, and as lean as a cowboy's wallet."

 ## SOME TRUTHS AND MISCONCEPTIONS ABOUT TEXAS BARBECUE

Most Texas barbecuers have several things in common. They are mostly men, with the exception of a few strapping women. They usually like the *thought* of hunting but prefer cooking meat to shooting it. They have a pretty good sense of humor about things—except when it comes to their own opinions about barbecue. (This trait seems to be a common denominator for barbecuers across the country. Maybe something in the smoke does it to them.)

The experts rally together on another point. Fewer professionals use mesquite than use hickory or oak. This runs contrary to the widespread belief that mesquite is the most common wood for barbecuing in Texas. Because it burns so hot and fast, mesquite is commonly used for high-temperature grilling, and for finishing off a piece of meat. But it is employed less often for slow barbecuing. The major exception is in the arid parts of West Texas, where mesquite is as common as weeds.

Most barbecue establishments we visited used large sticks of green hickory or oak (usually post, rather than live oak) and, on occasion, pecan. Green wood was preferred by some to dry wood soaked in water, since the green wood contained sap that allowed it to smolder at length, producing a continual stream of the smoke required for flavoring the meat. (However, since green wood is often hard to buy, we've provided information on how to prepare dry wood for barbecuing; see page 33.)

Another common misconception about Texas barbecue is that a red barbecue sauce is applied to the meat while it's cooking. Most barbecuers would never dream of doing this (although some purveyors, such as Dozier's Meat Market in Fulshear, Texas, baste their briskets with a "mop" of liquid marinade—vinegar and vegetable oil—while it's in the pit).

The red Texas-style sauce is different from the thick, richer midwestern variety, and is usually a dark, soupy concoction consisting of a tomato base such as ketchup, plus Worcestershire sauce, chili powder, sugar, spices, and often onions and vinegar. The mixture is usually served on the side for individualists who like to pour it on the meat themselves. Cumin and chili pepper are common seasonings.

As one barbecuer put it: "It's simply a matter of pride: if you put a red sauce on the meat when it's cooking, it's going to make the meat black. If you serve meat with sauce *already* on it, customers around here might think there was something wrong with the meat—otherwise why would you want to mask the taste?" This is an attitude that directly contradicts that of plenty of other barbecuers, particularly in the Midwest, who swear by a final coating of sauce, applied during the last half hour of cooking.

Although most Texans agree that sauce can and should be served on the side, anyone who asks for sauce at Kreuz Market in Lockhart, about thirty miles from Austin, is going to be disappointed. Meat is served here: period. And mostly it's hot spicy sausage, pork loin, prime rib, and juicy pork ribs. If you want sauce, you bring your own. For that matter, don't bother asking for beans, potato salad, or coleslaw either; they aren't offered, as a matter of principle. The only accompaniments are at the counter and include simple things like whole tomatoes, avocados, onions, and cheese. "We concentrate primarily on serving high-quality meat, says Rick Schmidt, who, along with his brother, Don, carries on the tradition passed down to them by their father, Edgar A. "Smitty" Schmidt, who acquired the place in 1948.

To enter Kreuz, you come in through the back door from the parking lot, past the old fire pit (which is hot enough to barbecue the customers). Your order is taken and the smoked meat is slapped down on brown butcher paper and weighed. You pay, grab your "plate," and enter the dining area, where you will find "trimmings" like tomatoes, dill pickles, and onions. And if you're a true urban cowboy, you'll purchase either a long-necked beer or a Big Red (a cherry-flavored soft drink bottled in Waco, Texas) to go along with your lunch.

People drive here from all over the country to sample the food, especially the link sausage that is a specialty of the German settlements found in the Texas Hill Country south and west of Fort Worth. In fact, the place is so popular that 4,000 pounds of shoulder clod (the top of the shoulder), 4,000 pounds of hot link sausage, 650 pounds of prime rib, 600 pounds of pork loin, and about 120 pounds of brisket are served here each week in the summer.

Whether central Texas epitomizes Texas barbecue depends upon your point of view. Some aficionados say that the best barbecue can be found in towns so old they resemble used saddlebags. Indeed, some central Texas restaurants are of the butcher-paper variety, complete with storefronts, peeling paint, and a taxidermist's treasure trove of stuffed game animals. And because health regulations in larger cities tend to be more rigid, mavens say that only in these smoke-encrusted establishments can you find the real "greats" of barbecue. But as we discovered in our travels across the country, small towns can also harbor well-scrubbed places that put out good food.

Take Rudy Mikeska's, for example. Located a few miles from Austin, in the German and Czech community of Taylor, Mikeska's is so clean a purist might pass it up, but then he'd miss the mouth-watering German-style potato salad. The Mikeska brothers have you covered when it comes to Texas barbecue, with additional family-run restaurants in Smithville, Columbus, El Campo, and Temple. There are subtle differences: Rudy Mikeska is the only one in the family who serves lamb ribs, while brother Clem, in Temple, prefers sirloin to brisket.

Rudy Mikeska's in Taylor is only a few steps away from Louie Mueller's, another butcher-paper establishment complete with ancient wooden tables, smoke-blackened walls, and typical Texas finger food: hot sausage, beef sandwiches, beef and pork ribs served along with a thin, sweet, soupy sauce laced with onions. Aside from hosting the famed International Barbecue Cook-Off, Taylor also hosts an annual fall Bratwurst Festival at its Lutheran church. Here visitors can sample the residents' German-style potato salad, sauerkraut, and noodles that sometimes take the place of the more traditional beans and coleslaw.

Other Hill Country barbecue spots include South Side Market in Elgin (pronounced *El-gun* by most Texans), which puts out fine hot link sausage, the City Market in Luling, the Settlement Inn in Leon Springs, and Hanson's Homestead Barbecue in Austin.

Austin also offers a number of typical barbecue eateries. Bill Miller's cafeteria serves great ribs, chicken, Polish sausage, ham, and brisket, plus the best barbecued chopped beef sandwich we found in Texas. At F. Weigl Ironworks, customers dine on picnic benches inside a corrugated tin–roofed building. The barbecued chicken is excellent, and as juicy and smoky as you'll ever find. This is a no-frills place, with rolls of paper towels instead of napkins on the picnic tables, alongside bowls of hot peppers intended for the strong of heart and stomach.

At Fuchak's Pit Bar-B-Q in San Marcos, the well-smoked barbecued meats were complemented by *fajitas*, iced tea served in large fruit jars, and some of the finest banana pudding this side of heaven. In fact, we found that

banana pudding was the most common dessert served in traditional barbecue restaurants in the Southwest and South. (Pudding and fruit pies were
favorites in about half the places we visited.)

The Spare Rib in Greenville, Texas, also featured another classic barbecue dessert, the "fried pie," a small deep-fried fruit turnover. We also
found one of the best and simplest recipes for coleslaw here. (In fact, the
variety of coleslaw recipes we collected from all over the Midwest, South,
and Southwest was staggering.) The Spare Rib's chef told us his secret:
"Chop a whole head of cabbage, mix water and vinegar half and half, add
salad dressing, salt, and sugar, toss and serve." We were served fancier and
more unusual slaws throughout the barbecue belt, but none better than
that.

In Brady, Texas, we sampled our first and best taste of mesquite-
barbecued *cabrito* at Mac's Bar-B-Q. We feasted on oak- and mesquite-
smoked miniature T-bone steaks from five-month-old goats, served with
excellent smoked Polish sausage, thick slices of onion, and jalapeño peppers. It was easy to understand why Brady, which hosts the annual World
Championship Barbecue Goat Cook-Off every September, calls itself "the
Goat Capital of the World."

The argument over what kind of meat is best rages hotter than a mesquite flame. Certain Texas restaurants wouldn't be caught dead serving
beef ribs, but that doesn't stop the folks who flock to places like Big Al's in
Dallas or the County Line in Austin. These restaurants have clones in other
parts of the state, and all of them serve thick and meaty smoked beef ribs the
size of dinosaur bones that are adored by fans, who prefer them to pork ribs.

County Line is definitely your high-end establishment: great upscale
barbecue for people who faint at the sight of butcher paper, and who
demand full table service along with a nice view of the outdoors.

At County Line they discard the "cap" or fatty top of the brisket and
serve only the lean heart of the meat. To brisket devotees like Darla Tinsley,
though, throwing away the top of the brisket is a sin. Tinsley owns Gaylen's
restaurant in Arlington, between Dallas and Fort Worth, and has a well-
deserved reputation for great barbecue, putting out a daily supply of superior brisket and pork ribs as well as smoked turkey and salami. She uses
every part of the brisket she can. She trims the fat off the cap and separates
the meat from it, and puts some of the fat in her baked beans instead of salt

pork. Tinsley cautions people to slice the brisket *against* the grain. "If you slice a brisket with the grain, it's stringy. The top cap has the grain running this way and that. I separate the top from the bottom and slice both against the grain."

"Chopped beef" sandwiches are popular in Texas, but Tinsley makes hers a special way. She'll take mostly lean pieces of hickory-smoked brisket, chop it up, mix it with sauce, and put it in a pan in the oven to let the fat melt. Then she puts the meat over a strainer to get the fat out, puts more sauce on it, and ladles it onto a bun. This Texas version of a sloppy joe is delicious.

Tinsley doesn't court the media, and she hasn't received the publicity that has followed some other Texas restaurateurs, but she's a dyed-in-the-wool purist who knows barbecue, and she can pit her pits against any man's, any day. Besides, any woman who can take on a wild boar with a 12-gauge shotgun has to have some kind of steel in her veins. Evidence of her hunting prowess lines the restaurant walls; trophies abound. But Tinsley really deserves a trophy of some sort for her prowess with pork ribs. She buys the biggest hogs she can, takes the best ribs with the most meat, and slow-cooks them for 5 to 7 hours. Once you try them, you'll be spoiled for anything else.

Down the road from Arlington, in Fort Worth, we found real pit barbecue at Jimmy Riscky's grocery store, which has served oak-smoked hams, turkeys, briskets, and link sausage since 1927. Another unsung hero of barbecue, Riscky is a one-of-a-kind entrepreneur. Aside from the tasty barbecue, his store holds just about everything you'd ever hope to find in one place: boxes of detergent and cases of soda pop sit side by side with stuffed deer and armadillos; old water pumps, coffee grinders, juke boxes, and toasters are wedged in between hippo and wild boar heads, saddles, and diapers. Riscky likes to brag about a customer who downed a half gallon of buttermilk and twenty-three chopped barbecue beef sandwiches at one sitting. "Guess he liked the food all right," Riscky quips.

Along with Riscky's, most travelers to Fort Worth like the taste of the barbecue served at Angelo's. You can't get their fine ribs here at lunch, but the green-hickory-smoked brisket makes for good sandwiches, and chugging down beer and barbecue at Angelo's is a longtime tradition. Owner Angelo George and his son, Skeet, cook about 3,500 pounds of ribs a week, along with 4,500 pounds of brisket. In addition to their ribs and brisket, they do a superior smoked bologna. Once you taste the meat, accompanied by spicy chili-flavored pinto beans, you'll understand why you'll need an icy schooner of beer by your side.

The Dallas–Fort Worth–Arlington triangle has produced a living legend in the form of William Jennings "Sonny" Bryan, Jr., probably the best-known barbecue man in Texas. Magazines have sung his praises; authors have written him up in books. Why? Probably because Sonny is an individualist who epitomizes Texas tradition: a loner who cranks out good barbecue and then closes shop when the food's all gone.

To eat at Sonny Bryan's is to be part of a ritual that's irresistible to people who love barbecue in the rough. They just belly up to the counter, which is already knee-deep in customers, grease, and grime, grab a bottle of sauce, and try to find a table, which is next to impossible. No matter what the temperature, people will take their plates outside and eat on the backs of their pickup trucks or BMWs. A tall, rangy Texan, Bryan has been serving barbecue out of the same shack for twenty-nine years. The fifty briskets he cooks daily are gone by 2 P.M., and so is Bryan. The moist and juicy beef sandwiches are his strong suit, along with his famous onion rings.

Of the many barbecue restaurants glutting Texas's major cities, many have established solid reputations that have grown over the years. Although they are too numerous to include all of the places here, the ones we've mentioned are definitely worth a visit.

Take the Swingin' Door in Richmond, a few miles southwest of Houston, where we found some of the best lean pecan-wood-smoked ribs we ever tasted. The Swingin' Door is a lively joint with country music bouncing off the walls on weekends. Owner Steve Onstad and his father built the old house-cum-restaurant nearly fifteen years ago and have added on to it since. The brisket, ribs, sausage, and chicken served here are excellent. Onstad uses a dry rub and pecan smoke to give his meat a wonderful flavor. He hangs the ribs perpendicular in the pit "so the juices run all through the meat." His side dishes are good examples of the slaw and potato salad so prevalent in the area.

The ambiance of this restaurant is nearly as much fun as the food. The restaurant is filled with rural and Texas memorabilia, from state flags to strings of garlic bulbs. Once you pass through its stained-glass portals, you won't want to leave.

But if you have room for more, head down the road to the southwest for a taste of Le Blanc's Barbecue and Lennox Barbecue near Fulshear. In Fulshear we also met Edward Dozier, whose restaurant continues to be one of the more popular in the area, although it has since been bought by the Evans family—father Gene and sons Scott and Smedley. Dozier demonstrated for us one of the unique qualities of pecan, which grows wild in this part of the state. He took us to one of his huge outdoor smokers, which had cooled down and was large enough for us to stand inside. He wiped down the walls with his hand, then showed us his palm. We expected it to be charcoal-black, but to our surprise it was clean. "There's very little soot from pecan smoke, which helps keep the meat sweet, not bitter," he explained.

One of the most popular barbecue places in sprawling Houston is Goode Co. Texas Bar-B-Q on Kirby Drive, with barbecue as down-home as it gets. We dined on fine mesquite-smoked chicken, brisket, and ribs, then retired across the street to the Goode Co. Grill, where we sampled the popular hamburgers.

About twenty minutes from Houston's Hobby Airport is Strack Farms Feed Store and Strack Farms Produce Market, on the same land the Stracks have been farming since 1845. The place is Texas-big, with three hundred seats to hold the enthusiastic crowds who come here to feast on authentic Texas pit barbecue and gargantuan chicken-fried steaks. (When Strack opened up a take-out department for their hickory pit barbecue, they even provided a heliport next to the restaurant, just in case a customer wants to fly in and pick up an order on his way home from work.)

On the way to San Antonio, we came to New Braunfels, where we discovered the New Braunfels Smoke House. We sampled many items on one of the largest menus in barbecue country, and every one was terrific. The Dunbar family founded this superb restaurant forty-two years ago. Sue (Dunbar) Snyder and her husband currently operate the place, which takes pride in preparing a wide variety of smoked and barbecued meats, as well as made-from-scratch salad dressings and soups such as smoked turkey, German potato, and thick split pea. Don't-miss desserts: German chocolate cake and a crusty bread pudding swimming in a cinnamon-butter sauce that is pure ecstasy.

★ OKLAHOMA

As we continued our quest for great barbecue, we found that brisket and sausage were abundant not only throughout Texas but in Louisiana and Oklahoma as well. Oklahoma, in fact, seems to have as many good barbecue spots per capita as Texas. Restaurants here favor hickory-smoked closed-pit barbecue, but generally tend to go with the thicker red sauces prevalent in the Midwest.

Oklahomans love their barbecue, and consequently the supermarket shelves offer more than one hundred and twenty sizes and flavors of barbecue sauces. Many are local brands. Latimer's, Martin's, and Hillbilly are favorites, with Cheeks and Head Country dominating the sales. The latter, a thick and spicy ketchup-based sauce, recently won the People's Choice award at the Tri-State Barbecue Cookoff in Bartlesville, Oklahoma.

While we found many similarities between the barbecued meats of Texas and Oklahoma, the side dishes and desserts were different, and the latter, in particular, were terrific in Oklahoma.

If you've never had huckleberry pie, for example, you've missed part of life. This sweet delight is a daily special during the Oklahoma summers, when the wild berries ripen in profusion in Delaware County. Small and bursting with intense flavor, tart and juicy huckleberries are coveted for the unique taste they impart to jams and jellies, pies, muffins, and pancakes. These little wonders command healthy prices when you can find them, but on the Fourth of July the small community of Jay, Oklahoma, shares its bounty with the rest of the world in an annual Huckleberry Festival. As the "Huckleberry Capital of the World," the town generously donated to us some of their favorite recipes.

Along with huckleberry pies, the fried pies we sampled all over the South were never better than those we had at Dan's Barbecue in Davenport, Oklahoma. The restaurant also served a unique peanut butter whipped dessert over crumbled graham crackers that was absolutely superb, as were the cinnamon rolls.

If you like the unusual, the Sooner Cafe in Davis offers a *mashed* potato salad made with sweet relish, mustard, salad dressing, and salt and pepper that is surprisingly tasty.

We also found a lot of "Texas toast" in Oklahoma, to our surprise. We particularly enjoyed the Texas toast at Van's Pig Stand in Shawnee and Dan's Barbecue in Davenport, where homemade white bread is sliced at least one inch thick, slathered with fresh butter, seasoned lightly, and toasted on a flat grill on both sides until it's crusty.

At Van's, along with the toast you get delicious hickory-smoked beef and pork ribs, and chopped pork shoulder sandwiches served with Susie Q's (ribbons of fried potatoes that are favorites in the Midwest and parts of the Southwest). Van's, which opened in 1930, also offers two versions of its popular sauces, which can be ordered by mail if you forget to take some back with you.

★ LOUISIANA

Louisiana has earned its fame as the Cajun capital of the country, and certainly some kinds of barbecue have been influenced by Cajun cooking.

Close to the Texas border, you're apt to find more brisket and beef, but in the eastern part of the state, pork is again a favorite. "Cochon de laits," a small whole hog roasted in an outdoor oven or open pit, with a vinegar baste containing Cajun seasonings poured into the belly during the last few hours of cooking, is the Cajun version of whole hog barbecue.

Just across the state line from Texas is Shreveport, Louisiana. At Leon's, Podnuk's, and Louis Cobbs's, we found barbecue similar to Texas's closed-pit hickory and oak barbecue, with red sauces predominating. We devoured the delicious hickory-smoked ribs, beef, and ham at Leon's, and finished off our meal with a taste of smoked turkey, a specialty of the house. Both Podnuk's and Cobbs's do a heavy carry-out business, with Cobbs's offering both a drive-in and inside pick-up counter.

Side dishes in Louisiana are different from those found in Texas and Oklahoma. Okra, usually served fried in Texas, is often pickled in Louisiana. Other favorite accompaniments are dishes made with pecans or yams, or both.

Seafood is also held in high esteem in this area, and barbecued oysters are found along the Gulf Coast all the way to Alabama. Some coast-dwellers go down to the water in the evening, pick the fresh oysters right out of the surf, and roast them fresh over charcoal, right on the beach.

As we explored, we tasted this region's cooking at its best, from Louisiana ribs to Texas brisket, and we never tired of the food. Traveling the back roads and highways, we found barbecue as engrained a part of the culture as blue jeans and cowboy boots. Once you try some of the following recipes, you'll understand why it's so easy to fall in love with the region's country-good barbecue—something that's as big here as the great outdoors.

 ## MEATS AND SAUCES

Sam Higgins's Barbecued Beef Brisket

Sam Higgins is the author of *I'm Glad I Ate When I Did, 'Cause I'm Not Hungry Now*. He was gracious enough to share some of his recipes with us. Sam adapted this barbecued beef brisket for *Bon Appétit* magazine, for people who don't really have a proper outdoor grill. He uses a double bathtub cooker and smokes several briskets at low temperatures for 20 to 24 hours. "In the early days, brisket was dirt cheap," Sam notes. "It was that part of the beef that nobody really knew what to do with. The meat was either ground up into hamburger or thrown away. But now brisket has gained a great amount of popularity, and the prices aren't dirt cheap anymore. A lot of people make a mistake by buying brisket with the fat trimmed off. The brisket needs the fat to keep it juicy as it cooks. If you don't keep the fat, you'll just wind up with a big old dry piece of leather."

6 cups mesquite chips
1 4-pound beef brisket, untrimmed

2 tablespoons Dry Rub (see below)
Gud BBQ Sauce (see below)

Soak mesquite in water to cover 1 hour. Drain.

Prepare a barbecue grill, lighting fire at one end only. Rub the brisket with Dry Rub. When the coals are white, place meat over coals and sear 5 minutes on each side. Move meat to side of grill away from fire. Spread 4 cups of the mesquite chips over coals. Cover grill and smoke brisket for 1 hour, maintaining the temperature at about 200°F and sprinkling the mesquite with water occasionally. Spread the remaining 2 cups mesquite over the coals and continue smoking meat 1 hour.

Preheat oven to 200°F. Wrap beef tightly in heavy-duty aluminum foil and bake for 8 hours. Slice the meat across the grain and serve with Gud BBQ Sauce.

SERVES 6.

Dry Rub

¹/₄ cup salt
1¹/₂ teaspoons freshly ground black
    pepper
1¹/₂ teaspoons cayenne pepper

Combine all the ingredients in a small bowl. Dry Rub can be stored for several weeks in an airtight jar.

Gud BBQ Sauce

¹/₄ cup meat drippings (rendered
    from brisket fat)
1¹/₄ cups ketchup
¹/₂ cup Worcestershire sauce
¹/₄ cup brown sugar

Juice of 2 lemons
¹/₄ cup minced onion
¹/₄ cup water
1 tablespoon Tabasco sauce

Combine all the ingredients and simmer for 30 to 45 minutes.

MAKES ABOUT 2 CUPS.

County Line Smoked Tenderloin

This is a "Blue Plate Special" at Austin's famous County Line restaurant. This tenderloin can be prepared on an enclosed smoke pit or a standard barbecue grill, preferably with a lid.

5 to 6 pounds choice whole beef
   tenderloin, peeled of membrane
2 tablespoons lemon pepper
   seasoning

1/2 cup (1 stick) butter, melted
1 teaspoon fresh lime juice
2 tablespoons pressed garlic

Sprinkle both sides of the tenderloin heavily with the lemon pepper seasoning. Place the seasoned meat on an aluminum foil "boat," which helps maintain juiciness. (If you wish a grilled effect, omit the foil and lay the meat directly on the rack.) Cook at a pit temperature of 225°F; the longer and slower you cook the meat, the better the flavor. After 1 hour, begin to check the temperature with a meat thermometer every 15 to 20 minutes. Overcooking can occur quickly, so be careful. When checking the meat, "dab baste" with a mixture of the butter, lime juice, and garlic, in proportions to taste. For medium-rare meat (internal temperature of 140°F), cooking time will be approximately 2 to 2 1/2 hours.

    SERVES 8 TO 10.

Sam Higgins's Barbecued Pork Ribs

1 12-ounce can light beer
Mesquite chips
2 sides of pork ribs, approximately
   6 pounds

Dry Rub (see page 124)
Sam's Special Sauce (see below)

Coat the ribs heavily with Dry Rub. Build a charcoal fire at one end of the cooker; when it starts to get white, add some mesquite chips to the coals.

Place the ribs at the opposite end of the cooker. (Ribs should never be cooked over direct fire.) Smoke them for 4 to 6 hours at about 200°F, then baste with Special Sauce.

EACH SIDE OF RIBS WILL FEED 1 ADULT MALE COYOTE, OR 2 TO 4 PEOPLE.

okay — nothing spectacular

Sam's Special Sauce

1 12-ounce can light beer
1 32-ounce jar prepared mustard
3 tsp chopped garlic

5 teaspoons Tabasco sauce
1 cup packed light brown sugar
1 tsp onion powder

Mix together all the ingredients in a heavy saucepan and heat until the sugar dissolves. *dash worchestershire*

MAKES ABOUT 3 CUPS.

Swingin' Door Barbecued Pork Ribs

This recipe comes to us courtesy of Steve Onstad of the Swingin' Door in Richmond, Texas.

1 slab "3 and down" ribs (3 pounds or under)
3 tablespoons salt

3 tablespoons pepper
3 tablespoons garlic powder
1¹⁄₂ tablespoons paprika

Mix together the seasonings and coat the ribs thoroughly with the mixture. Slowly smoke the ribs over seasoned pecan wood for 5 to 6 hours, using just enough heat (200°–225°F) to melt away the fat, leaving lean ribs with a nice pink color to the meat.

SERVES 2 TO 4.

Hot Texas Sausage

This is a very hot sausage, but a truly simple and delicious one. Reduce spices by one-fourth for a less fiery version.

5 pounds pork butt
2 tablespoons seasoned salt
2 teaspoons crushed red pepper
2 tablespoons cayenne pepper

2 tablespoons ground black pepper

Sausage casings

Grind the meat with the seasonings. Stuff into casing. Smoke 3 to 4 hours at low heat (225°F) over pecan wood. Cool, then serve as is, or grill or steam.

MAKES 5 POUNDS SAUSAGE.

Charlie and George's Mesquite-Smoked Bologna

Charlie Spaulding's and George Forrester's bologna is excellent, but salty, so serve with plenty of beer or soft drinks.

1 5-pound bologna
2 teaspoons paprika
2 teaspoons ground black pepper
3 tablespoons plus 1 teaspoon salt

1/2 teaspoon cayenne pepper
2 teaspoons chili powder
1 teaspoon garlic powder

Mix all the dry ingredients well and rub on bologna. Smoke over mesquite or bake for 3 hours at 250°F. Cool to touch and slice.

SERVES 15 TO 20.

J & R's Barbecued Chicken

J & R Manufacturing out of Mesquite, Texas, makes the Oyler commercial closed-pit barbecue unit, which is one of the best. They also publish a recipe booklet that is full of creative cooking ideas.

3 small chickens (2½ to 3 pounds each)	¼ cup lemon juice
	2 teaspoons celery salt
Salt	2 teaspoons garlic powder
Ground black pepper	2 teaspoons white pepper
	2 teaspoons paprika
Basting sauce	2 teaspoons onion powder
1 cup (2 sticks) margarine, melted	

Prepare your cooker for traditional closed-pit barbecue. Split the chickens down the back. Cut through top of breast just enough to break the breastbone. Spread the chickens and lay them skin side up. Lightly season the chickens with salt and pepper. Mix together all the ingredients for the basting sauce and brush the chickens with this mixture before placing them on the grill. (The basting sauce will help keep the skin tender and will retard wrinkling.) Cook at 225°–250°F until done, 2 to 3 hours. Twist the leg slightly to test for doneness (it should move easily). Refrain from piercing the chicken with a fork during cooking, as the juices will be lost. Chicken not served during the next few hours should be allowed to cool at room temperature, then wrapped tightly in aluminum foil and placed in the refrigerator. It can be reheated, wrapped in foil, at 250°F for approximately 30 minutes to 1 hour.

SERVES 3 TO 6.

County Line Smoked Quail

This is another favorite "Blue Plate Special" at the County Line in Austin. Smoke the quail on an enclosed smoke pit or on a standard barbecue grill (preferably one that has a lid), with the fire banked to one side, and soaked wood added for smoke.

4 quail (about 4 ounces each)	About 12 slices bacon
Lemon pepper seasoning	

Lightly season the quail with lemon pepper seasoning. Bind the legs together with kitchen string and wrap in bacon from ankle to neck. Place on a pit rack at a temperature of 225°F and cook for approximately 4 hours. During the last hour, begin checking the temperature of the quail every 15 to 20 minutes by inserting a meat thermometer deep into the meaty part of the breast without touching the bone. Remove the quail when the temperature reaches 165°F and the bacon is nicely browned. Serve immediately or hold at 140°F.

SERVES 4.

 ## FISH AND SEAFOOD

J & R's Barbecued Whole Salmon

1 4- to 8-pound dressed whole salmon (dressed weight)	1/4 cup lemon juice
Lettuce or celery leaves	4 crushed bay leaves
	1 tablespoon brown sugar
Marinade	1/2 cup (1 stick) butter or margarine, melted
1 teaspoon onion powder	1 tablespoon salt

Select a firm-fleshed fish; fresh salmon should have absolutely no fishy odor. Completely scale and wash thoroughly with cold water. Cut a slit on each side of the dorsal fins about 1/4 to 1/2 inch deep.

Mix together the marinade ingredients and apply to the fish inside and out, including the slits at the dorsal fins. Fill the cavity with lettuce or celery leaves to maintain the shape of the fish and let rest overnight.

Place the fish on a sheet of heavy aluminum foil and brush with more marinade. Place on rack and fold and crimp the foil on both sides, so as to block the fish as little as possible from smoke circulation. Cook at 250°F for 1 hour, then brush with additional marinade. Wipe off the white secretion from the slits at the dorsal fins, then carefully turn the fish over and remove the foil. Cook for 1 additional hour at the same temperature.

Note: This basic procedure can be used for other fish and fillets; reduce the cooking time for smaller fish.

SERVES 18 TO 25 AS AN APPETIZER.

J & R's Barbecued Shrimp in the Shell

These shrimp are messy to eat but delicious, and great with a chunk of crusty French bread and a nice dry, chilled white wine or icy-cold beer.

1½ pounds large fresh shrimp (21 to 25 count)

Marinade
½ cup (1 stick) butter or margarine, melted
1 cup tomato juice
2 tablespoons white vinegar
1 teaspoon liquid smoke

2 tablespoons Worcestershire sauce
½ cup lemon juice
2 tablespoons Louisiana hot sauce
1 teaspoon crushed red pepper
1 teaspoon paprika
1 teaspoon dry mustard
1 teaspoon garlic powder
1 tablespoon brown sugar

Remove the heads from the shrimp. Mix together the marinade ingredients and pour over the shrimp in an enameled or glass dish. Marinate in the refrigerator for 3 to 4 hours.

Pour off most of the marinade and place the shrimp in a shallow stainless steel pan on a trivet, if possible. Barbecue on the grill at 250°F for 45 minutes to 1 hour. Serve the shrimp in the shell, with plenty of French bread for mopping.

SERVES 4 OR 5.

J & R's Smoked Shrimp

1½ pounds large fresh shrimp (21 to 25 count)

Marinade
1 cup (2 sticks) butter, melted slowly (do not clarify)

½ teaspoon garlic powder, or to taste
¼ teaspoon cayenne pepper (more if you like 'em hot)
2 tablespoons dry sherry
1 tablespoon lemon juice

Remove the heads from the shrimp and peel off the shells, leaving the tail segments intact. Remove the sand veins. Rinse the shrimp in cold water and place in a large, non-corrodible bowl or dish. Mix together the marinade ingredients and pour over the shrimp. Carefully turn the shrimp until all are coated. Cover and place in the refrigerator if you aren't ready to cook.

Preheat your pit to 250°–275°F. Remove the shrimp from the marinade with a slotted spoon and place them in a single layer in a shallow pan that fits your pit racks. Place the shrimp in the hot pit and close lid. It is usually best to add a fresh piece of wood for heavy smoke at this time. Let smoke for about 15 to 20 minutes, depending on the size of the shrimp. Remove the shrimp and turn them over with a long-handled spatula. Close the oven doors and let smoke for about 15 minutes more. Test for doneness and remove. Cool and refrigerate until ready to serve.

SERVES 4 OR 5.

Serving suggestions: To serve as a cold appetizer, place the shrimp on salad plates on a bed of fresh Bibb lettuce, garnish with lemon wedges, parsley, and a dipping sauce (cold barbecue sauce is great).

For a buffet platter, form a sturdy cone of heavy-duty aluminum foil and place a bowl for sauce on top of the cone. Surround the cone with the shrimp, building in layers until the top layer is even with the top of the sauce bowl. Garnish as desired.

For a hot appetizer, spear the shrimp on small bamboo skewers and reheat on an electric pu-pu tray.

For kebabs, alternate the shrimp on skewers with scallops, chunks of green pepper and onion, and cherry tomatoes; reheat in broiler.

For soup, chop the shrimp and add to a chicken-base cream soup; season lightly with chives and garnish each serving with a whole shrimp, split lengthwise, and a tiny dash of paprika.

 **SIDE DISHES**

Dick Holt's Texas Chili

Texan Dick Holt has been barbecuing for years, and he makes a great chili, too. It's salty but if you want to cut back on the saltiness, use less beef bouillon.

1¼ pounds coarsely ground beef
¼ cup ketchup
¼ cup chili powder
2 tablespoons powdered beef
    bouillon (such as Herb-Ox)
2 tablespoons garlic powder
½ teaspoon dried oregano

1 tablespoon black pepper
2 tablespoons cumin
¼ cup flour
2 tablespoons paprika
½ teaspoon garlic salt
1 cup water

Brown the meat in a large heavy pot or Dutch oven. Stir in the remaining ingredients, bring to a boil, reduce heat, and simmer for 30 minutes.

SERVES 6.

Polly Haynes's Pickled Okra

This recipe is courtesy of Pat Baldridge, food editor of the Louisiana *State-Times Morning Advocate* and author of a cookbook, *Hot Off the Press*.

2 pounds tender fresh okra
5 cloves garlic, peeled
4 cups white vinegar

6 tablespoons salt
1 tablespoon mustard seed
2 tablespoons liquid crab boil

Wash the okra and pack it into 5 hot, sterilized pint jars. Put one clove of garlic in each jar. Bring the remaining ingredients to a boil. Pour over the okra and seal. Keep several weeks before serving.

MAKES 5 PINTS.

Darla Tinsley's Sweet Coleslaw

Darla Tinsley is the outspoken owner of Gaylen's Bar-B-Q in Arlington, Texas.

1 2¹/₂-pound head cabbage, chopped (about 5 cups)
¹/₂ cup sugar
¹/₂ cup mayonnaise
1 tablespoon celery seed
2 tablespoons diced sweet red pepper
¹/₂ teaspoon ground black pepper

Combine all the ingredients in a large bowl and mix well. Let the slaw sit overnight in the refrigerator before serving, to give the sugar time to dissolve.

SERVES 6.

Baldwin's Coleslaw

Johnnie Baldwin was still fixing great barbecue in a small concrete building on an Oklahoma back road when we passed through. She had a uniquely seasoned slaw and a potato salad typical of the area, and she was kind enough to share her recipes with us.

1 medium head cabbage, shredded (5 to 6 cups)
1 cup grated carrot
¹/₂ cup sugar
1¹/₂ teaspoons dried sweet basil
¹/₂ cup apple cider vinegar
1 cup mayonnaise or whipped salad dressing
Salt and ground black pepper to taste

Place the cabbage in a 3-quart bowl and add the carrot. Mix together the sugar, basil, and vinegar and pour it over the cabbage. Toss well. Add the mayonnaise or salad dressing and salt and pepper to taste and mix again. Refrigerate until serving.

SERVES 6 TO 8.

Dick Holt's Coleslaw

This is a sweet slaw, different and really good.

1 medium head cabbage, shredded
2¹/₂ cups diced carrots
¹/₂ cup diced celery
1 cup commercial whipped salad
    dressing

1¹/₂ teaspoons salt
¹/₂ teaspoon garlic salt
²/₃ cup sugar
1 teaspoon white vinegar

Place all the ingredients in a large bowl and mix well. Refrigerate until serving.

SERVES 6 TO 8.

Brannan's Potato Salad

Juanita and Isaac Brannan put out great closed-pit barbecue in Shawnee, Oklahoma. Their potato salad and baked beans were so good we asked for the recipes. Like many friendly Oklahoma folks, they were happy to share.

12 medium potatoes, boiled in their
    skins
2 green peppers, diced
2 stalks celery, diced
1 medium onion, diced
1 teaspoon garlic salt
¹/₂ teaspoon sugar

¹/₄ teaspoon salt
¹/₄ cup sweet pickle relish
Prepared mustard to taste
2 cups Miracle Whip (or other
    commercial whipped salad
    dressing)
Diced sweet pickle to taste

Peel and cube the potatoes. Combine with the peppers, celery, and onion, then sprinkle with the garlic salt, sugar, and salt. Combine the sweet pickle relish and prepared mustard, and add the Miracle Whip and diced sweet pickle. Add to the potato mixture and toss well.

SERVES 10 TO 12.

Baldwin's Potato Salad

10 medium potatoes, boiled, peeled, and diced
2 medium dill pickles (preferably Vlasic's), finely diced
1/2 cup diced celery

1 tablespoon prepared mustard
1 very small onion, chopped
1 hard-boiled egg, chopped
2 cups commercial whipped salad dressing

Combine all the ingredients and mix well. Refrigerate until serving.

SERVES 10.

Taylor Lutheran Church Potato Salad

This is a very different and delicious, sweet and tangy potato salad. It's served at the Taylor, Texas, Lutheran Church during its annual fall Bratwurst Festival.

1 tablespoon flour
3/4 cup white vinegar
1 cup sugar
1/2 teaspoon salt
1/2 teaspoon ground black pepper

1 1/2 cups water
1 tablespoon minced onion
1/4 cup (1/2 stick) margarine, melted
10 large potatoes (about 5 pounds)
Cooked bacon, crumbled, to taste

In a heavy saucepan, thoroughly blend the flour, vinegar, sugar, salt, pepper, water, onion, and margarine. Bring to a simmer and cook until the onion is tender, about 10 minutes.

Boil the potatoes in their skins until tender and drain. When they are cool enough to handle, peel and dice them. Pour the sauce over and mix well. Garnish with crumbled bacon bits. Refrigerate if not serving immediately.

SERVES 12.

Charlie and George's Potato Salad

Heavily smoked ribs and hot Polish sausage, along with smoked bologna, are specialties of Charlie Spaulding and George Forrester, who gave us this recipe for a simple but classic potato salad.

9 medium-large potatoes
3/4 cup plus 2 tablespoons chopped
    onion
1/4 cup chopped dill pickle
2 hard-boiled eggs, chopped
2 tablespoons prepared mustard

3 cups commercial whipped salad
    dressing
1 teaspoon salt, or to taste
1/2 teaspoon ground black pepper, or
    to taste
1/2 teaspoon paprika, or to taste

Boil the potatoes in their skins until tender. Drain, cool, and refrigerate overnight. When ready to use, peel and cube the potatoes. Mix together the remaining ingredients and add to the potatoes; blend well.

SERVES 10.

Darla Tinsley's Baked Beans

1 pound dried pinto beans
1/2 pound smoked sausage links
1/2 cup diced onion
1 tablespoon chili powder

1 teaspoon seasoned salt
1/4 cup seeded, diced jalapeño
    pepper

Measure the beans and place them in a pot with four times as much water. Bring to a boil. Meanwhile, slice the sausages and place them in a skillet with the onion. Sauté until the onion is transparent. Add the onion and sausage and the remaining ingredients to the beans and simmer until the beans are tender, about 4 hours.

MAKES 4 QUARTS, TO SERVE 10 TO 16.

Juanita and Isaac Brannan's Baked Beans

1 53-ounce can Van Camp's pork
   and beans
1 green pepper, finely chopped
1 stalk celery, finely chopped
1 medium onion, finely chopped

1 tablespoon brown sugar
3/4 cup ketchup
1/4 cup prepared mustard
1/4 teaspoon salt
1/8 teaspoon garlic powder

Preheat oven or barbecue cooker to 350°F. Combine all the ingredients in a large, heavy pot and smoke or bake for 1 hour.

    SERVES 8 TO 10.

Sam Higgins's Blue Ribbon Pinto Beans

2 pounds dried pinto beans
1 pound sliced smoked bacon, cut
   into 1-inch pieces
2 medium tomatoes, diced
1 1/2 tablespoons ground cumin

1 1/2 tablespoons chili powder
2 medium cloves garlic, minced
1 jalapeño or serrano pepper,
   minced
Salt

Place the beans in a large, heavy saucepan. Add water to cover and bring to a boil. Drain the beans and return to the pot. Add enough water to cover by 2 to 3 inches. Add all the remaining ingredients except the salt and bring to a boil. Reduce the heat to low and simmer, covered, until the beans are very soft, about 3 1/2 hours, adding more water as necessary to keep the beans submerged. Season with salt to taste and cook 15 minutes longer, uncovered if the liquid is runny.

    SERVES 10 TO 12.

Dick Holt's Barbecue Pinto Beans

4 cups dried pinto beans
¾ cup tomato-based barbecue
    sauce, any kind
1 cup maple syrup
¼ cup chili powder
2 tablespoons salt

1¼ tablespoons cayenne pepper
1½ tablespoons onion powder
2¼ teaspoons garlic powder
2 teaspoons Tabasco sauce
¼ pound fat from brisket or Boston
    Butt pork roast, diced

Wash the beans and place them in a large, heavy pot. Add water to cover and bring to a boil. Simmer slowly until tender, about 3½ hours. (You can also soak the dried beans overnight before cooking, if you prefer. In that case, they will take less time to cook.) Add the remaining ingredients to the cooked beans. Cover and bake in an oven preheated to 300°F until heated thoroughly, about 45 minutes.

    SERVES 9.

Sam Higgins's Black-Eyed Peas

1 pound fresh or frozen black-eyed
    peas
8 cups water
¼ cup bacon drippings

1 green onion, minced
1½ cups diced cooked ham
1 tablespoon beef bouillon

Combine all the ingredients in a saucepan and simmer until the peas are tender, about 45 minutes to 1 hour.

    SERVES 6 TO 8.

Taylor Lutheran Church Sauerkraut

This is a regional rarity served annually at the Taylor, Texas, Lutheran Church's Bratwurst Festival. It is also sometimes served as an accompaniment to barbecue.

¹/₂ pound thick-sliced bacon, diced
2 16-ounce cans sauerkraut
1 teaspoon ground black pepper

Sauté the diced bacon until brown. Remove the bacon from the pan with a slotted spoon and drain off all but a couple of tablespoons of the drippings. Place the sauerkraut in the saucepan and add the bacon to the sauerkraut along with the pepper. Heat through and serve.

S ERVES 6.

Smoked Nuts

Shelled nuts—almonds, pecans, and peanuts—are wonderful smoked. Place the nuts on wire mesh on your pit racks and barbecue for 1 hour at about 300°F. Remove and salt if desired. The smoke flavor strengthens if the nuts are kept in airtight containers. The following "soak sauce" does great things for peanuts:

¹/₂ cup water
¹/₂ cup tomato juice
1 tablespoon salt
1 tablespoon garlic powder

1 teaspoon ground cumin
3 tablespoons Louisiana hot sauce
1 teaspoon cayenne pepper
1 tablespoon olive oil or vegetable oil

Mix together all the ingredients. Place shelled roasted (or green) peanuts in a container and cover with the soak sauce. Let soak for 20 minutes, then drain, and barbecue as described above.

Hammond's Fried Stuffed Jalapeños

Linda Hammond is the owner of Hammond B-B-Q in Glen Rose, Texas. This makes a moderately hot fried pepper.

Cornmeal batter
1 cup flour
1 cup yellow cornmeal
1 teaspoon salt
1/2 teaspoon baking powder
1 egg
1 cup milk
2 tablespoons vegetable oil

1 12-ounce jar pickled jalapeño peppers
4 ounces Cheddar cheese, cut into 16 sticks
Vegetable oil for deep-frying

Make the batter: Combine the dry ingredients in a mixing bowl. Stir the egg, milk, and oil together; add to dry ingredients and blend until smooth.

Slit the jalapeños down the middle and remove the seeds, but leave the skins on. Divide the cheese among the peppers and close them up. Dip in batter and deep-fry in hot oil (350°F) for 4 to 5 minutes, or until golden. Drain on paper towels and serve at once.

MAKES 16 FRIED JALAPEÑOS.

New Braunfels Smokehouse Smoked Turkey and Bacon Salad

1 pound smoked turkey tidbits (picked from carcass)
1/2 pound smokehouse bacon, crisp-cooked and crumbled to bits

1/4 cup pickle relish
1/4 cup chopped celery
1/2 cup mayonnaise

Combine all ingredients in a large bowl and mix well. Refrigerate until serving.

SERVES 4 TO 6.

Mary Holloway's Piping Hot Oysters in the Shell

12 fresh oysters in the shell
1/2 cup (1 stick) butter or margarine
1 garlic clove, minced

1/2 teaspoon Worcestershire sauce
Dash Louisiana hot sauce

Scrub the oysters and place them on a grilling rack (or in a hinged grill) over a low (225°–250°F) charcoal fire. (See page 223.) While the oysters are cooking, sauté the garlic lightly in the butter and add the Worcestershire sauce and hot sauce. When the oysters pop open, coat them with the butter mixture and serve piping hot.

SERVES 2 OR 3 AS AN APPETIZER.

BAKED GOODS AND DESSERTS

Becky Higgins's Blueberry Buttermilk Biscuits

Becky and Sam Higgins love to create great food together. Maybe that's why they got married.

2 cups sifted all-purpose flour
1/2 cup sugar
1 tablespoon baking powder
1 teaspoon grated orange peel
1 teaspoon salt
1/4 teaspoon baking soda
1/3 cup Crisco (or other solid
   vegetable shortening)
3/4 cup buttermilk

1 egg, beaten
1/2 cup frozen blueberries (do not
   thaw)

Topping
3 tablespoons melted butter
3 tablespoons sugar
1/4 teaspoon ground cinnamon
1/8 teaspoon grated nutmeg

Preheat oven to 400°F. Lightly grease a baking sheet.

Combine the flour, sugar, baking powder, orange peel, salt, and baking soda in a mixing bowl. Cut in the shortening until the mixture resembles coarse meal. Combine the buttermilk and the egg and stir into the dry ingredients just until blended. Stir in the blueberries. Turn out the dough on a heavily floured surface and knead gently just until the dough holds together (5 or 6 times). Pat out to 1/2-inch thickness. Cut with a 4-inch floured cookie-cutter or a drinking glass. Arrange on the prepared sheet, 2 inches apart. Bake until light brown, about 20 minutes. Transfer the biscuits to a rack. Combine the topping ingredients and brush over the warm biscuits. Serve while still warm.

MAKES 6 TO 8 LARGE BISCUITS.

Huckleberry Muffins

Every Fourth of July, the small community of Jay, Oklahoma, holds its Huckleberry Festival. The following recipes, which came to us from the Jay Chamber of Commerce, are some of the best we ever tasted. If you can't get huckleberries, try substituting *blueberries* instead.

1 egg	3 teaspoons baking powder
³/₄ cup sugar	¹/₃ cup solid vegetable shortening,
1 teaspoon salt	melted
1 cup milk	1 cup fresh or frozen huckleberries
2 cups flour	(or substitute blueberries)

Preheat oven to 400°F.

Beat the egg with the sugar and salt. Add the milk. Combine the flour and baking powder and stir in. Add the melted shortening and the huckleberries and mix lightly. Fill 12 greased muffin-pan cups ²/₃ full and bake for 15 to 20 minutes, or until brown. Serve with sausages and scrambled eggs.

MAKES 12 MUFFINS.

Huckleberry Pancakes

For a special treat, add 1 cup fresh or frozen huckleberries per 2 cups of flour in your favorite pancake batter and cook as usual.

Huckleberry Dessert

16 graham cracker squares, crushed
³/₄ cup (1¹/₂ sticks) butter, melted
³/₄ cup sugar
2 eggs
1 8-ounce package cream cheese,
    softened

1 20-ounce can huckleberry (or
    blueberry) pie filling
Whipped cream or nondairy
    whipped topping

Preheat oven to 375°F.

Mix the graham cracker crumbs with the melted butter and ¹/₄ cup of the sugar. Pat into a 9-inch-square baking pan. Beat the eggs, add the remaining ¹/₂ cup sugar and the cream cheese, and beat well. Pour over the graham cracker base and bake for 20 minutes. Cool.

Pour the huckleberry pie filling into the prepared crust and refrigerate until ready to serve. Top with whipped cream or nondairy whipped topping.

Note: 1 pint fresh huckleberries, mixed with ³/₄ cup sugar, ¹/₄ cup water, and 2 tablespoons cornstarch and cooked until thick and soft, may be used instead of the canned pie filling. This is better tasting, too.

SERVES 9.

Fried Huckleberries

¹/₄ cup bacon or ham drippings
1 quart fresh huckleberries

1¹/₂ cups sugar
¹/₂ teaspoon salt

Pour the bacon or ham drippings into a skillet and add the huckleberries, sugar, and salt. Bring to a boil and cook for about 10 minutes, to a jamlike consistency. Fried huckleberries are best served hot on squaw bread, biscuits, pancakes, and other quick breads.

MAKES 1 QUART.

Cherokee Huckleberry Bread

1 egg
½ cup (1 stick) butter or margarine
1 cup sugar
1 cup milk

1 teaspoon vanilla
2 cups self-rising flour
2 cups fresh or frozen huckleberries

Preheat oven to 350°F.

Cream the egg, butter, and sugar together. Stir in the milk and vanilla. Sprinkle a little of the flour over the berries to prevent them from sinking to the bottom of the loaf. Stir the remaining flour into the batter and add the berries. Turn into a greased loaf pan and bake for approximately 40 to 50 minutes, or until a knife inserted in the center comes out clean.

MAKES 1 LOAF.

Extra Fancy Huckleberry Pie

1 8-ounce package cream cheese,
  softened
1 teaspoon vanilla
1 cup confectioners' sugar
2 cups whipped cream or 1 8-ounce
  container nondairy whipped
  topping

1 prebaked pie shell
1 20-ounce can huckleberry or
  blueberry pie filling

Combine the cream cheese, vanilla, and confectioners' sugar and mix well. Fold in the whipped cream or nondairy whipped topping. Pour half this mixture into the pie shell, then top with the pie filling. Pour the rest of the cream cheese mixture on top and chill until ready to serve.

MAKES 1 9- OR 10-INCH PIE.

Huckleberry Cobbler

1 quart fresh huckleberries
2 tablespoons flour
1¹/₂ cups sugar
¹/₂ teaspoon salt

2 tablespoons lemon juice (optional)
2 tablespoons butter, melted
1 recipe biscuit dough (homemade
    or from mix)

Preheat oven to 350°F.

    Place the huckleberries in a bowl and sprinkle with the flour, sugar, and salt. Stir to coat well. Pour into a 9x14-inch baking pan. (The fruit will make its own juice as it cooks.) Add the lemon juice, if used, and the melted butter. Top with biscuit dough and bake until crust is brown, about 20 to 30 minutes.

    SERVES 12.

Huckleberry Jelly

1 quart fresh huckleberries
2 cups water

1 package (1³/₄ ounces) Sure Jell
    (fruit pectin)
4¹/₂ cups sugar

Cook the huckleberries in the water until tender, about 15 minutes. Press through a sieve and measure; you should have about 3¹/₂ cups juice. (Add water to make up the difference if necessary.) Put the juice and Sure Jell in a 6-quart pot and bring to a rolling boil. Add the sugar and stir constantly until the mixture can't be stirred down. Boil for 1 minute more, then pour into hot sterilized jelly glasses and seal.

    MAKES ABOUT 5 CUPS.

Huckleberry Coffee Cake

¹/₄ cup solid vegetable shortening
3 tablespoons sugar
1 egg
1³/₈ cups sifted flour
1³/₄ teaspoons baking powder
¹/₂ teaspoon salt
¹/₂ cup milk
²/₃ cup huckleberries, fresh, frozen,
   or canned

Topping
¹/₂ cup sugar
1 teaspoon ground cinnamon
2 tablespoons melted butter
2 tablespoons milk

Preheat oven to 350°F.

Cream the shortening, then add the sugar and cream well. Add the egg and beat thoroughly.

Sift together the flour, baking powder, and salt. Add the flour mixture alternately with the milk, beating well after each addition. Add the huckleberries and mix. Pour the batter into a greased 9-inch layer cake pan and form deep ridges in the batter with a knife. Sprinkle with a mixture of the sugar and cinnamon. Bake for 20 minutes.

Mix together the melted butter and milk and pour over the cake. Bake 15 minutes longer, or until a knife inserted in the center comes out clean. Serve warm, cut in wedges.

SERVES 6 TO 8.

The Spare Rib's Apricot-Peach Fried Pies

Fried pie is an unusual treat we enjoyed throughout the South and Southwest. One of the best fried pies we came across was served to us at The Spare Rib in Greenville, Texas, and owner Dewey Fitzpatrick was kind enough to let us have the recipe.

Filling

²/₃ cup chopped dried apricots

¹/₄ cup fresh or frozen chopped
　peaches

¹/₄ cup (¹/₂ stick) butter

¹/₂ cup water

5 tablespoons cornstarch, dissolved
　in ¹/₂ cup cold water

1 cup sugar

Pastry

2¹/₂ cups flour

1 teaspoon salt

3 tablespoons sugar

1 cup solid vegetable shortening,
　softened

¹/₂ cup ice water

Vegetable oil for deep-frying.

Make the filling: Combine the apricots, peaches, butter, and water in a heavy saucepan and bring to a boil. Stir in the cornstarch mixture and cook, stirring, until thick. Add the sugar and allow to cool.

Prepare the pastry: Combine the flour, salt, and sugar in a mixing bowl and cut in the shortening until the mixture resembles coarse meal. Sprinkle with the ice water, stirring just until the dough holds together. Wrap in plastic and refrigerate for at least 1 hour.

Divide the dough into 16 equal portions. Roll out each piece of dough to a 5-inch circle. Place 1 tablespoon of the filling on each round and fold in half to form a half-moon shape. Crimp the edges with a fork to seal.

Heat 1 inch of oil in a large, heavy skillet. Fry the pies (no more than 2 or 3 at a time) until golden, about 2 to 3 minutes on each side. Drain on paper towels and serve hot.

MAKES 16 FRIED PIES.

Mitzi's Apple Pie

This recipe comes to us courtesy of Muriel Duncan of Arlington, Texas.

Pastry for a 2-crust pie

6 tablespoons sugar

6 tablespoons brown sugar

¹/₄ cup flour

1¹/₂ teaspoons ground cinnamon

¹/₄ teaspoon grated nutmeg

¹/₄ teaspoon salt

6 cups thinly sliced cored and peeled
　Granny Smith apples

Grated peel of ¹/₂ lemon

¹/₂ cup heavy cream

2 tablespoons butter

Milk

Additional granulated sugar

Preheat oven to 450°F.

Line a 9-inch pie pan with two-thirds of the prepared dough. Combine the sugars, flour, cinnamon, nutmeg, and salt. Add this mixture to the apples, and toss to coat them well. Spread the apple mixture in the unbaked pie shell. Sprinkle with the lemon peel and pour the cream over. Roll out the remaining pastry and cut into strips to make a lattice crust. Dot the holes with the butter (to make the crust flakier as well as to flavor the fruit). Brush the crust with milk and sprinkle with granulated sugar. Bake for 10 minutes, then reduce the heat to 350°F, cover the edges of the crust with aluminum foil, and continue baking for 30 to 40 minutes, or until the crust is browned and the filling is bubbling.

MAKES 1 9-INCH PIE.

Granny Manning's Peach Cobbler

Courtesy of Sam Higgins.

Filling
6 cups peeled, sliced (¹/₄-inch thick) peaches
1¹/₄ cups sugar

Pastry
2 cups all-purpose flour

1 teaspoon salt
³/₄ cup solid vegetable shortening
3 to 4 tablespoons cold water
¹/₂ cup (1 stick) butter, cut into small pieces
3 teaspoons sugar

Combine the peaches and the sugar in a large bowl. Let stand 4 hours or overnight, to allow the peaches to exude their juices.

Make the pastry: Combine the flour and salt in a large bowl. Cut in the shortening until the mixture resembles coarse meal. Mix in just enough water to bind the dough. Gather into a ball and divide in half.

Preheat oven to 350°F.

Pour the peaches into a 9x13-inch baking pan and dot with the butter. Roll out 1 portion of the dough on a lightly floured surface to a rectangle about ¹/₈ inch thick and 11 inches long. Cut into 1-inch strips. Arrange the pastry strips over the peaches diagonally, in one direction only, spacing them 1 inch apart; pinch off the excess dough. Bake until the pastry is just beginning to brown, about 35 minutes.

Meanwhile, roll out the remaining dough and cut into strips as above. Arrange the pastry strips over the peaches diagonally in the opposite direction, to form a lattice. Pinch off the excess dough, sprinkle with the remaining sugar and bake until golden brown, about 40 minutes more. (This gives the peach liquid a chance to thicken naturally.) Serve hot or warm, with vanilla ice cream.

SERVES 8 TO 10.

Dan's Bar-B-Q Pit Cherry Coconut Cobbler

This cobbler is courtesy of John W. Vandever, owner of Dan's Bar-B-Q Pit in Davenport, Oklahoma, home of fine barbecue and great desserts.

2 cups all-purpose flour
1¹/₂ cups sugar
4 cups grated sweetened coconut (1
   14-ounce package)

¹/₂ cup (1 stick) butter, melted
2 21-ounce cans cherry pie filling

Preheat the oven to 350°F.

In a large bowl, mix together the flour, sugar, and coconut until well blended. Add the melted butter and mix until crumbly. Pat 4 cups of the crumb mixture into a well-buttered 9x13-inch baking pan. Spread the pie filling over the crust and sprinkle with the remaining crumb mixture. Bake for 40 minutes. Serve hot or warm.

SERVES 12 TO 15.

Banana Pudding

Tom and Linda Hammond and Liz and H. A. Hammond of Glencoe, Texas, served us one of the best banana puddings we ever ate, and we're proud to have their recipe.

3/4 cup sugar
1/3 cup flour
Dash salt
4 eggs, separated, at room
    temperature
2 cups milk

1/2 teaspoon vanilla
35 to 45 vanilla wafers
5 or 6 medium-size ripe bananas,
    sliced
Additional crushed vanilla wafers
    and sliced bananas for garnish

Preheat oven to 425°F.

Combine 1/2 cup of the sugar with the flour and salt in the top of a double boiler. Stir in the egg yolks and milk and blend well. Cook over boiling water, stirring constantly, until thick. Reduce heat and cook, stirring occasionally, for 5 minutes. Remove from heat and stir in vanilla.

Place a third of the vanilla wafers in the bottom of a 1 1/2-quart baking dish and top with a third of the sliced bananas and a third of the hot custard. Repeat until you have three layers, ending with the custard. Beat the egg whites until soft peaks form, then add the remaining 1/4 cup sugar and beat until stiff. Spread on top of the pudding and bake for 5 minutes, or until the meringue is brown. Cool to room temperature and chill for several hours. Garnish with additional banana slices and crushed wafers around the edges.

SERVES 6 TO 8.

Jan Hartman's Yam Pecan Squares

Courtesy of Pat Baldridge.

1 9-ounce package yellow cake mix
1/4 cup (1/2 stick) margarine, melted
3 eggs
1 1/4 cups mashed canned yams (or
    1 1/4 cups mashed fresh yams plus
    1/3 cup sugar)
1/3 cup packed brown sugar
3/4 teaspoon ground cinnamon
3/4 teaspoon ground ginger

1/8 teaspoon salt
3/4 cup milk, scalded

Topping
1/4 cup (1/2 stick) margarine,
    softened
1/2 cup packed brown sugar
1 cup chopped pecans

Preheat oven to 350°F.

Make the crust: Combine the cake mix, margarine, and half of 1 egg, well beaten; mix well. Press into an 8-inch-square baking dish. Set aside.

Prepare the custard: Combine the yams, brown sugar, cinnamon, ginger, salt, milk, and the remaining 2 1/2 eggs in a heavy saucepan or the top of a double boiler set over boiling water. Blend well. Cook over medium heat, stirring, just until thick. (Do not let the custard boil or the eggs will curdle.) Remove from heat and let cool, then pour over crust. Bake for 20 minutes.

Make the topping: Combine the margarine, brown sugar, and pecans, and sprinkle over the custard. Bake for an additional 25 minutes. Cool and serve cut in squares, topped with whipped cream.

MAKES 16 2-INCH SQUARES.

Becky Higgins's Texas Pecan Praline

1 1/2 cups sugar
1 cup firmly packed light brown
   sugar
1 cup buttermilk

1 teaspoon baking soda
1/4 teaspoon salt
2 cups pecan halves
3 tablespoons butter

Grease two baking sheets. Combine the sugars, buttermilk, baking soda, and salt in a large, heavy saucepan. Cook over low heat, swirling the pan occasionally, until the sugar dissolves. Increase the heat to high and boil until the mixture registers 210°F on a candy thermometer, stirring frequently, about 5 minutes. Stir in the pecans and butter and boil, stirring constantly and scraping the bottom and sides of the pan, until the mixture registers 230°F (thread stage) on a candy thermometer, about 5 minutes. Immediately drop by tablespoons onto the prepared sheets. Cool completely. The candies should be wrapped individually and stored in an airtight container, where they will keep for up to 1 month.

MAKES 2 TO 3 DOZEN PRALINES.

Hammond's Caramel Pie

This one's courtesy of Hammond's Bar-B-Q of Glenrose, Texas.

Filling	*Meringue*
2 cups sugar	5 egg whites, at room temperature
5 tablespoons all-purpose flour	1 tablespoon cream of tartar
1/4 teaspoon salt	1 tablespoon cornstarch
5 egg yolks	1/2 teaspoon vanilla
2 cups milk	1 cup sugar
3 tablespoons butter	
1 teaspoon vanilla	1 9- or 10-inch prebaked pie shell

Make the filling: Melt 1 cup of the sugar in a heavy skillet, stirring constantly and being very careful not to let it scorch. Cover to keep warm and set aside. Mix the remaining sugar with the flour and salt in a bowl. In a separate bowl, beat together the egg yolks and milk. Add the egg-milk mixture to the dry ingredients and beat well. Very carefully pour this mixture into the melted sugar, a tablespoon at a time, being careful that the sugar doesn't spatter. When all is combined, place over medium heat and stir constantly until the custard is smooth and thick. Remove from heat and stir in the butter and vanilla, then pour into the prepared pie shell.

Preheat the oven to 350°F.

Make the meringue: In a clean, dry bowl, beat the whites until they are thick and foamy. Add the cream of tartar, cornstarch, vanilla, and sugar and continue beating until the meringue stands in stiff, glossy peaks. Cover the pie with the meringue. Bake for 10 to 15 minutes, or until the meringue is brown. Remove and let cool before serving.

MAKES 1 9- OR 10-INCH PIE.

Dan's Cinnamon Rolls

This recipe and the next come from Dan's in Davenport, Oklahoma.

2 envelopes dry, quick-rising yeast
¼ cup lukewarm water
1 cup milk
½ cup sugar
½ cup (1 stick) butter or margarine

1 teaspoon salt
3½ to 4 cups flour
2 large eggs, at room temperature
2 tablespoons cinnamon
¼ cup (½ stick) butter, melted

Dissolve the yeast in the water and set aside until bubbly, about 10 minutes. Scald the milk and add ¼ cup of the sugar, the ½ cup butter or margarine, and the salt. Stir until the butter or margarine is melted. Stir in 1½ cups of the flour, beating until well mixed. Add the eggs, beating well. Add the yeast mixture and beat again. Mix in as much of the remaining flour as is necessary to form a stiff dough. Place the dough in a well-greased bowl and cover with a towel. Let rise for approximately 1 hour, or until double in bulk.

Combine the remaining ¼ cup sugar with the cinnamon and set aside. Punch down the dough and divide in half. On a lightly floured board, roll out each portion of dough into a 9- by 16-inch rectangle. Brush with the melted butter and sprinkle with the cinnamon-sugar mixture. Roll up, jelly roll fashion, and slice each roll into 8 equal pieces. Lay the cinnamon rolls flat and let rise for 30 minutes more.

Preheat the oven to 400°F.

Place the rolls on a well-greased baking sheet, brush tops with additional melted butter, and bake for 20 minutes, or until nicely browned. Serve warm.

MAKES 16 ROLLS.

Dan's Peanut Butter Pie

1 8-ounce package cream cheese, softened
1 cup peanut butter
2 cups powdered sugar

3 cups prepared whipped topping
1 9-inch prepared graham cracker pie crust

Cream together the cream cheese and peanut butter until light and fluffy. Add the powdered sugar, ½ cup at a time, beating well after each addition. Fold in the whipped topping mixture until well blended. Pour this mixture into the prepared pie crust and refrigerate until firm, several hours or overnight. We liked it frozen, then sliced and served immediately.

MAKES 1 9-INCH PIE.

New Braunfels Smokehouse Bread Pudding

4 eggs
1 cup sugar
4 cups milk
2 teaspoons vanilla
1$^{1}/_{2}$ loaves home-style white bread,
   cubed

$^{1}/_{2}$ cup raisins
$^{1}/_{2}$ cup brown sugar
Butter Sauce (see below)

Preheat oven to 350°F. In a mixing bowl, beat together the eggs and sugar until light. Beat in the milk and vanilla. Add the bread and raisins and mix well. Pour into 2 9-inch square baking pans. Sprinkle evenly with the brown sugar. Bake for 30 minutes, or until pudding has risen to top of pan. Serve warm, topped with Butter Sauce.

SERVES 8 TO 12.

Butter Sauce

$^{3}/_{4}$ cup sugar
3 egg yolks, beaten
3 tablespoons butter, melted
2 tablespoons cornstarch, dissolved
   in $^{1}/_{4}$ cup cold water

1$^{1}/_{2}$ cups boiling water
2 teaspoons vanilla
$^{1}/_{8}$ teaspoon salt

In the top part of a double boiler, beat together the sugar, egg yolks, and melted butter until light. Add the cornstarch mixture. Slowly add the boiling water, whisking to combine well. Cook over hot water until thickened, stirring constantly. Remove from heat and stir in the vanilla and salt.

MAKES ABOUT 2$^{1}/_{2}$ TO 3 CUPS SAUCE.

Southeast

There may be religious, political, athletic, or sexual images that stir deeper emotions — *may* be, but nothing in the realm of southern food is regarded with more passionate enthusiasm by the faithful than a perfectly cooked and seasoned pork shoulder or slab of ribs.
—John Egerton, *Southern Food* (Knopf, 1987)

Take fork-tender barbecued pork, pulled or chopped, lace it with bits of crisp, crackling pork skins, season with a dash of hot vinegar-based sauce, put it on a bun or a slice of plain white bread, crown it with coleslaw and another piece of bread, and serve it up with hush puppies and potato salad. This southern-style feast may shock burly Texans who swear by brisket, ribs, and fries. But to Carolinians and Virginians, it's hog heaven.

Carolinians and Virginians have always been bullish about their pork. You'll never hear an unkind word about a pig in this part of the country. Come to think of it, you'd better watch your language around here — calling somebody a "pig-headed swine" won't go over well in these parts. Neither will the old cliché, "sweat like a pig." (Every Carolinian knows that pigs have no sweat glands.) Ranking seventh nationally in hog production, North Carolina has always considered itself first in barbecue cooking prowess. Of course, as far as barbecue is concerned, South Carolina thinks it outranks North Carolina. Having sampled the wares of both, we think each state has its good points.

While these southerners may not give a darn about what else they eat, when it comes to barbecuing they have definite, unshakable opinions. For every Carolinian who thinks he's 100 percent right about cooking pork, there's another Carolinian who thinks he's 100 percent wrong. And there are plenty of Virginians ready to settle the differences by telling their Carolina neighbors the *real* way to serve pork. Decades have passed, and still the great barbecue debate rages, smoldering hotter than a bed of hickory coals. The constant argument is usually over:

- which kind of Carolina barbecue is best, eastern or western? North Carolina or South?
- whether to cook the whole hog or just the shoulder
- whether to chop, shred, or pull (*no one* slices it)
- which sauce is best: vinegar-based, tomato-red, or golden mustard?
- what type of cooking method to use: gas, charcoal, or charcoal and wood; open-pit or closed-pit?

Outsiders won't much care whether their succulent, marvelous Carolina-style barbecued pork is chopped, minced, shredded, or chunked, or whether the sauce features vinegar, mustard, or tomato. To Yankee taste buds, pork barbecue served all these ways tastes great. But you'd better believe there *is* a difference to a southerner.

The only thing Carolinians will agree on is what to serve with their barbecue. Usually it's some variation on the same theme: potatoes or potato salad, coleslaw, hush puppies, sweet potatoes, and, in some areas, Brunswick stew (a soupy concoction of meat and vegetables). Sometimes, in South Carolina, a hot pork or liver hash is served over rice. You don't find the Texas and Kansas City favorite, barbecued baked beans, as often, but corn bread is as common in the Carolinas as it is in the Deep South.

A sentence like "Let's eat barbecued pork" would never be uttered in this part of the country. Instead, a Carolinian would simply say, "Let's eat barbecue," because "barbecue" in these parts always means pork—preferably whole hog or pork shoulder, occasionally a fresh ham, depending on the region you're from. Whole hog is found more often in the east, pork shoulder most frequently in the west (with some crossover, including the occasional fresh ham). There are various cooking methods for each cut, and who is to say which technique is the finest? Personally, we think it's all good.

"DOWN EAST" VERSUS WEST

In "down east" barbecue, which emanates from the Carolina coast (generally east of Raleigh), a whole hog is split and cooked for eight to twelve hours, traditionally over hardwood coals. (Recently, though, we've spotted a trend away from open-pit methods using charcoal to gas cookers and even some closed-pit cooking.) The meat is basted with a clear vinegar-based sauce seasoned with red and black pepper and salt. After it is cooked, the meat is shredded and mixed with more of the same sauce, until it is laced through and through with a tangy sweetness that's ecstasy to taste.

To easterners, like prizewinning barbecuer Willis Peaden, vinegar and pork go together like bread and butter. Tart in the bottle, vinegar becomes amiable, even lovable when added to pork, rendering the meat succulent and delicious. Served with hush puppies and a well-dressed coleslaw, this kind of meal brings people back for more. At restaurants like Bill's Barbecue and Chicken Restaurant in Wilson, North Carolina, where three hundred whole hogs are served in a week, a mix of charcoal and gas is used to cook the pork. The meat is then chopped and seasoned with a vinegar sauce and accompanied with Brunswick stew, coleslaw, and boiled potatoes. Owner Bill Ellis claims that the eastern open-pit method is authentic. "If you want to barbecue, you gotta cook a whole hog in an open pit. To me, baked shoulder cooked in a closed pit ain't barbecue."

But devotees of western-style barbecue disagree. Natives of the Piedmont region of North Carolina prefer pork shoulder to whole hog, and frequently cook the meat in a closed pit fired up with hickory and oak wood for flavor as they do in Lexington, North Carolina, a town of 15,000 residents.

This sleepy town has more barbecue restaurants per capita (thirteen, to be exact) than any other city. Lexington Barbecue is one of the largest restaurants here, serving 5,000 pounds of pork shoulder a week to happy and satisfied customers. (The other twelve establishments all offer the same general style of barbecue.)

Owned by Wayne Monk, the Lexington Barbecue uses hickory and oak for barbecuing. Creating a fire is a two-step process, according to John Williams, who has been an employee for seventeen years. Hickory logs are burned down to coals in a separate unit and the hot coals are then transferred to a closed pit cooker. "We cook shoulders," explains Williams, "because they're more fatty than the hams and give a more moist meat." The fat and skin are trimmed off after cooking and the skins are fried to a crisp and served as a delicacy. Slaw is automatically served on the sandwiches unless you notify them otherwise.

Lexington Barbecue gained fame in 1982 when the international summit meeting was hosted by President Reagan at Colonial Williamsburg. The restaurant was asked to furnish one of several native American dishes, so they cooked up some barbecue and slaw, plus chicken and whole beef tenderloin to boot. The food was whisked by private plane direct from Lexington to Williamsburg and arrived hot enough to serve at the table.

While Lexington Barbecue offers excellent examples of western-influenced North Carolina barbecue, for a rollicking good discussion, try starting a conversation with a "down east" man about which sauce is best, eastern or western style. Few self-respecting eastern Carolinians would eat a sauce blemished by tomatoes; they prefer their barbecue as it is prepared at North Carolina restaurants such as Melton's Barbecue in Rocky Mount or the Skylight Inn in Ayden, where the chopped meat is dashed with a clear, spicy vinegar and topped with a slaw made from white cabbage.

Those who live in the middle and western parts of the state love a thin, mild red sauce such as the hot ketchup-and-vinegar concoction served at Stamey's Old-Fashioned Barbecue in Greensboro, North Carolina. The sauce is poured liberally over the meat and is sometimes used to redden the coleslaw served on top (often called "barbecued" coleslaw in these parts). Hush puppies are usually served alongside.

So, with some exceptions, you could say it's vinegar and spices "down east," with mostly reddish vinegar sauces in the western areas. In the far western part of the region, though, where the smoke from backyard cookers wafts across the skies above Asheville, North Carolina, we found vinegar sauce still used for basting, with a ketchup-based "dippin' sauce" served alongside the meat.

★ SOUTH CAROLINA

Few North Carolinians share South Carolina's liking for golden mustard-based sauces (although Georgians sometimes do). But the debate doesn't stop there. According to Allie Patricia Wall and Ron L. Layne, authors of *Hog Heaven: A Guide to South Carolina Barbecue* (Lexington, S.C.: The Sandlapper Store, Inc., 1979). South Carolina can be divided into six regions as far as barbecue sauce is concerned, with three varieties of sauce —mustard-, vinegar-, or tomato-based—mingled throughout the state.

The central part of the state favors the mustard-based sauces served up in places like Shealy Bar-B-Q in Leesville. The southeastern area appreciates mustard, too, but often with the addition of some vinegar and a dollop of ketchup. The northeast area fancies vinegar and pepper, and also favors a delicacy called chicken "bog," which is found at restaurants such as Cain's Bar-B-Q outside Florence—barbecued chicken chunks mixed with rice. The state's south-central region uses sauces of half mustard, half ketchup, while the north-central area uses another "combination" sauce that leans more toward mustard. In northwestern South Carolina, which leans heavily toward a vinegar-and-ketchup sauce, redder means better. Such spicy fare is served up at Spartanburg's Beacon Drive-In, while a chili-sauce-with-relish mixture tops the deluxe pork sandwiches at the town's Old Hickory Restaurant. But it's mustard, vinegar, and tomato in the sauces at Yum Youngs and Sons Barbecue near Pawley's Island.

South Carolina also offers a *green* coleslaw, something we discovered on our visits to restaurants such as Wilber's, Gary Parker's BBQ, and Scott's BBQ in Goldsboro—shredded dark green cabbage leaves in a vinegar dressing that was sometimes spiked with mustard.

Commercial barbecuing methods range from gas/charcoal pits

(Shealy's), to large electric pits (Cain's), to the old-fashioned open pit still hand tended by restaurants such as Wilber's Barbecue in Goldsboro, where the chopped-with-a-cleaver pork sandwich still comes from a whole hog cooked for 12 hours over an open pit with oak coals, just the way restaurant founder Wilber Shirley did it in 1962. Open-pit cooking is also practiced by Lee Alfred, owner of Lee's Bar-B-Q in North Augusta, one of the smallest (two or three tables) restaurants we visited in this part of the country. The Varsity, a barbecue drive-in in Atlanta, Georgia, that claims to have served 17,000 customers in a day, may be the largest, although Bessinger's Piggy Park in Mt. Pleasant, South Carolina, reports having rung up one of the highest daily grosses ever recorded—$36,000 on a Fourth of July.

 ## VIRGINIA: THE BIRTHPLACE OF WHOLE HOG BARBECUE

Virginians seem to have a foot in each barbecue camp, using both open- and closed-pit cooking and red and vinegar-based sauces. And, as we've pointed out elsewhere, Virginia was the site of outdoor barbecue roasts in colonial times. Virginians were probably barbecuing long before they knew what the word meant. To give you an idea of how our American forefathers pigged out, Colonial Williamsburg hosts an actual re-creation of an eighteenth-century barbecue each Labor Day weekend. A whole hog is used, basted with the traditional mix of saltwater alternating with melted butter.

Some beef barbecue can be found in Virginia, but mostly pork reigns supreme, and it's usually oak- or hickory-smoked. The meat is piled on a plate after being chopped, minced, or sliced—which immediately sets the state apart from North Carolina, where the only thing sliced is the bread. In this state you may be served fried pie for dessert and, alongside the meat, you'll get chitterlings (fried hog intestines), and a Brunswick stew made with chicken, pork, and vegetables (which many Virginians will tell you originated in Brunswick County, Virginia, rather than Brunswick, Georgia).

The old methods have been passed down from colonial times, and today you'll still occasionally find barbecued whole hog in rural Virginia. But oak- or hickory-smoked shoulder and Boston butt are now more common in the state's restaurants.

To many Virginians, variety is the spice of barbecue. At Pierce's, in the Williamsburg and Norfolk areas, shredded pork is soaked in a reddish mixture of vinegar and spices in a tomato base. The Pierce family hails from eastern Tennessee, and their thin, ketchup-like sauce is not unlike that found in their home state. Heaped on a bun and served sloppy joe style, the sandwich is a celebration for the taste buds. S & S Barbecue in South Hill and Nottoway's Barbecue of Hopewell feature tart vinegar-based sauces, while King's Barbecue in Petersburg serves up mustard-style concoctions.

★ GETTING READY FOR A PIG PICKIN'

The argument over whether to chop or pull (pig pickin') is neatly summed up by a North Carolinian named Patrick Gorman, a "down east" man from Newport who has won several North Carolina barbecue contests. He contends that there is a big difference between "pickin' the pig" and chopping it up.

"To chop barbecue, you pull it apart in chunks and chop up the chunks, depending upon how fine you want to chop them. You can mix some of the fat up with the lean meat so you get a good moist feel, mix in some crispy skin to give you a good blend, and you've got what we call eastern chopped barbecue," says Gorman.

"If you're pickin' the pig, you pull it out in pieces, mostly lean, sprinkle some sauce on it, and eat it. You can put a knife and fork to it if you want, but fingers are better. I never use a plate. When I pick a pig, I just stand there at the cooker and eat what I want."

It takes finesse and experience to produce meat that is moist and tender without being mushy. Carolinians pride themselves on techniques and cookers that produce prize-winning results. While most agree that the meat should be slow-cooked at a distance from the heat, there are differences in flavor and taste depending on whether one uses portable gas ovens in closed pits or open-pit techniques utilizing charcoal and wood.

Technological advances in cookers have elevated barbecue contests to an art. And as competitions in Rocky Mountain, Greensboro, Raleigh, and Newport have begun to run into thousands of dollars, North Carolinians have entered into the sport at fever pitch. Ask any of the contestants the *right* way to cook a whole hog and you're bound to get a different answer. And if you really want to confound the issue, talk to a neighboring Virginian.

★ PIT TALK

Before you attempt whole hog pit barbecuing, have a heart-to-heart with yourself. We'd love to tell you it's easy, but not every person is equipped to try it. Don't be ashamed if you find you aren't up to the task. This stuff is hard physical labor that requires the proper man/womanpower, time, and tools, and the right mind-set. You have to be adventurous, a risk-taker, and someone who doesn't mind getting dirty. Not everyone succeeds the first time out. Be prepared to make mistakes. But if you do it right, there's nothing like it. And if you don't? Well, try again.

Following are basic how-to's for cooking whole hog over a closed pit or a traditional open pit. For those who'd rather deal with smaller quantities of meat, though, we have included many other ways to pig out on various cuts of pork. *Boston butt* is a lean portion of pork found where the shoulder and front leg of the hog "butt" up against each other. At the upper extreme end of the front leg is the *pork shoulder,* and at the top of the back legs are the pork *hams. Pork loins* run down the side of the hog between the Boston butts and the hams. And, if you want to bring home the *bacon,* you'll find it just below the loin, close to the underside or belly of the pig. (For a discussion of *ribs,* see page 29.)

MASTERING THE ART OF WHOLE HOG BARBECUING

As we've discussed, there are two basic methods for cooking whole hog: closed-pit and open-pit. The following are the most complete instructions we've seen on the art of open- and closed-pit whole hog barbecuing. With this information, you should be able to cook up a finger-lickin' pig pickin' just like the experts.

Before you start, here are some items you'll need to have handy:

- sturdy "catchall" table
- sturdy chopping table
- dependable oven and meat thermometers
- paper towels
- chopping block
- knife or cleaver for chopping
- container for sauce (a vinegar bottle with holes pierced in the lid is great)
- container of water to douse any flare-ups
- heat-resistant gloves for handling pork and rack
- apron
- shovel for shoveling coals
- chair to rest your weary body
- favorite beverages for calming effect
- moral support from good friends
- double dose of patience

Open-Pit Method

The Hog
You'll need to give your state-inspected-meat purveyor (or local butcher) a few days' advance notice when purchasing a whole hog for barbecuing. Unless he's been living on Mars, he should know how to prepare it for you.

Tell him to dress the pig, which means that the animal should come to you already cleaned, gutted, and split open so that it can be stretched flat on the grill, belly down, for the first part of the cooking process. (Take care not to puncture the back skin before you put the meat on the grill.)

The size of the pig you purchase depends on how many folks you want to feed. Allow 1½ pounds carcass weight per person to determine the amount of pork you will need, plus the estimated cooking time. As a general rule, a 75-pound dressed pig yields around 30 pounds of cooked, edible meat; a 100-pound pig, about 40 pounds of meat; and a 125-pounder, about 50 pounds of meat. A 100-pounder should satisfy the appetites of seventy to eighty hungry people. It takes *at least* 8 to 10 hours cooking time to barbecue a whole hog this size, following our directions. Pick your pig up the morning of the barbecue and take it directly from refrigerated storage to the barbecue site. (You may have to arrange for an early pickup before the butcher shop is open in order to get done in time for an evening barbecue.)

Building the open pit

There are a couple of ways to build an open pit. The first method is to dig a shallow 2-foot-deep pit in the ground and cover it with a grill the day before the barbecue. We prefer a simple concrete or cinder-block "pit" constructed on top of the ground, using 8-inch cinder or cement blocks laid

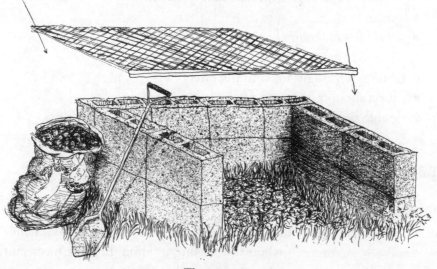

The open pit.

three high (2 feet) to form a U-shaped structure upon which to lay the hog. One end of the pit should measure 4 feet wide (inside measurement) for a pig of 100 pounds or more, 3 feet wide for a hog weighing under 100 pounds. The two adjoining sides should be approximately 5 feet long for the larger pig and 4 feet long for smaller pigs. Leave the fourth side open to shovel in new hot coals as needed.

The secondary pit

Since you don't want to add unheated charcoal directly to the pit fire, you need to prepare a second, smaller pit in order to have a continuous supply of hot coals available. About 10 to 15 feet from your open pit, clear and dig out a shallow pit, about 1 foot deep and 4 feet square. Keep coals going in the secondary pit throughout the day. You can also use a large barbecue cooker to keep a secondary bed of coals going.

Note: Your open pit will cover a lot of ground, so you need to choose a site with plenty of room. True outdoor whole hog barbecue is best done in the countryside, out of the way of houses and other structures. Before building your pit, we suggest that you check the local ordinances in your area to make sure that the building of such a structure is allowed.

The grill

Lay a series of strong, heat-resistant flat rods side by side, a foot apart, across the concrete blocks. On top lay heavy-gauge wire mesh upon which the entire pig will rest. (The size of the pig determines the size of the mesh, which should extend a good 6 inches beyond the pig on all sides.)

Have another sheet of open, heavy-gauge mesh of the same size handy to lay on top of the pig later, when you're ready to turn it over. Turning gets a little tricky. It takes one person on each end to lift the pig smoothly and quickly. (Be sure to use heat-resistant gloves.) Place the extra sheet of mesh over the pig. Place a rod on either side of the pig and weave the rods through the two pieces of mesh to hold them together. You can also use wire to tie the top and bottom pieces of mesh together at the edges. Both methods work well to ensure that the partly cooked hog won't come apart while it's being turned over for the final cooking process. Rehearse it first, before you start. It's even harder with the pig in there!

Turning a whole hog: Place a second sheet of wire mesh over the pig, "sew" the two sheets together on either side, using wire or heat-resistant rods, then—with one person on each end, wearing heat-resistant gloves—lift the pig smoothly and quickly turn it over.

The fire

Traditional open-pit barbecuc utilizes hardwood logs of hickory, oak, or pecan (or mesquite in the Southwest), which are allowed to burn down to coals before they are added to the pit. Never add whole logs to the pit fire for the same reason you don't add unheated charcoal: there will be flames using fresh wood or charcoal. Remember, flames are absolute no-no's in barbecue. You'll need about a third to a half a cord of wood for a 100-pound pig. For the purposes of this book, though, we'll build our fire using charcoal briquets, which are easier to obtain and provide a more even heat than logs.

It takes approximately 70 pounds of charcoal to cook a 100-pound carcass. Start the initial fire (either wood or charcoal) in the pit *before* the hog is placed on the grid. Begin with 20 pounds of charcoal in the pit. Pour a can of lighter fluid over the coals and ignite. The coals should be ready in about 45 minutes. (If you are using wood instead of charcoal, you'll need to allow 2 hours for the wood to ash down to embers.) Spread the coals out in a dumbbell shape, placing the highest concentrations of coals at the shoulder and butt ends of the hog. (Minimal coals are needed in the center or rib section of the hog, because it is much thinner and will cook much more rapidly.)

After turning the whole hog, pour basting sauce into the belly cavity and mop it all over the exposed meat surfaces. Repeat as needed until hog is done.

Place the hog rib side down, skin side up, on the grid (which should be 2 feet above the coals if you've stacked your cinder blocks correctly). Start your secondary pit fire 45 minutes after you light the first pit fire. (Allow 1 hour if you are using wood.) When these coals are red-white they can be added to the open pit as needed to keep the temperature at the cooking *surface* at 225°F for the first 2 hours and 250°F thereafter.

To help regulate the temperature, lay a good, accurate oven thermometer on top of the wire mesh at the source of the hottest fire (by the ham of the pig). If you see that the skin is starting to char or blacken, that means the fire is too hot. Cool the fire down by removing some of the charcoal. If the fire starts to wane, add more charcoal to build it back up. Your fire should never vary more than 10 to 15 degrees from the suggested temperature.

Cooking method
A 100-pound dressed hog will require at least 8 to 10 hours cooking time. Allow approximately 1 hour cooking time per 10 pounds for larger hogs.

There is no need to baste the hog during the first 5 to 6 hours. After turning, remove the top piece of wire mesh and pour a vinegar-based sauce (see pages 173 and 176) into the belly cavity, which is now facing up, until the sauce is about 1 inch deep. Mop the sauce all over the exposed meat surface. Baste again if necessary to keep the meat from drying out during the last few hours of cooking.

Place a meat thermometer into the ham section (the thickest part of the pig) without touching the bone. The pig will be done when the thermometer reaches 170°F. Place the cooked hog on a sturdy slicing or "pulling" table and let it stand for 20 minutes to allow the juices to reabsorb. The serving temperature should be approximately 130°F.

Pickin' the pig

Remove the skin of the pig and save the crisp cracklings, which can be mixed in with the meat later or served separately. Remove the fat and discard. Chop the pig into large chunks, sectioning out the leg, shoulder, and loin, and further chop or "pull" into eating pieces. Bits of meat from the jowls (if the head is left on), backbone, and ribs are often the juiciest and most prized for their flavor. You can eat the meat as is, or serve with additional sauce on the side. Pick and pull until either you or the hog are done for!

Closed-Pit Method

Courtesy North Carolina Pork Producers Association.

1 75- to 100-pound dressed hog
1/2 pound salt
Barbecue sauce (see recipes this
   section)
60 pounds charcoal briquets

Have the backbone of the pig split so that it will lie flat, and be careful not to pierce the skin. Trim and discard any excess fat. Sprinkle the salt inside the cavity and set the pig aside.

Place 20 pounds of the charcoal in a pork cooker. A 55-gallon drum will hold a small whole pig (see page 221). Pour 2 quarts of charcoal lighter fluid over the coals and ignite. Let the charcoal burn until it turns ash-gray, then spread out the coals, concentrating them at the shoulder and butt areas. Place heavy-gauge wire mesh about the size of the pig on the grill, about 14 inches from the coals.

Place the pig flat, skin side up, on the wire mesh. Cook at 225°F for 6 hours, adding additional lighted coals as needed to maintain the temperature in the cooker. Close the lid but do not add soaked woods, since this is not intended to be heavy-smoked, Texas-style barbecue.

Place a second piece of mesh over the pig, fastening the two layers of mesh with rods or wire as described above. Turn the pig over and remove the top piece of mesh. Insert a meat thermometer into the ham section without touching the bone.

Baste the meat with a vinegar-based sauce as described above. Close the lid and cook at 225°F for 2 more hours, or until the meat thermometer registers 170°F and no pink meat is visible when the hams and shoulders are cut. Slice and chop the meat or allow guests to "pull" the meat from the bones. Serve with additional barbecue sauce.

Note: Leftover cooked meat may be frozen for up to three months.

 **MEATS**

If you don't have time to fix up a whole hog, here are some delicious alternatives.

Southern-Style Barbecued Pork Shoulder

This recipe, from the North Carolina Pork Producers Association, can be prepared using a standard round kettle barbecue unit. Allow about 8 hours for the entire cooking process, including the time it takes to build the fire and let it ash down.

Marinade
2 cups cider vinegar
1 tablespoon Worcestershire sauce
1 tablespoon Tabasco sauce
1 tablespoon chili powder
2 tablespoons paprika
3 tablespoons ground black pepper

3 tablespoons salt
1 cup water

8 to 10 pounds boned and tied fresh
    pork shoulder (Boston butt)

Place the roast in a large, heavy plastic bag. Combine the marinade ingredients and pour half of it over the roast. Seal the plastic bag and place the roast overnight in the refrigerator. Reserve remaining marinade for basting and as a table sauce.

Pyramid 15 to 20 charcoal briquets to one side of the cooker, light, and let ash down (30 to 45 minutes). When the fire is ready, remove the roast from the marinade, sprinkle with salt, and place on the *opposite* side of the cooker from the coals. Close lid. (Do not add wet wood for smoke since this is an adaptation of an open-pit process.)

Baste the roast with the reserved marinade every 30 minutes, turning it occasionally for even cooking but being careful not to pierce it. Control the temperature by adding charcoal, keeping the heat at approximately 200°–225°F throughout the cooking process. Cook for 5 to 6 hours, or until a meat thermometer shows 170°F.

Remove the roast and let it cool, then discard the fat and chop the meat in 1/2-inch or smaller chunks, or shred by pulling. To serve, place a handful of meat on white bread and sprinkle with a Carolina barbecue sauce. Top with coleslaw if desired. Serve with hush puppies and potatoes.

SERVES 10 TO 15.

North Carolina Roast Pork

The following recipe is one of the least complicated ways of preparing a pork roast with juicy results. The recipe is courtesy of chef Brad Nordgulen of the K.C. Masterpiece Barbecue and Grill. It's different in that a dry rub, as well as a vinegar sauce, is used.

1 whole boneless pork roast, bottom or butt (4 to 6 pounds)

Dry rub
1/4 cup sugar

1/4 cup salt
1/4 cup paprika
1/4 cup ground black pepper

Vinegar-Pepper Sauce (see below)

Mix together the dry rub ingredients and coat the roast generously with the mixture on all sides. Barbecue at 200°F until done, approximately 4 to 6 hours. Baste every 30 minutes with Vinegar-Pepper Sauce. Let stand 15 minutes before chopping.

To serve, chop or shred the meat and mound it on a plate. Douse with additional sauce. For sandwiches, pile the meat on plain white or wheat bread, douse generously with sauce, and top with coleslaw and another slice of bread.

SERVES 8 TO 10.

Vinegar-Pepper Sauce

3 quarts cider vinegar
1 cup crushed red pepper

1 cup sugar
4 tablespoons salt

Place all ingredients in a gallon jug and shake to mix well. Store any left-over sauce in the refrigerator, where it will keep indefinitely.

MAKES ABOUT 3 QUARTS SAUCE.

Southern-Style Indoor "Barbecue" Sandwich

1 3-pound boneless pork shoulder
    roast (Boston butt)
1 small onion, thinly sliced and
    separated into rings
1 teaspoon salt
1/4 teaspoon ground black pepper

Eastern-style barbecue sauce (see
    pages 173–177)
Coleslaw
8 or 9 hamburger buns, split

Cut the pork shoulder into 3 or 4 pieces. Place the pork, onion, salt, and pepper in a Dutch oven. Add 1/2 inch water, cover tightly, and cook slowly 2 to 2 1/2 hours, or until pork is tender. Let the meat cool slightly in its juices.

Shred with two forks and mix it with barbecue sauce. Heat 4 to 5 minutes, stirring occasionally.

Place an equal amount of the pork mixture on the bottom half of each bun; top with an equal amount of coleslaw. Close sandwich with bun top.

SERVES 8 OR 9.

Stove Top Barbecue

If you can't get outdoors to cook, here's an indoor recipe for western North Carolina barbecue that's hard to beat, courtesy of the North Carolina Pork Producers.

1 4- to 6-pound boneless pork
   shoulder roast (Boston butt)
2 tablespoons vegetable oil
1½ cups water
1 8-ounce can tomato sauce
¼ cup white vinegar
¼ cup Worcestershire sauce

¼ cup packed brown sugar
Salt and ground black pepper to
   taste
1 teaspoon celery seed
1 teaspoon chili powder
Dash hot pepper sauce

Randomly pierce the surface of the roast with a sharp knife. In a Dutch oven, brown the roast on all sides in hot oil. In a mixing bowl, combine the remaining ingredients and mix well. Pour this sauce over the roast and bring to a boil. Reduce heat, cover, and simmer for 2 hours, or until the pork is fork tender. Baste with the sauce occasionally during cooking. Slice or chop and serve with sauce of your choice.

SERVES 8 TO 10.

The Basic Carolina-Style Chopped Pork Sandwich

8 slices plain white or wheat bread,
   or 4 sliced buns
1 to 1⅓ pounds chopped barbecued
   pork shoulder roast (see recipes
   this section)

Vinegar-based barbecue sauce to
   taste (see recipes this section)
1 cup coleslaw (see recipes this
   section)

Divide the chopped pork evenly among half the slices of bread or the bottom halves of the buns. Sprinkle generously with barbecue sauce. (Use a hot and spicy vinegar sauce for east-coast style, and for west-coast style a Piedmont or tomato-based peppery vinegar sauce. You can also use a South Carolina yellow mustard-vinegar sauce.) Place about 3 level tablespoons of coleslaw on top of each sandwich, top with the remaining slices of bread or bun halves, and give your taste buds a treat.

SERVES 4.

 ## NORTH CAROLINA BARBECUE SAUCES

North Carolina barbecue sauce recipes are plentiful and as distinctive as seasoning preferences of barbecuers across the state. The predominant sauce used in the east is a clear vinegar-based variety to which pepper and salt are added in various proportions. Western sauces use ketchup, sugar, and spices in addition to generous quantities of vinegar and pepper. The best way to select a sauce is to find one that suits your own taste.

For a sweet sauce you can use brown or white sugar, honey, molasses, ketchup, or sherry. For sour, use vinegar or lemon juice. Hot sauces usually include black or cayenne pepper, or crushed dried red pepper flakes. Mustard, onion, garlic, and Worcestershire sauce give a spicy kick. And soy sauce or salt provide a salty taste. Our thanks to the North Carolina Pork Producers, the National Pork Producers Council, and the South Carolina Pork Producers, who graciously shared several of the following recipes with us.

Eastern Pig Pickin' Sauce

This sauce is used for basting a whole hog. Additional sauce is served with the cooked meat. The recipe can be cut in half for a smaller quantity.

1 gallon white vinegar
1/4 cup salt
2 tablespoons cayenne pepper

3 tablespoons crushed red pepper
1 cup firmly packed brown sugar
   (1/2 cup dark corn syrup)

Combine all the ingredients and mix well. Allow to stand 4 hours before using.

   MAKES ABOUT 1 GALLON.

Piedmont/Lexington Sauce

1 1/2 cups white or cider vinegar
10 tablespoons ketchup
Salt and ground black pepper to
   taste

1/2 teaspoon cayenne pepper
Pinch crushed red pepper
1 tablespoon sugar
1/2 cup water

Combine all the ingredients in a small saucepan and bring to a simmer. Cook, stirring, until the sugar dissolves. Remove from heat and let stand until cool. Spoon a small amount of the sauce over barbecued meats.

   MAKES 3 CUPS.

Western Ketchup-Based Barbecue Sauce

1 cup ketchup
1 cup packed brown sugar
1/2 cup lemon juice
1/4 cup (1/2 stick) butter

1/4 cup minced onion
1 teaspoon hot pepper sauce
1 teaspoon Worcestershire sauce

Combine all the ingredients in a heavy saucepan and bring to a boil. Reduce heat and simmer for 30 minutes. Use as a dipping sauce.

   MAKES 3 CUPS.

Carolina Red Barbecue Sauce

2 tablespoons brown sugar
¼ teaspoon chili powder
½ teaspoon salt
2 tablespoons Worcestershire sauce
1 cup tomato sauce
¼ cup water

1 tablespoon paprika
1 teaspoon dry mustard
⅛ teaspoon cayenne pepper
¼ cup white vinegar
¼ cup ketchup

Combine all the ingredients in a small, heavy saucepan and simmer for 10 minutes. Refrigerate for at least 12 hours before using.

MAKES ABOUT 1½ CUPS.

 ## SOUTH CAROLINA BARBECUE SAUCES

In South Carolina there are three major sauce variations: tomato, mustard, and vinegar. The following typical recipes were given to us by C.C. Moorhead, Jr., of Blacksburg, South Carolina, the South Carolina Pork Board, and the North Carolina Pork Producers Association.

C.C.'s Favorite Barbecue Sauce (Tomato Style)

2 tablespoons brown sugar
1 tablespoon dry mustard
1 tablespoon celery salt
1 tablespoon cayenne pepper
1 tablespoon ground black pepper
1 tablespoon paprika

2 tablespoons cornstarch
½ teaspoon ground allspice
4 cups tomato juice
1½ teaspoons Worcestershire sauce
1 cup white vinegar
1 tablespoon grated onion

Mix the brown sugar, mustard, celery salt, cayenne, black pepper, paprika, cornstarch, and allspice in a heavy saucepan. Combine the tomato juice, Worcestershire sauce, and vinegar. Add a small amount to the dry ingredients to form a paste, to prevent lumping before adding the balance of the liquids. Add the grated onion. Cook on very low heat until thickened, about 2 hours, stirring frequently in the beginning.

MAKES 4 CUPS.

Note: You can substitute 4 cups canned tomatoes, puréed in the blender, for the tomato juice, in which case reduce the cornstarch to 1 tablespoon.

Mustard-Based Barbecue Sauce

1/4 cup (1/2 stick) margarine
1 tablespoon mayonnaise
4 to 5 tablespoons prepared mustard
1 tablespoon ketchup
2 to 4 tablespoons dark brown sugar

1 to 2 teaspoons white vinegar
Hot pepper sauce to taste
Dash salt
Dash ground black pepper
Garlic powder to taste

Melt the margarine in a saucepan. Add the mayonnaise and stir until liquified. Add the mustard, ketchup, and sugar, stirring until dissolved. Add the vinegar, hot pepper sauce, salt, pepper, and garlic powder. Heat thoroughly.

MAKES 1 CUP.

Hot Vinegar Barbecue Sauce

8 cups cider vinegar
1/2 to 3/4 cup crushed red pepper

1/4 cup salt
3 tablespoons ground black pepper

Mix all the ingredients well. Use for basting a whole hog, then reserve the remaining sauce in small jars to serve with cooked barbecue.

MAKES 10 CUPS.

Variation: You can make up a smaller quantity to serve with pork shoulder, using the following proportions:

2 cups cider vinegar

2 to 3 tablespoons crushed red
   pepper

1 tablespoon salt

2¹/₂ teaspoons ground black pepper
   to ³/₄ cup crushed red pepper

MAKES ABOUT 2¹/₂ CUPS.

Colonial Williamsburg Barbecue Baste

2 tablespoons salt

1 quart water

Melted butter

Mix the salt with the water and stir until well dissolved. Use this mixture as
a baste for any barbecued meat, such as a large roast or chicken, basting
alternately with the melted butter, every 15 to 20 minutes.

 **SIDE DISHES**

Eastern-Style Slaw

This slaw and the one that follows are courtesy of the North Carolina Pork
Producers Association.

1¹/₂ medium heads cabbage,
   shredded (about 9 cups)

¹/₄ cup minced green onion

2 cups mayonnaise

2 tablespoons plus 2 teaspoons sugar

2 tablespoons plus 2 teaspoons white
   vinegar

1¹/₂ tablespoons plus ¹/₂ teaspoon
   celery seed

¹/₂ tablespoon salt

In a large bowl, combine the cabbage and green onion. In a small bowl,
blend the mayonnaise, sugar, vinegar, celery seed, and salt. Mix well. Driz-
zle the mayonnaise mixture over the cabbage mixture and toss lightly to mix
well. Refrigerate until serving.

SERVES 6 TO 8.

Red Slaw (Piedmont/Style Barbecued Slaw)

Prepare the Eastern-Style Slaw above, omitting the green onions and celery seed, and adding 1½ tablespoons ketchup, plus any Piedmont/Lexington barbecue sauce to taste (see recipes this section).

Wilber's Green Coleslaw

This recipe was given to us by Wilber Shirley, the owner of Wilber's Barbecue & Restaurant in Goldsboro, North Carolina.

5½ cups shredded cabbage (use
   bright green leaves only)
1 cup commercial whipped salad
   dressing

2 tablespoons white vinegar
1 tablespoon prepared mustard
1 tablespoon sugar
Salt to taste

Place the cabbage in a large bowl. Mix together the remaining ingredients and pour over the cabbage. Mix thoroughly. Chill and serve cold.
    SERVES 10.

Melton's Coleslaw

The large quantity of mustard in this recipe makes for an unusual, distinctly pungent slaw that is excellent. Our thanks to Ms. Pattie L. Smith, owner of Melton's Barbecue in Rocky Mount, North Carolina.

Dash dry mustard
½ teaspoon celery seed
1 cup sugar
½ cup white vinegar

1 cup prepared mustard
½ cup mayonnaise
1½ pounds cabbage, shredded

Combine all the ingredients in a large mixing bowl and mix well.
    SERVES 4 TO 6.

C.C. Moorhead's Barbecue Slaw

This is the quickest "barbecue" slaw we know.

1/2 medium head cabbage, shredded
2/3 cup ketchup
1/3 cup white vinegar

6 to 8 drops Tabasco or Texas Pete
  hot sauce

In a large bowl, mix together all ingredients. Serve.
  SERVES 3 OR 4.

Carolina-Style Potato Salad

Courtesy North Carolina Pork Producers Association.

1 1/2 to 2 pounds potatoes
4 hard-boiled eggs, chopped
6 stalks celery, chopped
1/2 cup minced sweet salad pickles
  (or sweet pickle relish)
1 4-ounce jar pimentos, drained and
  chopped

1 small onion, chopped
1 small green pepper, chopped
2 teaspoons salt
1/2 teaspoon ground black pepper
1/2 cup mayonnaise
2 tablespoons prepared mustard

Wash the potatoes and place them in a large pot. Add water to cover, bring
to a boil, and cook for 30 to 40 minutes, or until tender. Drain potatoes and
let cool, then peel and dice. Mix the potatoes with the eggs, celery, pickle or
relish, pimentos, onion, green pepper, salt, and pepper. Blend the mayonnaise and mustard and add to the potato mixture; blend well. Chill for at
least 1 hour to permit flavors to mingle.
  SERVES 6 TO 8.

Moree's Sweet Potatoes

Courtesy of Rachel Moree, owner of Moree's Bar-B-Q in Andrews, South Carolina.

3 pounds sweet potatoes, boiled and peeled (or use canned)
3/4 cup granulated sugar
1 1/4 cups water
1 1/2 tablespoons cinnamon
3 tablespoons margarine

Preheat the oven to 250°F. Slice the sweet potatoes thickly and place them in a baking pan. Mix 1/2 cup of the sugar with the water and cinnamon and pour over the potatoes. Cut the margarine in chunks and dot the potatoes with it. Bake for 2 hours. Remove from oven, mash the potatoes, and top with the remaining sugar. Serve at once.

SERVES 6 TO 8.

Low Country Bar-B-Q's Liver Hash

We're grateful to Gene and Debra Baker and Eddie and Jennie Dingle for giving us their recipe served at Low Country Bar-B-Q in Georgetown, South Carolina.

1/2 pound pork fatback, diced
3/4 pound onions, finely chopped
5 pounds pork shoulder, finely chopped
2 tablespoons salt
3 tablespoons ground black pepper
2 1/2 pounds fresh pork liver, cut into 2- or 3-inch chunks
2/3 cup ketchup
3/4 cup Worcestershire sauce
2 teaspoons hot sauce

Sauté the fatback and onions together until onions are golden. Add the pork shoulder. Sauté together, stirring frequently, until meat is done, about 30 minutes. Add the salt and pepper.

In a separate pot, place the pork liver, add water to cover, and boil until done, about 20 to 30 minutes.

Put the cooked liver through a meat grinder, discarding the broth. Add the sautéed pork mixture and mix well. Add the ketchup, Worcestershire sauce, and hot sauce, and blend well. Serve hot, over boiled rice.

SERVES 24.

Mary Johnson's Hush Puppies

1 cup cornmeal	¹/₂ teaspoon salt
1 cup flour	¹/₄ cup butter or lard
1 teaspoon baking powder	1 medium onion, finely chopped
¹/₂ teaspoon baking soda	1 cup buttermilk
1 tablespoon sugar	Vegetable oil for deep frying

In a mixing bowl, combine the cornmeal, flour, baking powder, baking soda, sugar, and salt. Add the butter or lard and cut in as for pie crust, until the mixture resembles coarse meal. Add the onion and buttermilk and mix well. The batter will be thick.

In a large heavy pot or Dutch oven, heat 2 to 3 inches of oil to 325°F. Shape the batter into 2-inch balls and deep-fry, a few at a time, until golden brown, 3 to 4 minutes. Drain well on paper towels and serve hot.

MAKES ABOUT 30 HUSH PUPPIES.

Sausage Spoon Bread

Courtesy North Carolina Pork Producers Association.

1 pound breakfast sausage links	2 tablespoons chopped onion
4 cups milk	1 tablespoon prepared mustard
1 cup yellow cornmeal	¹/₂ cup grated Cheddar cheese
2 tablespoons butter	4 eggs, well beaten
¹/₂ teaspoon salt	

Preheat oven to 425°F.

In a frying pan, brown the sausage on all sides. Remove to paper towels to drain. In a heavy saucepan, heat the milk until it steams. Gradually stir in the cornmeal and cook, stirring constantly, until the mixture is the consistency of mush, about 10 to 15 minutes. Add the butter and salt, and mix well. In a mixing bowl, combine the onion, mustard, and cheese with the beaten eggs. Gradually stir in the cornmeal mixture. Pour into a greased 1 1/2-quart ovenproof baking dish. Top with the sausages and bake for 45 minutes.

SERVES 6.

Best Ever Brunswick Stew

Courtesy North Carolina Pork Producers Association.

1/2 pound country ham, chopped
1 pound ground chuck
1 small chicken (2 pounds)
1 jalapeño pepper, sliced
1 14-ounce bottle ketchup
1 28-ounce can crushed tomatoes
1 6-ounce can tomato paste
1 10³/4-ounce can condensed tomato
   soup
Dash Worcestershire sauce
Dash hot sauce
Salt and ground black pepper

1/2 cup (1 stick) butter
1 10-ounce package frozen corn
1 10-ounce package frozen butter
   beans
1 10-ounce package frozen green
   beans
2 large onions, sliced
1 pound Great Northern white
   beans, cooked, drained, and
   mashed (optional)
4 large potatoes, cooked and mashed

Cook the ham, chuck, and chicken together in a large stewing pot over medium heat until tender, about 1 hour. Remove the chicken, bone it, and cut it into small pieces and return to pot. Add the jalapeño pepper, ketchup, tomatoes, tomato paste, tomato soup, Worcestershire sauce, and hot sauce, and add salt and pepper to taste. Add the butter, corn, butter beans, green beans, and onions. Cook over low heat for 1 1/2 hours, stirring occasionally. Add the white beans, if using, and the potatoes.

SERVES 12.

 **DESSERT**

Town Point Club Lemon Chess Pie

This recipe is from the private Town Point Club, Norfolk, Virginia. Manager Dick Pfaff kindly shared this simple, delicious classic with us.

5 eggs
2 cups sugar
Juice of 3 large lemons

Grated peel of 1½ lemons
1 tablespoon cornmeal
1 unbaked 10-inch pie shell

Preheat oven to 350°F.

Beat the eggs until light, then add the sugar, lemon juice, grated lemon peel, and cornmeal, and mix lightly. Pour into the pie shell. Bake for 35 to 40 minutes, or until the pie is a light golden brown. Chill well before serving.

MAKES 1 10-INCH PIE.

South

 THE BARBECUE BELT

Tennessee, land of Elvis and W.C. Handy, where blues and barbecue reign supreme. In Memphis, which boasts more than eighty barbecue restaurants (and that's more than any other city its size), crisply braised pork shoulder and crusty-but-tender ribs have put this southern metropolis on the barbecue map.

The power of pork is especially strong once you get out of the mountains into the rolling hills of the middle part of Tennessee, where restaurant hickory pits turn out goodly amounts of pulled shoulder and succulent ribs. West of Memphis is the tiny town of Mason and Bozo's Pit Bar-B-Q, a place pit mavens consider to be a shrine. Here, delicious pulled pork chunks on toasted buns are crowned with a mound of slaw and served with hot or mild sauce on the side.

Memphis is the gastronomic mecca where the devout gather to experience the revelation of the city's renowned barbecue. Coupled with nearly two hundred contestants who come to claim prizes at the annual Memphis in May International Barbecue Festival, you have a city which has earned a righteous claim to the title "Pork Barbecue Capital of the World."

Memphis's pathways of pork go in many directions, beginning with the most venerable establishment of them all: Leonard's, at 1140 South Belleview. Although the current ownership has expanded its customer base to four locations around Memphis, the pork sandwiches remain as good as they were when the original restaurant opened more than sixty years ago. That's because the principal pit men on the premises have been working here for nearly half a century. The senior cook, James Willis, continues to barbecue pork shoulder, ribs, chicken, and brisket with the same finesse he had back in 1938 when he hired on as a helper.

Actually, the legend of Leonard's began in 1922, when Leonard Heuberger opened a sandwich stand, delivering barbecue by bicycle. In 1933 he moved to the location at 1140 South Belleview and, according to some, originated the granddaddy of the Memphis pork barbecue sandwich that is still the standard today: pulled or chopped pork shoulder piled on a *toasted* hamburger bun, topped with coleslaw and a sweet, potent red sauce.

"Just say 'give me a barbecue' and I guarantee that you'll get the same thing anywhere in town," says Dan Brown, the restaurant's general manager. "Every Memphian knows what 'a barbecue' means, and it's always pork shoulder." According to Brown, you can always tell tourists from the locals: the tourists are the ones who get the mixed pork shoulder platters because they don't know they have a choice of meats. The wall over the door of Leonard's sports a neon pig decked out in tuxedo, top hat, and cane, legs moving and cane twirling. Under the sign, in bold letters, are the words "Miss White and Mr. Brown." The sign's meaning is simple: when you cook a whole pork shoulder over direct fire, the outside gets dark and crusty. Memphians call that delicious crispy exterior "brown meat." The inside of the pork shoulder stays tender and light; that's the "white" meat. Therefore, if you're speaking proper Memphian, you'll order your barbecue mixed, white, or brown. In some places, such as Leonard's, you can further specify whether you want the meat "pulled" (in stringy chunks) instead of chopped. And you must tell the waitress to "hold the slaw" if you don't want this garnish. Otherwise, you'll wind up with the 75 percent of the local population who love the tangy, mustardy cabbage concoction piled on top of their pork.

Remember not to ask for "a barbecue" (pork sandwich) when you really mean ribs. Furthermore, you have to decide whether you want Memphis's famed pork spareribs served "dry" or "wet." Both versions are rubbed with a dry seasoning of herbs, spices, and sometimes brown sugar before cooking, but "wet" ribs are basted in a sweet, pungent sauce in the last stages of the 4- to 5-hour cooking process. To get "dry," you go to Charlie Vergos's Rendezvous, a downtown rib joint that serves charcoal-cooked ribs coated with a dry seasoning of herbs and spices. If you want sauce here, you have to ask. John Willingham's World Champion Bar-B-Que on South Perkins offers a version halfway between dry and wet. Both restaurants are among those that ship their ribs express mail all over the country. For "wet" ribs, it's all four locations of Gridley's. This is Memphis's largest barbecue establishment, which collectively seats 1200 hungry eaters, who bathe knuckle-deep in juicy ribs smothered in a baked-on sweet sauce.

At the Bar-B-Q Shop (formerly Brady and Lil's), there are other perks aside from the ribs and sandwiches. Owner Frank Vernon serves a barbecued spaghetti that Memphians crave. A thin, sweet barbecue sauce laced with chunks of Boston butt is ladled over pasta for a creation that has fans flying in from all over the country for carry-out. Unfortunately, when it comes to sharing barbecued spaghetti recipes, Memphis restaurateurs are silent as clams. So we tried barbecuing a Boston butt, chopping it into bite-size pieces, mixing it together with our favorite barbecue sauce, and spooning it over freshly boiled noodles. It was surprisingly good.

If the thought of barbecued spaghetti is strange to you, the idea of barbecued pizza may seem positively kinky. But the thin-crusted pizza crowned with cheese, tomato sauce, and bits of barbecued pork shoulder smothered in a tangy barbecue sauce is a highly prized side dish at Coletta's.

Another Memphis favorite is barbecued bologna, like that found at John Wills's Bar-B-Q Pit. The whole stick of bologna is scored every inch or so on all sides so that the smoke can penetrate, rubbed with seasoning, and slow-smoked over hickory wood, then glazed with a sweet sauce. "I eat it all the time," says John Wills, the winner of the 1980 and 1981 coveted grand championships at the famed Memphis in May International Barbecue Festival, "not because it's cheap, but because it's *good*."

Wills is an acknowledged expert on Memphis barbecue, known especially for the excellent quality of his ribs and pork shoulder. Wills employs a basic three-step method for barbecuing. First, he rubs dry seasonings on the meat. Then he places it in the smoker. Once the fat has begun to drip onto the coals and the meat starts to "sweat," he mops basting sauce generously over the food every 30 minutes or so. Many barbecuers do not use any oil, tomato bases, or sugar to baste, claiming that these cause the meat to burn. But Wills glazes the meat with a sweet sauce about a half hour before it's ready to be served, and deliberately "chars" the meat by slow-smoking it over direct heat. He prefers the combination of a succulent, tender inside and a dark, crunchy outside, which he says is "synonymous with real barbecue."

Like some other Memphis barbecue pros, Wills cooks in a closed brick pit, using hickory wood, oak and hickory briquets, and lump charcoal directly under the meat. Using a damper that he can open and shut at will, he can keep the temperature at the 200°–250°F required for the 12 to 14 hours it takes to cook a 15-pound pork shoulder.

Wills's side dishes are typical Memphis fare: barbecued baked beans laced with molasses and chunks of pork; coleslaw in a mustard-based dressing flavored with vinegar, sugar, pickles, and pickle juice; onion rings; french fries; and a vermicelli pasta in a meatless tomato sauce. "We serve something called 'half and half.' It's half barbecued pork and half spaghetti and it's one of our biggest sellers," says Wills.

But the more than 350,000 tourists who flock to the annual Memphis in May barbecue contest don't come for the spaghetti. Memphis in May is serious business. For over a decade, the event has been a two-day celebration of the food for which Memphis is famous. Teams have come from as far away as Ireland to compete in whole-hog, pork shoulder, and pork ribs categories, with names like "The Pit and the Pigulum," "Swine Lake Ballet," "Raiders of the Lost Pig," "Oink, Inc.," and "Pepto Porkers." The music as well as the food is a big draw, with stars such as "Blues Brother" Dan Ackroyd flying in to perform. The success of the contest has had a major impact on the city's image. When it began in 1977, there were relatively few good barbecue restaurants in town. But the publicity has helped support more commercial pits to feed the thousands of customers who flock here like homing pigeons in the spring, and with all the quantity, there is quality, too.

Memphis in May contest winners don't necessarily hail from Memphis. In fact, Darrell Hicks, whose Cajun Country Cookers won the Memphis in May Grand Prize in 1987, hails from Dexter, Missouri.

To Hicks the difference between Memphis and Midwest barbecue lies in the seasonings. "Memphis barbecue is a dry-base barbecue, with the seasoning applied to the meat before cooking it over hickory or oak," Hicks comments. "Midwestern-style barbecue uses lots of sauce."

Another Memphis in May contestant, Jim Quessenberry, who lives in Cherry Valley, Arkansas, cites even more differences between Tennessee barbecue and other regions. He calls Tennessee barbecuers "smokers," northern barbecuers "saucers," and southern barbecuers "spicers." Midwestern barbecue (which he fits neatly in the northern category) is simply a "mishmash."

Quessenberry, who has barbecued in contests from Cleveland to San Antonio, has participated in the Memphis in May contest for ten years. His group, the Arkansas Trav'lers, won the Irish Cup in Ireland's famed barbecue contest in 1985 and 1987. The man is literally a walking compendium of delicious recipes, from brisket and chicken to sauces and salads.

Tennessee ribs are cooked by traditional methods: usually hickory wood is used in closed-pit barbecue units; the meat is seasoned with a dry rub and brushed with a home-made sauce. There's nothing all that different about the Tennessee way to prepare a Boston butt or a fresh ham, either. The basic methods outlined in the Southeast section of this book are similar to the recipes in many parts of Tennessee. So rather than repeat ourselves, we've chosen to concentrate on Tennessee's famed dry rubs and sauces.

Using these dry rubs and sauces to cook a fresh pork shoulder roast over hickory in a closed pit will give you the flavor and taste of great mid-South barbecue. Since many of the Memphis in May barbecue contest winners are actually from states other than Tennessee, we managed to collect a rather eclectic group of down-home recipes for this book.

★ KENTUCKY

While Tennessee is a prime contender for the barbecue championship of the south, Kentucky can hold its own as far as barbecue lovers are concerned. The western part of the state is laced with barbecue pits that sell hickory-smoked pork shoulder, ribs, mutton, and red sauces. Kentucky barbecue tends to differ from that found elsewhere. For example, we found our pork served up on cornbread rather than on a bun, and sandwiches were likely to include a dill pickle or onion. Instead of Brunswick stew, we found a hearty, peppery dish called burgoo.

Burgoo is a stew that includes everything but the proverbial kitchen sink. The main ingredient is mutton, and since farmers around Owensboro used to raise plenty of sheep back around 1830, it came to pass that the town's church socials always included a barbecued mutton as the main course. The zeal for summer barbecucs spread to various religious and political groups, and by the late nineteenth century Owensboro became famous for its celebrations. Memphis may call itself the "Pork Barbecue Capital of the World," but Owensboro has tried to capture the limelight by calling itself the "Bar-B-Q Capital of the World."

Certainly Owensboro deserves recognition. The town's International Bar-B-Q Festival held each summer attracts thousands of people, who come to town to dine on mutton barbecue and burgoo. Owensboro is a tough act to follow, but the town still has a way to go before it reaches the size and scope of the Memphis in May contest. Meanwhile, the town's fame is spreading as its restaurants cater each year to the growing clientele who've heard about the food and want to taste it for themselves.

The Moonlite Bar-B-Q Inn has gained respect for the quality and quantity of its food. The place can serve over a thousand people daily and cooks about 4,000 pounds of meat and 200 gallons of burgoo a day in the summer. Besides barbecue, the Moonlite offers ham, catfish, and a fabulous barbecue buffet that includes mutton, pork, beef, burgoo, and plenty of veggies, breads, drinks, and dessert.

Chopped or sliced mutton is the main attraction at the Old Hickory Bar-B-Q. The place was opened in 1918 by Charles Foreman, an Owensboro blacksmith, who passed the mutton mantle down five generations to the present owner, Harl Foreman.

Foreman cuts a whole sheep into seven pieces, then barbecues it over hickory coals in a closed pit for 16 hours. Along with the mutton, Foreman serves chopped or sliced Boston butt, chicken and ribs, and, of course, burgoo. Foreman gave us his recipe for the burgoo, which called for church social proportions: 100 pounds of meat (90 percent of which is comprised of mutton flanks and necks) and about 40 gallons of water, plus gallon quantities of vegetables and sauces. (For our home-sized version, see the recipe for burgoo in this section.)

While Owensboro takes center stage when it comes to barbecue, Paducah, about 150 miles downriver from Owensboro, boasts Starnes Barbecue. In operation for nearly half a century, Starnes prides itself on serving up fine brisket, ribs, and pork shoulders. West of here is Leigh's Barbecue in Heath, which serves excellent sandwiches of pork shoulder accented with a vinegar-tomato barbecue sauce.

ARKANSAS

While Kentucky and Tennessee retain their southern influence, it's in the state of Arkansas that the Midwest and South meet head to head.

In the northwest corner of the state, where narrow roads curve and dip through the hills along U.S. 12 and 62, the meat is still hickory-smoked pork, mostly chopped, with spareribs and a little beef brisket thrown in for diversion. The Arkansas sauces we sampled had a definite midwestern influence; they were thicker than the thin and vinegary concoctions we found in Tennessee and elsewhere in the South. Subtly flavored, the brown, sweet Arkansas sauces were served on the side, along with typical accompaniments of coleslaw, baked beans, and french fries.

At Froggies in Eureka Springs, hickory-smoked chopped pork on a bun is laced with a sweet, thick sauce. Further south in Hot Springs, brisket laced with a peppery but sweet hot sauce is offered at McClard's Barbecue, probably the single most popular barbecue enterprise in the state. The place serves nearly 4,000 pounds of hickory-smoked beef and pork a week, and the sauce is so popular that owner J.D. McClard ships it all over the country.

A barbecue bonanza can also be found in northeast Arkansas, at Couch's Bar-B-Q in Jonesboro, where hickory-smoked beef and pork bathed in a spicy, vinegary sauce draws customers from around the state. And, for dessert, there are always fried pies.

★ DEEP SOUTH

There are hundreds of good city and roadside barbecue spots throughout the Deep South whose only claim to fame is the food they serve. In Georgia and Alabama the crosscurrents of various influences intermingle so that surprises appear around every corner, in sauces, cooking styles, and side dishes. Yellow, sweet red, and hot-as-fire orange sauces pop up unexpectedly from county to county to delight the palate, much as they do in parts of South Carolina. Barbecuers in these parts use both open- and closed-pit methods, fueled with hickory and oak.

In Georgia, barbecue is featured on the menus of steakhouses in the western part of the state and seafood restaurants near the Gulf; in eastern Georgia, it is offered along with chicken. In fact it isn't at all unusual to find restaurants that advertise "chicken, seafood, barbecue, and steaks."

In Brunswick, the Choo-Choo Bar-B-Q offers pork butt, ham, and spareribs, along with barbecued sirloin roasts and chicken. The beef is sliced, the pork chopped, and there are three house sauces, ranging from mild to fiery hot. At Boyd's Bar-B-Q in Statesboro, chicken is barbecued inside brown paper bags, the only place we found this method used. Pork and beef are prepared in the usual manner, using oak to flavor the meat. In Jackson, the Custom Fresh Air BBQ offers smoky chopped pork sandwiches, served with a warm vinegar-and-oil-based barbecue sauce and a tasty Brunswick stew that warms the innards. In Atlanta several barbecue places offer the unusual: the Flying Pig's Texas toast grilled over live coals; the thick and hearty Brunswick stew at the Old Hickory House; the "come back" sauce at Aleck's BBQ Heaven, where meat is cooked on cobblestone pits.

Yet no food we tasted matched our delight over the white corn bread laced with crisp ham skins served at Harold's BBQ southwest of downtown Atlanta, founded by Harold Hembree and his wife in 1947. When Harold died in 1957, Mrs. Hembree took over the operation, keeping the friendly atmosphere intact. As a sign on the wall states, "There are no strangers here, only friends we haven't met." Harold's serves pork, as well as a marinated eye of round roast and Brunswick stew. The meat is encased in grilled toast, and can be livened up with a swipe of the hot red vinegar sauce. From Mrs. Hembree we learned that Atlanta barbecue had its roots in dirt-floor carry-out places such as Mobley's, Lefty's, Harold's, Old Hickory, Southern Gold, and the Flying Pig.

Georgia is Brunswick stew country, and if you make the mistake of telling Georgians that Brunswick stew originated in Virginia, you'll be regarded as an extraterrestrial. In truth, the soupy, rich concoction of meat and vegetables developed all along the coastal regions of Georgia, North Carolina, and Virginia, changing form slightly in Kentucky, where it evolved into the similar dish called burgoo, which is made with mutton.

In Newnan, Georgia, which has more sumptuous residences than any other small town we've ever visited anywhere, we gobbled down pulled and chopped barbecued pork shoulder sandwiches at a popular restaurant called Sprayberry's. Sprayberry's is fried pie heaven, with peach and apple versions in perfect flaky crusts. Columbus has thirty-some barbecue spots, and most of them offer Brunswick stew, with barbecued beans running a close second as a side dish. People here like the orange mustard- and vinegar-based barbecue sauces (see the Southeast section for recipes), and many restaurants take them a step further, producing a raging-hot sauce for intrepid connoisseurs of cayenne. While ketchup and sugar aren't big on the barbecue list of Columbus citizens, we did find both mild and hot red tomato-based sauces at the Hamilton Road BBQ, not to mention the most beautiful heavy-smoked ribs we had encountered since we left the Swingin' Door in Richmond, Texas.

Savannah is no slouch when it comes to barbecue, either, and you won't find the usual creosote-covered chimneys and concrete-block construction at Johnny Harris's place. The circular, domed dining room is paneled in a rich knotty pine, and there is a parquet dance floor. Lightly smoked leg of lamb was wonderful, as were the chicken, ribs, and pork.

Ditto for dessert: cheesecake, custard, Key lime pie, and trifle proved great ways to end a barbecue feast.

Outside Savannah on Highway 17 South we found Mammy's Kitchen, an older establishment serving unusually delicious barbecued baked beans along with beef, pork, and ham. Every day, owner Arthur Klees and his wife prepare award-winning batter-dipped french fried potatoes that are simply seasoned and utterly delicious. Beautifully prepared fresh vegetables, buttery pound cakes, and traditional pecan pie round out the fare served here.

We couldn't leave Georgia without a visit to Vidalia onion country, where we collected recipes and information on how to use the sweet, mild onions.

The Vidalia onion is a special variety of hybrid onion grown near the small town of Vidalia, Georgia, located west of Savannah on Highway 280. The soil and climate here produce the wonderfully sweet taste for which these onions are famous. True Vidalia onions are harvested from May until the middle of June, yet unlike many other onions, Vidalias are often planted in September for a May harvest, taking eight months to mature.

In *Georgia Cooking with Sweet Vidalia Onions* by Evelyn Carroll Rogers, published in 1984, we found some creative recipe ideas using these wonderful vegetables. We've included two barbecue sauce recipes from the book in this section, but if you want to know more about preparing Vidalias, from dips to entrees, write to Ms. Rogers at P.O. Box 736, Vidalia, Georgia 30474.

If you're looking for a blazing brand of sauce that's sure to incinerate the insides, Alabama is the state to find it in. At Cromwell's Bar-B-Que in Phenix City (formerly Chicken Comer's), an off-the-beaten-path pit, the crusty pork shoulder is cloaked in a fiery mustard-based sauce and served with enough white bread to extinguish the flames. The restaurant's current owner, May Cromwell, heads up an all-female staff (except for the pit master) that serves the customers gathered at noon inside the simple concrete building.

Phenix City also boasts the "scramble dog," a large steamed hot dog crowned with chili, onions, slaw, and pickles and sometimes served with barbecued coleslaw. The scramble dog has been popular here for twenty-five years and is found only within a fifty-mile radius of town. We also discovered two unique pies at Country's in Phenix City: "goober" pie, with a smooth, creamy peanut butter filling, and a scrumptious chocolate chess pie with pecan topping that is the downfall of chocoholics. Country's also makes their own scalloped apples and packages their own products, from hot chowchow and green tomato relish to spring onion, muscadine, and jalapeño jellies. You can't imagine a tastier treat than some of these spread on their fresh garlic-sesame toast. Fortunately for those who don't get to Phenix City, there are Country's branches in Montgomery, Alabama, and Columbus, Georgia.

Twixt and Tween in Montgomery serves an unusual barbecue sauce that tasted to us like a mix of mustard, ketchup, and dill pickle juice. The french fried onion rings were dipped in a seasoned pancake batter that made them extra-crusty.

Heading south from Montgomery to the Gulf we reached Mobile, where we discovered two unusual barbecue restaurants that are worth the trip. At elegant Fletcher's, owner Dick Lewis (a first cousin of the grand-daughter of founder Fletcher Harvey, Sr.) oversees an ambitious and sophisticated establishment, but open-pit smoked pork shoulders and butts are still his mainstay. The house barbecue sauce is a distinctive thick, brown, gravylike affair that tastes of apples, and desserts included out-standing rich coconut and lemon ice-box pies, along with delicious peanut butter and chocolate pies.

Kirkland's Texas-Style BBQ in Mobile serves barbecued shrimp, peeled raw and smoked for a good 20 minutes over hickory, then doused with Kirkland's special sauce. Unusual dishes such as deep-fried corn on the cob and fine-textured barbecued beef sausages complement the more standard fare. The owner claims his iced tea is the best in the South. It was outstanding—freshly brewed and a fine way to wash down barbecued shrimp!

In nearby Tuscaloosa, University of Alabama students favor the simple but basic barbecue served up at small, classic joints like Dreamland Drive-Inn just south of Tuscaloosa, and Archibald's in Northport. These restau-rants and many more are evidence that traditional pit barbecue is still going strong along the old southern barbecue belt.

★ MEATS AND POULTRY

Jim Quessenberry's Prime Rib

Arkansan Jim Quessenberry and his Arkansas Trav'lers have participated in the Memphis in May contest for over a decade. They have twice been awarded the grand prize at the Irish Cup Invitational Barbecue Festival in Ireland, and this prime rib won first place at the contest in 1985. Timing is important on this one; practice makes perfect!

1 5-pound standing rib roast, nicely marbled
1 teaspoon garlic powder

¼ cup olive oil
Freshly cracked black peppercorns

With a boning knife, carefully separate the rib bones from the roast, keeping them in one piece. Then remove the lip, or fat, layer in one piece. This will leave you with three pieces of meat: the ribs, the lip, and the ribeye. Sprinkle the ribeye with the garlic powder, then reassemble the three pieces and tie them tightly with butcher's string, binding at each rib. Brush the roast generously on all sides with the olive oil, then cover the entire surface with cracked pepper. Insert a meat thermometer in the center of the roast.

Cook in a closed barbecue unit (Quessenberry prefers the Weber kettle) over medium (250°F) indirect heat. Cook for 2 to 3 hours, checking frequently after 2 hours, to an internal temperature of 140°F for medium rare. Then wrap the roast tightly in foil and head for the kitchen; it's carving time. (The foil wrap is important, as it allows the roast a little extra steaming time.) Carve into slices at least ½-inch thick. There should be a slice to fit everyone's preference, from the well-done outside to the rare center. Serve with a hot white sauce seasoned with prepared horseradish and salt and pepper to taste, or with a cold sauce of sour cream flavored with prepared horseradish, salt, pepper, and lemon juice to taste.

SERVES 10.

Jim Quessenberry's Beef Brisket

1 7-pound beef brisket, trimmed | 4 tablespoons salt
2 tablespoons ground black pepper

Dry rub
6 tablespoons chili powder | Texas Sauce (see below)

Rinse the meat and pat it dry. Mix the dry rub ingredients together and rub the roast thoroughly with this mixture. Cook slowly over indirect heat (225°–250°F) until a meat thermometer reaches 165°F, about 3 to 4 hours. Wrap tightly in foil and continue cooking for an additional 3 hours, or until tender. (The long cooking tenderizes the brisket, while the foil holds in the moisture.)

Serve with buns, slaw, and Texas Sauce.

SERVES 15 TO 20.

Texas Sauce

2 cups white vinegar | 1 tablespoon chili powder
2 cups ketchup | 1 teaspoon salt
1 cup packed brown sugar | 2 teaspoons ground black pepper

Combine the ingredients in a heavy saucepan and bring to a boil over medium heat. Simmer for 30 to 40 minutes, or until thick and smooth. Serve warm or cold.

MAKES ABOUT 5 CUPS.

Kirk Kirkland's Beef Sausage

Voris E. Kirkland supplied us with this recipe from Kirk Kirkland's Bar-B-Q in Mobile, Alabama.

1¼ pounds ground chuck

¼ pound ground pork

8 saltine crackers, crumbled

1½ teaspoons granulated garlic

1½ teaspoons ground black pepper

2 tablespoons salt

½ teaspoon cayenne

½ teaspoon paprika

½ teaspoon sodium nitrate
   (saltpeter) (optional)

Mix together all ingredients and put through a meat grinder on the finest grind. Kirkland stuffs the sausage into casing, making 1 long roll of sausage or 18-inch loops tied at the ends. He also recommends hanging the sausage from bars in a drum-style cooker. However, we tested this recipe another way, forming the meat into 6 ¼-pound patties, each 1-inch thick. We laid them flat on the grill and cooked them, as Kirkland suggests, for 1½ hours over indirect coals at 225°F. They came out fine.

Note: If you prepare the sausage and cook it the same day, you don't need to add the sodium nitrate.

MAKES 1½ POUNDS SAUSAGE.

John Wills and the Tennessee Playboys's Prize-Winning Baby Loin Back Ribs

John Wills and the Tennessee Playboys, a Memphis team, won the Memphis in May grand prize in 1981 and the year before, too. Here's how to prepare their famous baby loin back ribs.

3 to 4 pounds baby loin back ribs
   (2 slabs)

Dry Rub

2 tablespoons paprika

2 teaspoons seasoned salt

2 teaspoons ground black pepper

2 teaspoons granulated garlic

1 teaspoon cayenne pepper

1 teaspoon MSG (monosodium
   glutamate) (optional)

1 teaspoon dried oregano

1 teaspoon dry mustard

½ teaspoon chili powder

Basting Sauce
4 cups red wine vinegar (preferably
    Regina)
4 cups water
1/2 cup packed brown sugar
1 5-ounce bottle Worcestershire
    sauce (preferably Lea & Perrins)

1 teaspoon Tabasco sauce
1 bay leaf
3 tablespoons dry rub (above)
Sweet Sauce (optional; see below)

Place the ribs in a large, shallow pan. Combine the dry rub ingredients and rub the mixture all over the ribs. Cover and refrigerate at least 3 hours.

Mix together the ingredients for the basting sauce and let sit several hours or overnight. (Remember that a basting sauce is not supposed to taste good by itself.)

Cook the ribs over slow coals (225°–250°F) for 3 hours, basting them sparingly with the basting sauce (just enough to keep them moist) and turning them occasionally. You can also cook them on the grill for 1 hour, then finish them in a 250°F oven for 1 1/2 to 2 hours. If you like your ribs "wet," glaze the ribs with the following Sweet Sauce during the final 30 minutes of cooking.

SERVES 4.

Sweet Sauce

1/2 cup (1 stick) butter
2 cups ketchup (preferably Heinz)
1 15-ounce can tomato sauce
2 cups red wine vinegar (preferably
    Regina)
1 10-ounce bottle Worcestershire
    sauce (preferably Lea & Perrins)
1 8-ounce bottle hot, sweet mustard
1 2-ounce bottle Tabasco sauce

1/4 cup packed brown sugar
2 tablespoons paprika
1 tablespoon granulated garlic
2 tablespoons seasoned salt
2 tablespoons lemon juice
Dash chili powder
Dash ground black pepper
Dash cayenne pepper

Melt the butter in a large, heavy saucepan over medium heat. Add the ketchup, tomato sauce, vinegar, barbecue sauce, and Worcestershire sauce, stirring constantly. Add the remaining ingredients, bring to a simmer, and cook gently for 30 minutes, stirring occasionally.

MAKES 8 CUPS.

Choo Choo Barbecue Ham

This one's courtesy of Steve Rawl, owner of the Choo Choo Barbecue in Waverly, Georgia. To ensure proper moisture and taste, Choo Choo's hams are cooked on a wood cooker, using hickory and live oak only.

1 10- to 12-pound *fresh* ham
Salt and ground black pepper to
   taste

Choo Choo's barbecue sauce (or
   substitute your favorite barbecue
   sauce)

Prepare a heavy bed of coals, and regulate cooker temperature to 200°F. Cover the grill rack with aluminum foil. Salt and pepper the ham and place it on the foil; cover it tightly with additional foil. Cook for 7 hours, then uncover and cook for 3 more hours, or until tender. Remove immediately. Slice or pull the meat, add barbecue sauce, and serve. (The ham skins can be cut up and deep fried for a delicious side dish.)

SERVES 15 TO 20.

John Wills's Barbecued Bologna

This was the best bologna we've ever eaten.

1 2-pound stick good-quality
   bologna

Dry Rub (see page 124)
Sweet Sauce (see page 199)

Score the bologna lengthwise every inch or so on all sides, so that the smoke will be able to infiltrate. Rub the entire stick with the dry rub. Slow-smoke (225°–250°F) for about 2 to 3 hours with hickory wood. Glaze with the sauce during the last 30 minutes of cooking. Cut in cubes or slice to serve.

SERVES 6 TO 8 AS AN APPETIZER.

Johnny Harris Restaurant's Barbecued Lamb

Courtesy of Norman Heidt, owner of Johnny Harris Restaurant in Savannah, Georgia.

1 4- to 6-pound leg of lamb, bone in

Sauce
1 14-ounce bottle ketchup
$1/2$ cup packed brown sugar
$1/4$ cup lemon juice
$1/4$ cup white vinegar

$1/4$ cup liquid smoke
$1/2$ cup water
1 teaspoon hot pepper sauce
1 tablespoon garlic powder
2 tablespoons Worcestershire sauce
1 tablespoon salt
1 tablespoon soy sauce

Combine the sauce ingredients in a large bowl and blend well. Baste the lamb with the sauce and place it, fat side up, in the cooker. Slowly smoke (at 225°–250°F) over hickory and oak wood, fat side up, for 6 to 8 hours without turning, or until the internal temperature reaches 170°F. Continue to baste the lamb with the sauce during cooking; baste once again right after removing from the cooker.

S E R V E S 6 T O 8.

Jim Quessenberry's Chicken Oregano

3 $2^{1}/_{2}$- to 3-pound chickens,
    quartered
1 cup lemon juice
4 cups olive oil

2 teaspoons salt
1 teaspoon garlic powder
1 tablespoon dried oregano

Place the chicken in a non-corrodible bowl or dish. Combine the remaining ingredients and pour over. Cover and let marinate in the refrigerator for several hours.

Cook the chickens over charcoal at 200°–225°F in a covered grill. Turn and baste often with the reserved marinade until done, about 2 hours.

S E R V E S 6 T O 8.

Jim Quessenberry's Roast Turkey

1 10- to 12-pound turkey
Lemon juice to taste
Garlic powder to taste
Paprika

Sauce
1 cup mayonnaise

1 6-ounce can tomato paste
1/4 cup lemon juice
3 tablespoons Worcestershire sauce
1 tablespoon grated onion
1 tablespoon prepared horseradish
1 teaspoon salt
1 teaspoon cayenne pepper

Rinse and dry the turkey. Rub generously with the lemon juice, sprinkle with garlic powder, and let stand until dry. Then coat thoroughly with paprika. Roast over slow coals (225°–250°F), using indirect heat, until the meat thermometer registers 195°F, about 6 hours. (Be sure to place a drip pan underneath the turkey.)

Meanwhile, make the sauce: In a mixing bowl, combine all ingredients and blend well. Refrigerate until serving. (This sauce is best if made a day in advance.)

SERVES 10 TO 12.

 ## RUBS AND SAUCES

Darrell Hicks's Cajun Country Dry Rub

Darrell Hicks, whose Cajun Country Cookers won the Memphis in May grand prize in 1987, hails from Dexter, Missouri.

3 tablespoons rubbed sage
1/4 cup salt
2 tablespoons brown sugar
2 1/2 tablespoons MSG (monosodium
  glutamate) (optional)

2 1/2 tablespoons garlic powder
1/4 cup cayenne pepper
1 1/2 tablespoons celery salt

Combine all the ingredients and store in an airtight container.

MAKES ABOUT 2 CUPS, ENOUGH FOR SEVERAL SLABS OF RIBS, OR 2 WHOLE BRISKETS.

Darrell Hicks's Championship Whole Hog
Table Sauce

$^{1}/_{2}$ cup lemon juice
1 cup packed brown sugar
1 cup (2 sticks) margarine
$^{1}/_{4}$ cup prepared mustard
1 cup white vinegar
1$^{1}/_{2}$ teaspoons salt

3 8-ounce cans tomato sauce
1 14-ounce bottle ketchup
1$^{1}/_{2}$ teaspoons liquid smoke
4 teaspoons Cajun Country Dry Rub
  (optional)
1 clove garlic, minced (optional)

Combine all the ingredients in a large, heavy saucepan. Bring to a simmer
and cook gently until thick, about 30 minutes. Stir occasionally.

MAKES 4 CUPS.

Donna's Whiskey-a-Go-Go Sauce

This is an excellent table sauce, courtesy of Donna Quessenberry of Bird-
eye, Arkansas. It can also be used as a final basting sauce for pork or beef.

1 teaspoon dry mustard
2 cups ketchup
$^{1}/_{2}$ cup bourbon, or to taste
$^{1}/_{2}$ cup sorghum molasses
$^{1}/_{2}$ cup cider vinegar
2 tablespoons Worcestershire sauce
2 tablespoons Pickapeppa sauce

2 tablespoons lemon juice
1 tablespoon soy sauce
2 cloves garlic, crushed
$^{1}/_{2}$ teaspoon coarsely ground black
  pepper
1 tablespoon dried parsley

In a saucepan, make a paste of the dry mustard and a little of the ketchup.
Gradually add the rest of the ketchup, stirring constantly. Stir in the rest of
the ingredients. Bring to a boil over medium heat and simmer for 10 minutes. If you prefer a hotter sauce, add Tabasco sauce to taste.

MAKES 4 CUPS.

Chuckwagon Barbecue Team's Barbecue Sauce

This is a salty sauce with an unusually fine flavor, courtesy of Ronald Turnbow and the Chuckwagon Barbecue Team.

$2/3$ cup commercial barbecue
   seasoning
$1/2$ cup cider vinegar
2 cups water
1 5-ounce bottle Pickapeppa sauce
2 tablespoons Kitchen Bouquet
   (or other commercial gravy
   seasoning)

$3/4$ cup Kraft barbecue sauce (or
   other tomato-based barbecue
   sauce)
6 tablespoons soy sauce
$2/3$ cup packed brown sugar
$1/2$ teaspoon onion powder
$1/4$ cup honey

Combine all the ingredients in a heavy saucepan and bring to a simmer. Cook gently for 15 minutes, stirring occasionally.
   MAKES 4 CUPS.

Star Boars Sauce

Lee Thompson, Jr., a Memphis in May contestant from Mississippi, says this sauce tastes better "after sitting three days."

4 cups ketchup
4 cups water
$1/4$ cup Worcestershire sauce
3 tablespoons soy sauce
10 dashes Tabasco sauce
$1/4$ cup white vinegar
$1/4$ cup chili powder

$1/2$ tablespoon garlic salt
$1/2$ tablespoon celery salt
1 teaspoon ground black pepper
Dash salt
1 tablespoon paprika
2 tablespoons granulated garlic
2 tablespoons prepared horseradish

Combine all the ingredients in a heavy saucepan and mix well. Cook slowly on a low temperature for about $2\frac{1}{2}$ hours.
   MAKES 8 CUPS.

Bay of Pigs Sauce

This sauce, courtesy of Judy Cooper, has a heavy Worcestershire sauce flavor.

1/2 cup (1 stick) butter
1 6-ounce bottle hot, sweet mustard
1 1/2 cups tomato sauce
2 cups ketchup (preferably Heinz)
2 cups red wine vinegar (preferably Regina)
2 1/2 cups Worcestershire sauce (preferably French's)
4 teaspoons brown sugar
2 teaspoons paprika

2 teaspoons Lawry's seasoned salt
1 teaspoon garlic powder
1/4 teaspoon chili powder
1/4 teaspoon ground black pepper
1/4 teaspoon cayenne pepper
2 tablespoons liquid smoke (preferably Colgin's)
2 teaspoons lemon juice
1 teaspoon Tabasco sauce

Melt the butter in a heavy saucepan. Add the mustard, tomato sauce, and ketchup, stirring constantly. Add the vinegar and Worcestershire sauce. Stirring constantly, add the remaining ingredients. Simmer for 30 minutes.

MAKES ABOUT 8 CUPS.

Joe Kilgo's Sweet Barbecue Sauce for Boston Butt Roast

This is a tangy sauce with the taste of Worcestershire.

1/2 cup (1 stick) butter
1 cup ketchup
3/4 cup tomato sauce
1 cup red wine vinegar
1/2 cup Worcestershire sauce
2 tablespoons hickory liquid smoke
1/4 cup hot, sweet mustard
1 1/2 teaspoons Tabasco sauce

2 tablespoons dark brown sugar
2 tablespoons paprika
1 1/2 teaspoons garlic powder
1 tablespoon seasoned salt
1 tablespoon lemon juice
Dash chili powder
Dash ground black pepper
Dash cayenne pepper

Melt the butter in a heavy saucepan. Add the ketchup, tomato sauce, vinegar, and Worcestershire sauce, stirring constantly. Add the remaining ingredients and simmer for 30 minutes.

MAKES 4 CUPS.

Mrs. Kerr's Secret Sauce

This sauce, given to us by John Cooper of Greenville, Mississippi, resembles a salad dressing. We found it surprisingly good when used that way, but Mrs. Kerr uses it as a basting sauce for barbecue.

¹/₄ cup salt	1 tablespoon poultry seasoning
1 teaspoon garlic salt	1 tablespoon ground black pepper
2 cups white vinegar	1 egg, beaten
1 cup vegetable oil	

Mix together all the ingredients and bring to a boil. Simmer for 10 minutes.

MAKES 3 CUPS.

Evelyn's Barbecue Sauce

This recipe and the one that follows come to us courtesy of Evelyn Carroll Rogers, author of *Georgia Cooking with Sweet Vidalia Onions*, which you can order by writing to her at P.O. Box 736, Vidalia, Georgia 30474.

¹/₃ cup chopped onions	2 teaspoons prepared mustard
¹/₃ cup chopped celery	2 tablespoons lemon juice
1 garlic clove	2 tablespoons Worcestershire sauce
2 tablespoons corn oil	2 tablespoons brown sugar
1 6-ounce can tomato paste	4 teaspoons paprika
1 10³/₄-ounce can tomato soup	1 teaspoon salt
¹/₈ teaspoon Tabasco sauce	¹/₈ teaspoon ground black pepper

Sauté the onions, celery, and garlic in the corn oil until brown. Stir in the remaining ingredients, bring to a boil, and simmer for 10 minutes. Use immediately or bottle; store in the refrigerator.

MAKES ABOUT 2 CUPS.

Evelyn's Vidalia Onion Barbecue Sauce

¹/₂ cup (1 stick) butter
¹/₂ cup finely chopped Vidalia onion
¹/₂ cup white vinegar
1 cup water
2 teaspoons prepared mustard
4 tablespoons Worcestershire sauce
4 tablespoons sugar

1 teaspoon ground black pepper
¹/₂ teaspoon cayenne pepper
2 teaspoons salt
¹/₂ cup ketchup
¹/₂ cup steak sauce (such as A-1)
1 lemon, sliced

Melt the butter and add the onion, vinegar, water, mustard, Worcestershire sauce, sugar, peppers, and salt. Bring to a boil and simmer for 30 minutes, uncovered. Add the remaining ingredients and simmer for 5 minutes more. Use immediately or bottle and store in the refrigerator.

MAKES ABOUT 3 CUPS.

 **SIDE DISHES**

Old Southern Brunswick Stew

Courtesy of Pat Baldridge, author of *Hot Off the Press*.

1 3-pound hen
1 chicken bouillon cube
1 green onion
Several sprigs celery leaves
Salt
Ground black pepper
1 medium onion, chopped
3 14½-ounce cans whole tomatoes
 with juice
2 10½-ounce cans tomato puree

1 cup (2 sticks) butter
3 17-ounce cans white cream-style
 corn
1 8-ounce package instant mashed
 potatoes, prepared according to
 manufacturer's directions
1 tablespoon Worcestershire sauce
4 ounces smoked ham, sliced
 (optional)
Cayenne pepper

Place the hen in a large pot and add cold water to cover. Bring to a boil over medium-high heat and skim. Add the bouillon cube, green onion, celery leaves, and salt and pepper to taste. Reduce heat and simmer until tender, 2 to 3 hours. Let cool, and refrigerate overnight.

Skim off the fat from the chicken broth and discard. Remove the hen and discard the skin and bones. Dice the boned chicken and place it in a large, heavy pot. Add the onion, tomatoes, tomato puree, and butter. Cook slowly for about 30 minutes. Add the corn and cook for several minutes, then add the prepared instant mashed potatoes, Worcestershire sauce, and ham if used. Season with salt, black pepper, and cayenne pepper to taste. Simmer for about 30 minutes more, stirring constantly.

SERVES 10.

Old Hickory Bar-B-Q Burgoo

This recipe, which comes to us courtesy of Harl Foreman, was broken down to home kitchen proportions from the quantities prepared at Harl's Old Hickory Bar-B-Q in Owensboro, Kentucky. The original recipe calls for 100 pounds of meat and 40 gallons of water, among other ingredients.

2 pounds lamb shanks
1/2 pound pork steak (or 2 small chops)
2 chicken thighs, skinned
3 tablespoons tomato paste
2 8-ounce cans whole tomatoes, with juice
1 cup drained canned corn

1 cup Piedmont/Lexington (Carolina) barbecue sauce (see pages 174)
3 cups diced potatoes
2 1/4 cups chopped cabbage
3 cups chopped onions
1 tablespoon salt
1/2 teaspoon ground black pepper

Place the meat in a large pot and add water to cover. Bring to a boil and cook over medium-low heat for 2 hours. Skim. Remove the meat and bone it, discarding the bones and fat. Set aside.

Add to the broth the tomato paste, tomatoes, corn, barbecue sauce, potatoes, cabbage, onions, salt, and pepper. Bring to a boil and simmer for 1 to 2 hours. Add the reserved meat, heat through, and serve.

Serves 8.

John Wills's Coleslaw

1/2 cup prepared mustard
1/2 cup sugar
1/4 cup white vinegar
1/4 cup sweet pickle juice
1 teaspoon celery seed
Salt

White pepper
1/4 cup chopped sweet pickle
1 2 1/2- to 3-pound head cabbage, shredded (about 6 cups)
Chopped pimentos for garnish

Whisk together the mustard, sugar, vinegar, and pickle juice until the sugar dissolves. Add the celery seed and salt and pepper to taste. Place the cabbage and chopped pickle in a bowl, pour the sauce over, and toss well. Garnish with chopped pimentos.

SERVES 6.

Donna Quessenberry's Rainbow Macaroni Salad

1 12-ounce package rainbow (multi-colored) rotini
1 cup sliced celery
1/2 cup sliced green onion,
1/2 cup chopped green pepper
1/2 cup sliced green olives with pimentos
1/2 cup chopped pitted black olives
2 tablespoons finely chopped parsley
1 1/2 cups mayonnaise
2 to 3 tablespoons wine vinegar, to taste
Salt and freshly ground black pepper to taste

Cook the rotini according to the package directions, being careful not to overcook. Drain and place in a large bowl. Add the celery, green onions, green pepper, green and black olives, and parsley and toss well. In a separate bowl, mix together the mayonnaise and vinegar until smooth. Add to the macaroni mixture along with the salt and pepper to taste. Toss well. Refrigerate several hours before serving.

SERVES 8.

Kirk Kirkland's Fried Corn on the Cob

This tasty treat comes to us courtesy of Kirk Kirkland's Bar-B-Q in Mobile, Alabama.

Fresh or frozen ears of corn, preferably halved
Vegetable oil for deep frying
Melted butter or margarine

Thaw the corn if using frozen ears. Heat the oil in a large, heavy pot or deep fryer to 350°F. Add the corn, only a few ears at a time, and fry until the kernels begin to brown around the edges, about 4 minutes. Drain on paper towels and serve with the melted butter or margarine for dipping.

Jim Quessenberry's Perfect Corn on the Cob

Only sweet butter will do for this recipe; it makes the corn sweet.

4 ears fresh corn
2 tablespoons sweet butter

Shuck the corn. Wrap the ears in a foil packet with the butter. Seal tightly so the butter will not run out. Place on the grill and cook for 30 to 45 minutes, depending on how hot the fire is. Turn several times during cooking to spread the butter around.

SERVES 2 TO 4.

Jerry Roach's Bacon-Wrapped Chicken Livers

These are great appetizers to make and serve while ribs are cooking.

2 pounds chicken livers
1 pound sliced bacon, cut in half
1 10-ounce bottle soy sauce

Rinse the livers and pat them dry. Cut the larger ones in half. Wrap each piece of liver in a half slice of bacon and secure with a toothpick. Place in a non-corrodible dish and pour the soy sauce over. Marinate overnight in the refrigerator.

Drain the livers and place them on a piece of foil on a grill or on the hot end of a barbecue pit. Cook for about 15 minutes, turning once.

MAKES ABOUT 24 HORS D'OEUVRES.

Country's Skillet Apples

Country's Restaurant in Columbus, Georgia, shared with us this recipe and several others.

15 small to medium apples   ¼ cup cornstarch
1 cup packed brown sugar   3 cups water
1 teaspoon cinnamon   6 tablespoons margarine

Preheat the oven to 350°F. Wash the apples, then halve and core them; do not peel. Place them in a 9- by 13-inch baking dish or in a large cast-iron skillet, cut-side up. In a bowl, combine the brown sugar, cinnamon, cornstarch, and water. Pour this mixture over the apples. Cut the margarine in small pieces and dot the apple mixture with it. Cover with aluminum foil and bake for 1¼ hours. Serve warm.

SERVES 8 TO 10.

 ## DESSERTS

Country's Buttermilk Pie

2 eggs, separated   1 teaspoon vanilla
⅓ cup margarine, softened   1¼ cups buttermilk
1 cup white sugar   1 9- or 10-inch unbaked pie shell
3 tablespoons flour

Preheat the oven to 350°F. In a clean, dry bowl, beat the egg whites until stiff; set aside in the refrigerator. In a separate bowl, blend the egg yolks, margarine, sugar, flour, and vanilla until smooth. Add the buttermilk and blend well, scraping the sides of the bowl. Fold in the beaten egg whites. Pour into the pie shell and bake for 45 to 50 minutes. The pie will puff up.

MAKES 1 9- OR 10-INCH PIE.

Country's Chocolate Chess Pie

1¹/₃ cups sugar
4 tablespoons cocoa powder
1 teaspoon vanilla
Dash salt
4 tablespoons (¹/₂ stick) margarine,
    melted

2 eggs, well beaten
¹/₂ cup evaporated milk
¹/₂ cup pecan pieces
1 9- or 10-inch unbaked pie shell

Preheat the oven to 350°F. In a large bowl, thoroughly blend the sugar and cocoa powder. Add the vanilla and salt and blend well. Blend in the margarine. Add the eggs and evaporated milk and blend well. Mix in the pecans. Pour into the pie shell and bake for 45 to 50 minutes. The pie will puff up and the top will crack when it is done.

MAKES 1 9- OR 10-INCH PIE.

Country's Goober Pie

We froze one of these pies, then sliced it straight from the freezer. It was a sensation—almost like a peanut butter ice cream pie.

Crust
1 cup crushed vanilla wafers (about
    30 wafers)
¹/₃ cup sugar
4 tablespoons (¹/₂ stick) margarine,
    melted

Filling
8 ounces cream cheese, softened
2 cups powdered sugar
1 cup peanut butter
1 cup prepared whipped topping,
    chilled
2 tablespoons pulverized peanuts

Prepare the crust: Preheat the oven to 350°F. Mix the vanilla wafer crumbs well with the sugar. Pour the melted margarine over and blend well. Press into a 9- or 10-inch pie pan and bake for about 7 minutes, until set but not browned.

Prepare the filling: Blend the cream cheese, powdered sugar, and peanut butter until smooth and fluffy. Fold in 1 cup of the whipped topping. (Do not blend completely; you should still be able to see white streaks in the filling.) Pour into the prepared pie crust, sprinkle with the peanuts, and refrigerate for several hours or overnight before serving.

MAKES 1 9- OR 10-INCH PIE.

Johnny Harris's Key Lime Pie

6 egg yolks, beaten
1 7½-ounce can sweetened
   condensed milk
½ cup lime juice

Sugar to taste (optional)
1 9-inch prebaked graham cracker
   pie crust

Blend the egg yolks with the condensed milk. Quickly blend in the lime juice. Add sugar to taste (we didn't add any when we tested this recipe). Pour into the pie crust and refrigerate for at least 2 hours before serving.

MAKES 1 9-INCH PIE.

Pecan Pie

This recipe comes from *The Williamsburg Cookbook*, published by the Colonial Williamsburg Foundation.

4 eggs
¾ cup sugar
½ teaspoon salt
1½ cups light corn syrup

1 tablespoon melted butter, cooled
1 teaspoon vanilla
1 cup pecan halves
1 9-inch unbaked pie shell

Preheat the oven to 400°F. In a bowl, beat the eggs lightly and add the sugar, salt, corn syrup, melted butter, and vanilla. Blend well. Spread the pecan halves on the bottom of the crust and cover with the filling. Place in the oven and immediately reduce the heat to 350°F. Bake for 40 to 50 minutes, or until the filling is firm in the center. Cool before serving.

SERVES 6 TO 8.

Equipment and Supplies

Barbecuing is like learning how to drive a car. Once you've got the basics, the rest is relatively easy. As one Kansas City aficionado put it, "Barbecuing is easy. All you need is one lesson and forty years of experience."

To begin with, you'll need the right type of equipment.

BARBECUE UNITS

Barbecue units range from gas grills, hooded braziers, and square-covered cookers to water smokers, portable grills, and kettle cookers, plus hundreds of homemade varieties made out of everything from bathtubs to refrigerators to oil barrels. If you aren't a do-it-yourselfer, you can choose from a variety of name brands on the market. The right unit depends upon your life-style and the type of cooking you plan to do.

Barbecue units usually contain a grid that holds the meat, often called a grill. Frequently used to quick-cook steaks and hamburgers, the "grill" can be utilized for barbecuing only if the entire unit meets certain criteria: the ability to separate meat and fire so that a cooking-level temperature of 200°–250°F can be maintained, and (for closed-pit barbecuing), the ability to close the unit for heavy smoking. By reading the manufacturer's directions, you'll learn how to maneuver the air vents, adjustable grids, fire pans, and covers.

The open brazier

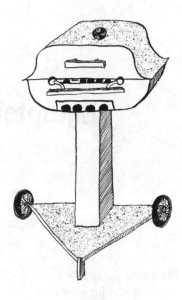

A covered cooker

The *open brazier* is really nothing more than a shallow metal pan with a grid on top. Some braziers have half-hoods, covers, or battery-operated rotisseries. Tabletop *hibachis* are also considered open braziers. These are fine for grilling hamburgers, steaks, poultry, and fish, but are not suited for serious slow-smoking.

Covered cookers come in all shapes and are quite versatile. When you take the cover off, the smoker acts as a grill. These types of cookers occasionally come with adjustable fire pans or grids, and vented covers for controlling heat. With dampers to control fire temperature, you can cook larger pieces of meat. When the cookers are covered, they can be used to barbecue closed-pit style. Some units (such as the Hasty-Bake) allow for lowering the fire source, or for raising the grilling grid.

While some covered cookers come with a thermometer in the lid, they aren't always dependable. It's a good idea to insert a regular meat thermometer in the meat to avoid mistakes. Don't confuse a meat thermometer with an oven thermometer. A standard *oven* thermometer with a hook for hanging on the grill is best for determining the temperature at meat level. Place it where you can see it easily when opening the hood. (You can also lay it on the grill.) You can adjust the distance between the food and coals by raising or lowering the fire grate. Some models also have a fire door that allows you to add more fuel without opening the lid.

Expensive wagon models are usually made of heavy metal, coated with a heat-resistant finish. You can buy accessories for these, including rotisseries, extra grills, smoking equipment, and detachable shelves as well as utensil racks.

The *Japanese kamado* is new to this country. It is ceramic and looks like a big egg, with the small end anchored by a metal bracket to make it stand upright. It boasts a controllable smoke vent and a draft door. The top acts as a lid. When the lid is open, you can grill. Closed, the smoker becomes an excellent oven.

A firebox at the bottom has an iron grate that holds the charcoal. Remarkably small amounts of charcoal will produce adequate heat. You

The Japanese kamado

can barbecue with charcoal alone or add water-soaked hardwood chips to provide smoke. There is a Chinese oven similar to the kamado, but it is barrel-shaped rather than egg-shaped. Both have inspired people to make their own ovens, often incorporating the pull-out firebox that makes it easy to add charcoal and wood in small amounts throughout the cooking process.

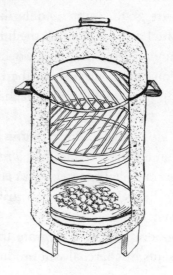

A water smoker

Water smokers have heavy dome-shaped tops with handles and built-in water pans. Many outdoor enthusiasts use these ovens for cooking game and fish. The water smoker is a three-tiered device, as shown, with the fire at the bottom, a water pan above, and above that the grill for the meat.

You can slow-cook food in these ovens, flavoring them with your favorite woods and letting the meat automatically baste and bathe in the moisture. But some serious barbecuers don't like this method because the meat is permeated by the water and doesn't get the hard, crusty finish it does with dry smoking. Simply remove the water pan for the last hour of cooking, and this shouldn't be a problem. These ovens should also have a side door large enough to add fuel and more soaked wood below, as well as water to the water pan.

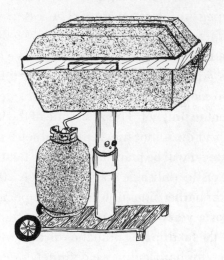

A gas grill

Although barbecue purists cook with nothing but hardwoods or hardwood charcoal, *gas and electric units* are becoming more popular in the backyard because of their convenience and time-saving features. There are a wide variety of these units available. Some of the more expensive ones come complete with rotisseries; you can place an aluminum foil drip pan underneath the meat in any of the models to catch fat and deflect direct heat, as well as to prevent flare-up. Cookers that can be lit automatically, providing instant heat, have their advantages: they are more economical to operate than charcoal barbecues, are ready to use in a short time, and cleaning is a breeze. Electric units are easier to use in that no matches are required and there are no flames to keep lit. But electric units produce a drying, non-smoky heat, so they are best for *grilling*. Gas units, too, are at their best when *grilling* foods. Their disadvantage for barbecuing is that they cannot provide the intense smoky flavor a traditional smoker gives, since it is difficult to maintain low temperatures or to create a smoky environment in the continuous draft absolutely essential to maintain the gas flame. (And flames are bad news to barbecue purists!)

Many professional barbecuers will argue about whether it is orthodox even to *ignite* hickory or oak logs with gas, let alone cooking the meat over gas or electric heat. But if you do choose this type of unit, make sure it's capable of maintaining the low temperatures necessary for slow cooking. In most gas units, the fire source and the grill are at a fixed distance from each other and there is a fixed minimum temperature. We always recommend the two-burner gas grills, so that you can shut off the heat on one side, allowing the meat to cook more slowly on the other side. First turn on both burners, to get the entire unit hot. Then turn one of the burners off. Wait 10 minutes, then place an oven (not meat) thermometer on the unlit side, at the level where the meat will be placed. Adjust the heat on the lit side until the cooking surface on the unlit side is approximately 200°–225°F, the optimum temperature for barbecuing (unless your recipe notes otherwise).

Some of the flavor you do get from cooking with gas comes from the smoke produced by the fat dripping onto the volcanic rock set in the bottom of the grill. However, for barbecuing we definitely prefer wood smoke. To get natural wood smoke in a gas unit, place a well-soaked chunk of your favorite wood on a piece of heavy-duty aluminum foil, wrap it tightly, and pierce several holes in the top. Add it to the preheated unit at least 10 minutes before cooking, arranging the wood over the lava rocks on the lit side so that it doesn't obstruct the flame. As the wood gets hot, it will smoke, but the foil will keep it from flaring up or from clogging the vents with ashes. (Foil melts if it touches an electric coil directly.)

Some additional reminders when cooking with a two-burner gas unit:

Don't light the grill with the lid closed. Open the lid and light the burners with a butane wand specifically designed for this use, rather than with a match. If the flame is too yellow, adjust according to the manufacturer's instructions.

You can slow the buildup of grease and char by alternating burners and grids each time you barbecue. It is also helpful to clean the grill with a metal brush after using. An occasional "burn off" will get rid of the buildup when it does get to the black, crusty stage: turn the grids upside down and turn on both burners full tilt. Leave them on for an hour or two, until the accumulated layers burn off. Rotate the "briquets" until the char is gone on all sides. See the manufacturer's instructions for information on cleaning a gas unit and the lava rocks.

Homemade smokers are for those inventive and intrepid enthusiasts who prefer to create their own wood or charcoal smoke ovens out of everything from refrigerators and barrels to electric cookstoves and cement blocks. Sam Higgins of Arlington, Texas, uses two matching porcelain bathtubs, hinged together to form a closed pit! Such ingenious devices are in constant use in backyards and at barbecue contests. If you are serious about barbecue, you might want to try making your own. While we can't give you detailed instructions here, we recommend that you attend some national or regional barbecue contests where these types of smokers are in use (see page 229). Some contestants even offer their ovens for sale, and others sell instruction kits. The basic elements of an efficient smoke oven are: a fire pan to create heat and smoke; an area to confine the smoke; racks or hooks to hold the meat; an adequate draft and controllable air inlet near the source of the smoke; and adjustable air outlets at the top of the smoker.

Here are a few models from folks who've come up with their own versions of the perfect smoker. The varieties available are nearly endless. (See also the instructions on building an open pit, page 165-167.)

Paul Kirk's "The Pig." This variation on a chemical-free 55-gallon drum can smoke 22 slabs of pork ribs or 90 pounds of brisket at a time.

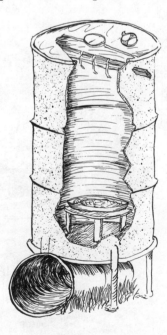

Paul Kirk's "The Pig"

John "Buffalo" Gattenby's "Ice Box Smoker." Buffalo says his meat smoker can be built from an old refrigerator of any size. Refrigerators are well insulated and hold heat, save fuel, and provide a full-length door for convenient loading and unloading. To convert a refrigerator into an oven takes some work, and we definitely don't advise building one yourself unless you've talked with experts. You can find them at barbecue contests and cook-offs around Missouri, however. (*Warning*: Old refrigerators can be a hazard for small children and may contain residues of freon gas. Caution and safety features are essential.)

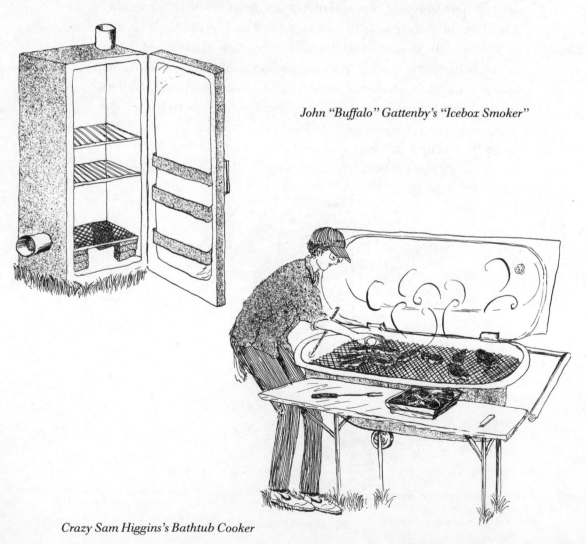

John "Buffalo" Gattenby's "Icebox Smoker"

Crazy Sam Higgins's Bathtub Cooker

★ ACCESSORIES

To produce good barbecue, you'll need the right accessories, tools that are easy to clean and to handle. A utensil rack on the grill keeps them handy when they're needed.

A *meat thermometer* comes in handy for gauging the doneness of large cuts of meat. An ordinary *oven thermometer* is ideal for monitoring the cooking temperature at meat level.

You'll need two sets of *tongs:* one for coals, the other for food. (*Never* use forks to test or turn barbecue; they pierce the skin, allowing precious juices to escape. Use tongs or a spatula instead.) A *long-handled meat spatula, fork,* and *basting brush* are essential—the spatula for turning food, the fork for spearing vegetables and to hold the finished meat while slicing, and the basting brush to spread the basting liquid, if used, and to brush on any sauce applied during the last part of the cooking process.

You should have heavy-duty *gloves, mitts,* or *hot pads* to protect your hands from high heat and hot surfaces. Extra-long mitts are preferable for handling hot grills and for avoiding splatters.

A *spray bottle* for water and *baking soda* should be on hand to extinguish flare-ups. Ordinary plastic spray bottles for house plants work beautifully; you want a spray, not a hard stream of water, to avoid stirring up too much ash over the meat.

Hinged grill baskets, with space to secure the food between two grids, are ideal for cooking foods such as fish, vegetables, hamburgers, pork

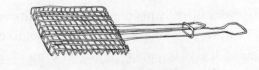
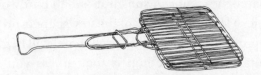

Hinged grill baskets

chops, and other delicate, sticky, or smaller foods (such as shrimp) that tend to fall between the grids or fall apart when turning. You turn the basket, not the food, which is why we recommend this device for cooking fish. (If you don't have a grill basket, be sure to oil both the fish and the grill when grilling or barbecuing fish.)

Long-handled skewers are perfect for kebobs. (Don't use round skewers because the food will spin loosely on them; the best are the broad, flat skewers that have a handlelike device for turning.)

 # STARTING A PROPER CHARCOAL FIRE

For a small barbecue, build twelve to twenty briquets into a pyramid to one side of the grill and ignite. They should remain in a mound throughout the cooking process. (If you are *grilling* steaks, fish, etc., however, determine the amount of briquets needed by spreading out the unlit charcoal in a single, closely packed layer that extends an inch beyond the surface of the food to be grilled. Then pyramid the charcoal back up and light it. You'll have the correct amount of fire when you spread the nearly-ready charcoal out evenly just before grilling.)

Knowing the number of ways and products available to start an outdoor fire for barbecuing goes along with learning the principles of good barbecue. Here are several methods to use:

1. Newspapers and kindling. One of the most common and simplest ways to start your barbecue is the way people have started fires in their fireplaces for generations. Twist some newspapers into long, loglike cylinders. Make two crossed layers of the newspaper "logs." On top of them, place some small twigs as dry kindling. Place the charcoal briquets on top of the kindling. (In big pit barbecues you can substitute small hardwood logs for the charcoal if you prefer.) Light the edges of the newspapers on all sides. If the fire has been built properly, before long the charcoal will begin to get white.

One disadvantage of this method is that unless you make a slight indentation in the middle of the newspaper-kindling area, the charcoal will scatter about the cooking unit as the paper and twigs eventually burn away, making this method less effective than some others.

2. Electric fire-starters. A simple way to start a fire is by using an electric fire-starter. Place it in the center of your cooker, and pile the briquets on top according to the manufacturer's directions. When the briquets begin to turn red (around 10 to 20 minutes, depending upon the unit and the outdoor temperature), turn off the electrical apparatus. Remove it when the charcoal is ready, but remember, *it is still hot.* Place accordingly.

The major hazard with this method is forgetting about the unit and having it get too hot for too long, which will damage it or the oven. Inserting a timer between the electrical outlet and the plug for the starter is a good idea. Set the timer according to the instructions on the electrical starter, and be sure to follow the other instructions carefully as well.

3. Liquid fire-starters. *Never* use kerosene, gasoline, or other quick-igniting fuels when starting a barbecue fire. Instead, start your fire by stacking briquets in a pyramid (as described above), then pour or spray on a liquid fire-starter specifically designed for barbecuing. These commercial preparations have a much lower flashpoint and are much safer than ordinary liquid fuels.

The disadvantage of this method is the lingering chemical odor of the starter, which can attach itself to the food if the food is put on before the charcoal ashes down properly. The fire may also go out if you have used too small an amount of starter fuel. Never try to restart a fire that has already been lit by trying to soak the coals with more fuel, since there may be live coals hidden from view that can flare up and burn you, or cause an explosion. Liquid fire-starters are meant to be used on charcoal *before* it is ignited. If instructions are followed and proper precautions are taken, however, both these problems are avoidable and this is a safe means of starting your fire.

4. Fuel-coated substances. These range from fuel-soaked barbecue briquets to wood products or sawdust compressed into sticks and permeated with an igniter fluid. Fire-starter sticks can be inserted in the middle of the cooker and the briquets piled on top. With the help of a match and adequate ventilation, they catch fire and burn long enough to ignite the charcoal before burning themselves out. Again, fumes and odors can result from this method, *unless the chemicals burn down completely before food is placed on the grill.* Sometimes these coated sticks don't catch on fire as easily as liquid fire-starters, particularly if they are old or have been left uncovered for a while. However, some of the newer briquet products do light easily and, once they are red-white, can be counted on not to produce fumes or to affect flavor. They are the simplest, easiest way of all to start a fire.

5. Jelly fire-starters. These thick compounds are considered safer than liquid fire-starters, although because they age and lose their effectiveness over time, they have never been quite as popular. Simply spread them over the charcoal as directed and light.

6. Metal "chimney" fire-starters. This is one of the safest and cheapest methods of all. The "chimney" is simply a large, round tube of metal about 6 to 12 inches in diameter and 8 to 15 inches high, much like a large tin can with both bottom and top removed. Partway up, there is a grid that separates the newspaper from the charcoal. A chimney-type fire-starter obviously has no chemical odor or taste to impart to the food, nor does it involve the expense of fuel other than charcoal.

Place the chimney starter in the fire box or grill. Below the latticelike insert toward the bottom of the chimney, insert crinkled newspaper, which serves as the fire source. Punctured holes around the bottom allow ventilation as the newspaper burns, igniting the charcoal above. Fill the chimney with charcoal and ignite the newspaper. Once the coals are reddish in color, they can be dumped out into the barbecue unit.

Make sure your unit has enough space to enable you to utilize your chimney effectively. Also be sure that you use gloves or mitts to protect yourself from the hot handle—which should, preferably, be insulated or wooden. (The best units have a wooden handle, and a shield between the handle and the hot unit to protect your knuckles when you pick it up.) Another potential disadvantage of this method is that it limits the size of the fire you can start.

In general, starting a barbecue fire is a simple procedure. Follow the instructions carefully for whatever method you choose and you'll be able to start a fire safely and effectively every time. For the novice griller or barbecuer, the briquets already permeated with a lighter fluid (Kingsford's Match-Lite, for example) are easiest, cleanest, and best. Obviously, precautions should be taken to ensure that the fire is a safe distance from houses, trees, and shrubbery, and to protect small children and pets from it. Just look around you and be sure you've done everything necessary to ensure that your barbecue will turn out to be fun and enjoyable. Exercise good common sense, and you should have no problems at all.

Be prepared for a flare-up, particularly when grilling. Plenty of water will stop any ordinary charcoal fire. If you have a flare-up, don't panic. This usually indicates that your fire is too hot for closed-pit barbecuing. It could also mean that the meat is directly over the briquets and is dripping fat into the fire. Be sure to have a ready means of dousing flames fast. A plastic plant sprayer filled with water works well in emergencies. Be careful to spray the water on gently so it won't shower the meat with ashes. (You may have to spray a surprising amount of water to stop some flames.) Correct the problem (by removing dripping meat to one side of the fire, etc.) before resuming. Remember, we're not grilling!

Well, friends, those are the basics of barbecue. Just remember—cook it low and smoke it slow and you'll be a pro in no time. We can't think of a tastier way to have fun with friends and family.

Barbecue Cookoffs

We compiled this selective list of barbecue cookoffs with major assistance from Ardie Davis, who helped found the Diddy Wa Diddy Barbecue Sauce Contest and the Kansas City Barbecue Society.

Mid-South (Arkansas, Kentucky, North Carolina, Tennessee, Virginia)

Name/Location	1988 Date(s)	Meats	Contact
CRITTENDEN COUNTY FESTIVAL West Memphis, Arkansas MIM Sanctioned	Sept. 9–10	Pork: whole, shoulder, ribs	David Peeples (501) 735-5500
ST. FRANCIS RIVER BOAT FESTIVAL/WALLACE MARTIN BBQ CONTEST Parkin, Arkansas	Oct. 7–8	Pork	Ms. Gayle Cameron (501) 755-5401

ARKANSAS STATE BARBEQUE CHAMPIONSHIP & CHILI CONTEST Ft. Smith, Arkansas	June 17–18	Beef, pork	Vic Forgren (501) 782-1061
SPRING RIVER BARBECUE COOKOFF Hardy, Arkansas MIM Sanctioned	May 28–29	Pork	Danny Barton (501) 856-3249
WYNNE FUN FEST BARBECUE CONTEST Wynne, Arkansas MIM Sanctioned	June 11	Pork	Chamber of Commerce (501) 238-2601
RAZORBACK STATE CHAMPIONSHIP BARBECUE COOKOFF Blythesville, Arkansas	April 29–30	Pork Misc.	P.O. Box 568 Blythesville, AR 72316
HOG HAPPENIN' Kinston, North Carolina	May 21	Hog	Lenoir County Chamber of Commerce (919) 527-1131
CLARKSVILLE JAYCEES COOKOFF ON THE CUMBERLAND Clarksville, Tennessee	Mid-August	Whole hog, shoulder, ribs	Dudley Griffin (615) 552-5602
RIVERFEAST INVITATIONAL BARBECUE CONTEST Knoxville, Tennessee MIM Sanctioned	Oct. 7–8	Pork	Tisha Skleenar (615) 523-7543
McKENZIE PORK FESTIVAL BARBECUE COOKING CONTEST McKenzie, Tennessee	Oct. 1	Pork Misc.	Joel Washburn (901) 352-3323

MEMPHIS IN MAY WORLD CHAMPIONSHIP BARBECUE COOKING CONTEST Memphis, Tennessee	3rd weekend in May	Pork: whole, shoulder, ribs	MIM Ida Notowitz (901) 525-4611
ANNUAL VIRGINIA STATE CHAMPIONSHIP BARBEQUE COOKOFF Fairfax, Virginia	June 18	Beef, pork	Rick Dygve (703) 830-3219

Deep South (Alabama, Florida, Georgia, Louisiana, Mississippi, South Carolina)

SLOSHEYE TRAIL BIG PIG JIG Vienna, Georgia	2nd weekend in October	Pork: whole, shoulder, ribs, ham	Stanley Gambrell (912) 268-4554
LOUISIANA STATE BARBECUE CHAMPIONSHIP Shreveport, Louisiana	May 6–7		Jim Ewoldson (318) 797-8206
DELTA JUBILEE ANNUAL MISSISSIPPI CHAMPIONSHIP PORK BARBECUE COOKING CONTEST Clarksdale, Mississippi	June 24–25	Pork: whole, shoulder, ribs	Buddy Hitt (601) 627-7337
ANNUAL SOUTHHAVEN SPRING FESTIVAL BARBECUE COOKING CONTEST Southhaven, Mississippi	April 21–23	Pork: whole, rib, shoulder	Margie Haberstoh (601) 342-1752
POSSUM TOWN PIG FEST Columbus, Mississippi	August 26–28	Pork: whole, shoulder, ribs	Edwin Norris (601) 328-4532

Southwest (Arizona, New Mexico, Oklahoma, Texas, Utah)

ANNUAL TRI-STATE BARBECUE COOKOFF Bartlesville, Oklahoma	May 21	Brisket, beef, pork, fowl, game, ribs	Len Silver (918) 333-4555
WILL ROGERS BARBEQUE COOKOFF Claremont, Oklahoma	Oct. 29	Open	Gary Benfield (918) 341-2541
ARDMORE'S ANNUAL CHILI, RED BEAN & BARBEQUE COOKOFFS Ardmore, Oklahoma	April 9	Brisket, ribs, specialty	Billy Bean (405) 226-0421
MUSKOGEE ANNUAL AZALEA BARBECUE & CHILI COOKOFF Muskogee, Oklahoma	April 16	Whole hog, brisket, open	Richard Black (918) 683-6611
CHILI COOKOFF IX (Chili & Barbecue) Lawton, Oklahoma	Labor Day Saturday	Open	Rhonda Griffiths (405) 248-8195
ANNUAL TAYLOR INTERNATIONAL BARBECUE COOKOFF Taylor, Texas	August 20	Beef, lamb, poultry, pork, goat, wild game, seafood	Chamber of Commerce (512) 352-7071
TOP OF TEXAS 9TH ANNUAL CHILI & BARBECUE COOKOFF Dallas, Texas	May 22	Brisket, ribs (sales to guests encouraged)	Harvey West (214) 422-2677
DO DAT BARBECUE Nacogdoches, Texas	Sept. 24	Beef, pork, poultry	Jeannie Hensley (409) 564-8361

ANNUAL CACTUS JACK CHILI & BAR-B-QUE Uvalde, Texas	Oct. 15–16	Open	Cindy Logsdon (512) 278-3361
ANNUAL CALIENTE CLASSIC BBQ & CHILI COOKOFFS Big Lake, Texas	Mid-October	Brisket	Hope Tinney (915) 884-2467
SAN ANTONE ROSE ANNUAL BARBECUE & CHILI COOKOFFS Houston, Texas	July 3	Brisket	San Antone Rose Sandy, Al, or Cecil (713) 977-1843
10TH ANNUAL TEXAS STATE CHAMPIONSHIP BARBEQUE COOKOFF Smithville, Texas	July 15–16	Brisket, pork butt	Mandi Brown (512) 237-4888
ANNUAL WORLD CHAMPIONSHIP BBQ BEEF COOKOFF Pecos, Texas	1st weekend in October	Beef	Chamber of Commerce (915) 445-2406
INTERPLANETARY CHILI & B-B-Q CHAMPIONSHIP College Station, Texas	Nov. 12	Brisket	Richard Conole

Midwest (Illinois, Indiana, Iowa, Kansas, Michigan, Minnesota, Missouri, Ohio, Wisconsin)

RIBFEST Chicago, Illinois	Late Sept.	Ribs	Inc. staff (312) 222-3232
OHIO RIVER ARTS FESTIVAL BARBECUE CONTEST Evansville, Indiana	2nd weekend in May	Pork: whole, ribs, shoulder	Mike Shoulders (812) 423-7729

THE GREAT LENEXA BARBEQUE BATTLE–KANSAS STATE CHAMPIONSHIP Lenexa, Kansas	June 25	9 categories	Jennifer (913) 541-8592
AMERICAN ROYAL Kansas City, Missouri	Oct. 6–8	6 categories	Paulette (913) 221-9800
ANNUAL BLUE SPRINGS BBQ BLAZE OFF Blue Springs, Missouri	Sept. 9–10	Brisket, ribs, poultry	Pam Buck (816) 228-0187
ANNUAL GLADFEST BBQ COOKOFF Gladstone, Missouri	Sept. 30– Oct. 1	5 categories	Ed Wegner (816) 436-2200
SHOW ME STATE CHAMPIONSHIP BARBECUE COOKOFF Kennett, Missouri	June 24–25	Pork: ribs, whole hog, shoulder	Frank Carter III (314) 888-4923
NATIONAL RIB COOKOFF Cleveland, Ohio	May 26–30	Ribs	Gary M. Jacob (216) 241-3888
MEAT ON THE MISSISSIPPI Caruthersville, Missouri MIM Sanctioned	August 5–6	Whole hog, shoulder, ribs	Parker Mehrle (314) 333-1386
DIDDY WA DIDDY NATIONAL BARBECUE SAUCE CONTEST Kansas City, Missouri	Oct. 6–8	Commercial sauces	Ardie Davis (913) 831-3635 Paulette (913) 221-9800

West (Alaska, Colorado, Idaho, Nevada, Oregon, Washington, Wyoming)

CHILIALLUP WASHINGTON STATE BBQ CHAMPIONSHIP & PUGET POD CHILI COOKOFF Puyallup, Washington	Sept. 24	Brisket	Bob Whiteside (206) 483-7532
WASHINGTON MEN'S CHAMPIONSHIP Winthrop, Washington	May 7	Brisket, pork ribs	Bob Lyon (206) 643-0607
10TH ANNUAL NORTHWEST OPEN BBQ CHAMPIONSHIP & WASHINGTON STATE CHILI COOKOFF Seattle, Washington	Memorial weekend Sunday	Brisket	Michael Baldwin (206) 282-8338

Index

About the Authors

RICH DAVIS, leading barbecue authority and creator of K.C. Masterpiece barbecue sauces, learned the homespun art of barbecuing as a youngster growing up in southern Missouri and Kansas City, where he now resides. A noted food historian, Davis has written numerous barbecue articles for magazines such as *Playboy* and *Ladies' Home Journal* and earned kudos with his first book, *All About Bar-B-Q: Kansas City-Style*, co-authored with Shifra Stein. In addition Davis has served as a technical consultant for the barbecue scene in the recent Sally Field and James Garner movie, *Murphy's Romance.* He has been guest chef on *Good Morning America,* and is the host-chef of a popular video, *The Secrets, Sauces and Savvy of American Barbecue*, available from Serendipity Communications, 1-800-451-7000.

SHIFRA STEIN's love for good barbecue began in her hometown of Kansas City, Missouri, and has expanded along with her waistline as she's traveled the country in her capacity as an award-winning travel and food writer. A syndicated broadcaster whose popular radio show, *TravelTalk*, is heard throughout the Midwest and Sunbelt states, Ms. Stein is the former restaurant critic of the Kansas City *Star* and co-author of *All About Bar-B-Q: Kansas City-Style* with Rich Davis. She is also the creator of the acclaimed *Day Trips America* series for Globe Pequot Press, and is the author and publisher of several regional guidebooks.